DISGUISE AND RECOGNITION
IN THE *ODYSSEY*

DISGUISE

AND RECOGNITION

IN THE

ODYSSEY

Sheila Murnaghan

PRINCETON

UNIVERSITY

PRESS

Published by Princeton University Press, 41 William Street,
Princeton, New Jersey 08540
In the United Kingdom: Princeton University Press, Guildford, Surrey

Library of Congress Cataloging in Publication Data will be
found on the last printed page of this book

ISBN 0-691-06716-3

Publication of this book has been aided by a grant from the
Paul Mellon Fund of Princeton University Press

This book has been composed in Linotron Galliard

Clothbound editions of Princeton University Press books
are printed on acid-free paper, and binding materials are
chosen for strength and durability. Paperbacks, although satisfactory
for personal collections, are not usually suitable for library rebinding

Printed in the United States of America by Princeton University Press,
Princeton, New Jersey

To Hugh

Contents

Acknowledgments

MY WORK on this project both began and ended at the Center for Hellenic Studies, and I would like to thank the then Director, Bernard Knox, and the Senior Fellows for allowing me the use of the library when I was a graduate student and for electing me to the unique pleasures and privileges of a Junior Fellowship for 1984–1985. My work was also supported by a Mellon Fellowship at the Whitney Humanities Center at Yale during 1982–1983 and by a Morse Fellowship during 1984–1985, for both of which I am very grateful. The dissertation out of which this book grew was directed by George Kennedy, whose advice and support meant more than he may have realized at the time, and was given exceptionally careful and helpful readings by Kenneth Reckford and Peter Smith. Since then, this text has been woven and unwoven more times than Penelope's web, and I have benefited at every stage from the moral support and the substantive suggestions of numerous friends and colleagues who took the time and trouble to read and comment on all or part of the manuscript. For their generous help I would like to thank Victor Bers, Peter Bing, Thomas Cole, Kevin Crotty, Lars Engle, Giovanni Ferrari, John Herington, Gregory Nagy, Seth Schein, Laura Slatkin, and, above all, Hugh Gordon. Finally, I would like to express my gratitude to Joanna Hitchcock of Princeton University Press for her excellent advice and welcome encouragement during the process of bringing the book to publication.

DISGUISE AND RECOGNITION
IN THE *ODYSSEY*

Introduction

IN BOOK 13 of the *Odyssey*, when Odysseus finally sets foot on the shore of Ithaca again, he takes, with the aid of his divine patroness Athena, the decisive step that will assure that his homecoming is successful: he adopts a disguise. This disguise, which involves his transformation into an old man as well as the clothes of a beggar, is at once a sign of divine protection and a physical manifestation of Odysseus' character. In the complex negotiations that lead up to this moment, Odysseus shows his inherent inclination to disguise when he responds to finding himself in unfamiliar surroundings by concealing his identity. Meeting Athena, who is herself in disguise, he tells one of his false tales. She is delighted with his deviousness and with his continued cautiousness even after he has realized that he is in Ithaca, and she proclaims that these qualities earn him her constant support and set him apart from all other men.

αἰεί τοι τοιοῦτον ἐνὶ στήθεσσι νόημα·
τῷ σε καὶ οὐ δύναμαι προλιπεῖν δύστηνον ἐόντα,
οὕνεκ᾽ ἐπητής ἐσσι καὶ ἀγχίνοος καὶ ἐχέφρων.
ἀσπασίως γάρ κ᾽ ἄλλος ἀνὴρ ἀλαλήμενος ἐλθὼν
ἵετ᾽ ἐνὶ μεγάροις ἰδέειν παῖδάς τ᾽ ἄλοχόν τε·
σοὶ δ᾽ οὔ πω φίλον ἐστὶ δαήμεναι οὐδὲ πυθέσθαι,
πρίν γ᾽ ἔτι σῆς ἀλόχου πειρήσεαι, . . .

Always the same, and always so clever!
That is why I never can desert you, even when you are
    wretched,
for you are politic, and sharp-witted, and resourceful.
Any other man happily coming home from such wanderings
would be eager to see his children and wife in his house.
But it doesn't suit you to expose yourself by asking questions
until you test your wife. . . .
        (*Od.* 13.330–336)[1]

[1] Quotations in Greek from the Homeric epics are taken from the edition of

3

Odysseus is distinguished from other heroes by his willingness to defer the reunions with members of his family through which his homecoming will receive its full expression. He is able to endure a period of disguise during which his achievement in reaching home at last goes unrecognized. And this is what allows him to achieve the greatest success possible for a Homeric hero: *nostos*, "return home," after winning *kleos*, "glory," in the war against Troy. This capacity for disguise distinguishes him from the other great Achaean warriors: Achilles, the hero of the *Iliad*, who is defined by a character that makes him incapable of disguise[2] and a fate that precludes the achievement of both *kleos* and *nostos*; and Agamemnon, whose story of failed *nostos* and lost *kleos* provides a contrast to Odysseus' throughout the *Odyssey*, and who does just what Athena here praises Odysseus for not doing (as Odysseus himself notes soon afterwards, *Od.* 13.383–385).[3] It is because he disguises himself that Odysseus' story departs from the larger pattern of "the Achaeans' bitter homecoming" (*Od.* 1.326–327).

The pivotal episode of Odysseus' encounter with Athena is a

---

the *Iliad* by Thomas W. Allen and David B. Munro and from the edition of the *Odyssey* by Thomas W. Allen in the Oxford Classical Texts series. The English translations are my own, with some borrowings from the versions by Richmond Lattimore and improved by many helpful suggestions from Seth Schein.

[2] Achilles expresses his hostility to the duplicity inherent in disguise at *Il.* 9.312–313. His own attempt to employ a disguise, when he allows Patroclus to enter the battle wearing his armor, is a complete failure. Virtually no one is deceived, and Achilles' impossible aim of gaining glory while avoiding risk (cf. *Il.* 16.80–86) is thwarted as he is drawn back into battle to avenge Patroclus' death.

[3] This distinction between Odysseus and Agamemnon continues in later tradition. The story of Clytemnestra's beacons found in Aeschylus is another way of expressing an essential fact about Agamemnon, that he is incapable of concealing his return. There control over events is transferred to his wife, but her perfidy and his incaution are inextricable notions. Similarly, Odysseus both disguises himself, unlike Agamemnon, and does not need to disguise his return from his wife, also unlike Agamemnon. Penelope's faithfulness and Odysseus' disguise might seem mutually exclusive from the point of view of logical plot making (see the discussion of this point in Chapter 4), but they are also mutually supportive ways of saying the same thing about Odysseus and his family.

4

highpoint of the *Odyssey*'s self–consciousness as a narrative. This episode builds two features of the poem's narrative organization into its action: the singling out for special treatment of one hero who succeeds where others fail and the constructing of a plot designed to forward his interests. Odysseus' assumption of a disguise initiates an extended narrative in which a widespread and traditional plot type, the hero's return in disguise, is used to describe the highest achievement possible within the specific values of the Homeric epics.[4] This study is an account of the intersection of that plot with those values, an examination of how the working-out of the *Odyssey*'s plot defines and articulates that particular brand of achievement.

Odysseus' affinity to disguise is related to the capacity for endurance that is expressed in his characteristic epithet, "πολύ-τλας," "much-enduring." It represents the ability to endure a suspension of recognition—both in the narrow sense of recognition of identity, and in the broader sense of recognition of achievement and status—that other Homeric heroes are unable to tolerate. In the world of the Homeric epics, the recognition of identity also involves recognition in this broader sense, because there identity is bound up with honor and prestige. In the aristocratic society that these poems portray, the chief sources of a hero's identity—his lineage and his home—are also the sources of his heroic status. His capacity to secure constant ac-

---

[4] An assumption of this study is that the *Iliad* and *Odyssey* belong to the same culture and tradition and can profitably be discussed together. Thus, although the discussion focuses on the *Odyssey*, parallels from the *Iliad* are frequently used to illuminate specific points. Underlying this assumption is the belief that the differences the two poems display are primarily due to the differences between their settings. This hypothesis not only serves well in explaining specific points of difference, but it also coheres with one of the main thematic preoccupations of the epics themselves. The *Iliad* and the *Odyssey* are both centrally concerned with the effects of different settings on human experience. The *Iliad* is pervaded by a sense of its battlefield setting as different from that of peacetime and home, and its hero's story is shaped by the need to choose whether to remain in that setting or not. The *Odyssey* explores the meaning of setting by presenting similar sequences of action (for example, the reception of a stranger, a recurrent action that serves as a test for the poem's civilized values) taking place in a range of different settings.

knowledgment of that status through his own accomplishments is understood by his contemporaries to be a reflection of his birth and station. Thus, an assertion of identity is not simply a statement of fact but is also a claim to a certain status. A name is not simply a name but a kind of title, and it carries with it a certain entitlement. For that reason, names are not given neutrally but with a verb, *euchomai*, which means to say something in a particularly assertive or contentious way.[5]

A hero's status, although it derives from an association with the gods that may manifest itself in his ancestry or in divine support for his actions, is expressed, even constituted, through the honor he receives from other men. This is one aspect of the often-noted other-directedness of the Homeric self.[6] Homeric characters do not display the elaborate inner consciousness of characters in later classical and modern literature; rather they find their sense of self in their relations with the world outside

[5] Leonard Charles Muellner, *The Meaning of Homeric EYCHOMAI Through its Formulas*, esp. p. 99, where the definition "say (proudly, accurately, contentiously)" is proposed for εὔχομαι when used in secular contexts. The connection between name and status is well illustrated in the first episode of name giving in the *Odyssey*, the exchange in which Telemachus asks the disguised Athena who she is, and she ostensibly tells him, a conversation that is self-consciously typical in that both participants are trying to act like full-grown human heroes, although that is not what either of them actually is (*Od.* 1.170–188). Telemachus asks a series of questions that suggest that knowing his visitor's identity involves knowing where he comes from, who his parents are, and how and with whom he is traveling. These questions call forth a survey of the ways in which "Mentes'" honored status is expressed. He touches on his illustrious parentage, the home in which he bases his power, and his well-established relationship to another great hero, in this case Odysseus. Telemachus' question about how he came to Ithaca allows him to establish that he is traveling, not as a homeless wanderer but as the master of a ship full of followers, and that he is engaged in the properly heroic purpose of adding further to his already substantial fund of possessions. Because identity is so closely bound up with the status that derives from these sources, Homeric characters often identify themselves simply by referring to their ancestry or to their homes without mentioning their names. See Bernard Fenik, *Studies in the Odyssey*, 18–19.

[6] See Hermann Fränkel, *Early Greek Poetry and Philosophy*, 75–85; Alasdair MacIntyre, *After Virtue*, 114–122; James M. Redfield, *Nature and Culture in the Iliad*, 20–23.

them. Their identities are largely congruent with a social role that is determined by their valuation in others' eyes. Thus, they are sustained by the possession of outward signs of honor (mostly material possessions and social privileges) and are deeply threatened by the loss of those signs. For this reason, solitude is an especially harrowing experience; this can be seen from the first trial of Odysseus' endurance in the *Odyssey*, his journey from Calypso's island to Scheria in *Odyssey* 5 (the sole account in the Homeric epics of a character totally alone).

The intensity with which heroes feel threatened by a loss of honor lies behind the quarrel at the opening of the *Iliad*: the Achaeans find themselves without sufficient prizes to honor everyone, and neither Agamemnon nor Achilles can tolerate the suspension of honor that doing without a prize would mean. Neither can support the resulting disjunction between his merit, as he perceives it, and its outward expression; their view of the world does not allow for such a contradiction. Consequently, each takes drastic and eventually self-destructive action to eliminate that disjunction. Agamemnon insists on appropriating Achilles' prize, complaining that it would be unfitting for him alone of the Achaeans to be unhonored. Achilles responds more categorically by denying the capacity of this society that has diminished his own honor to confer honor properly. Proclaiming that he does not need the other Achaeans at all, since he is honored by Zeus, he withdraws from Achaean society altogether.

Throughout the *Iliad* heroes are provoked to action by threated suspensions of their honor. Such threats come either in taunts by gloating enemies[7] or in rebukes by generals who call the honor of their subordinates into question in order to spur them on to further action.[8] In such speeches a hero's defeat or inactivity is interpreted as a sign that he can no longer claim the

---

[7] E.g., *Il.* 8.161–166, where Hector, having put Diomedes to flight, taunts him by reminding him that the Achaeans used to honor him with the first place at feasts and predicting that they will no longer do so.

[8] E.g., *Il.* 4.338–348, where Agamemnon accuses Odysseus and Mnestheus of enjoying the privileges of heroic status without really earning them.

honor that has defined his position. These speeches generate a sense of crisis and provoke action because they question the connection between identity and evaluation implicit in an aristocratic society. This questioning is very clear when Athena goads Diomedes into fighting harder by suggesting that she is not really sure that he is the son of his father (*Il.* 5.800–813). The need to maintain their honor, of which such speeches are constant reminders, keeps heroes constantly performing the actions that honor rewards: it keeps them constantly risking their lives. The capacity of heroes to be provoked in this way is what helps to make them heroic; it is no accident that the *Iliad*'s greatest hero is noted for his quickness to anger.

Odysseus' distinguishing capacity for disguise marks him out as a hero of a different kind, a hero who not only endures but also embraces the obscurity that comes when either misfortunes or the challenges of rivals deprive him of the outer marks of heroic status. In Phaeacia, where he arrives without any emblem of his proper status, knows no one, and has no means of returning to his home (where his power is based), he chooses to suppress his name and to remain anonymous until he has again attained a position commensurate with that name.[9] On Ithaca, he responds to the usurpation of his home by younger and more numerous rivals by adopting the powerless persona of an old and homeless wanderer, and he remains unprovoked by the aggressive dishonor offered by his enemies.

Odysseus' willingness to undergo the humiliation involved

---

[9] For a thorough discussion and critique of attempts to explain Odysseus' seemingly illogical suppression of his name in Phaeacia, see Bernard Fenik, *Studies in the Odyssey*, 7–18. Fenik's own view (which is in part a development of the discussion of irony and disguise in the *Odyssey* by Uvo Hölscher, *Untersuchungen zur Form der Odyssee*, 58–72) is that the poet is less interested in giving Odysseus a logically satisfactory motive than in developing the rich and characteristically Odyssean irony that pervades the episode as a result of Odysseus' secrecy. I would simply add that part of what that irony is about is the gap between Odysseus' actual reputation and the anonymous status he has among the Phaeacians. For the view that Odysseus does not give his name when Arete asks him to because he is not at that time fully himself, see Wilhelm Mattes, *Odysseus bei den Phäaken*, 133.

especially in his Ithacan disguise suggests an appreciation of the inescapable forces that can prevent even the greatest hero and most privileged aristocrat from maintaining his eminent status. The history he adopts along with his disguise involves a fall from a position of prominence and prosperity through misfortune, and in that persona he speaks eloquently of the subjectedness of all humans to fortune and the necessity for endurance (most notably in his famous warning to Amphinomus, *Od.* 18.125–150).

But while Odysseus' disguise testifies to the limitations of human fortune, it also denies them. Because Odysseus' poverty and even his old age are represented as parts of a disguise, they are not inescapable conditions imposed on him by fortune but temporary and inessential states that he can shed at will. His apparent decline does not represent susceptibility to the changes that come with time, but rather a deliberately manipulated falsehood. Odysseus' disguise testifies to the reality of the suitors' challenge, but also belittles it; it is a sign of their temporary ascendance, but also a resource that assures his eventual and inevitable triumph over them. Thus the weakness to which Odysseus' disguise testifies is cast in an ironic light; its significance is always tempered by the audience's awareness of the reality that will be revealed when Odysseus' true identity becomes known.

Odysseus' disguise allows him to turn the humiliation imposed on him by his enemies into a defense against them. More broadly, the idea it dramatizes—that seeming debilities can be seen as part of a deliberately assumed disguise—offers a defense against the painful experience of powerlessness. The representation of weakness as a disguise implies that people are not themselves unless they are at their most impressive. In the specific context of the Homeric epics, the strategy of disguise overcomes the problem experienced by Achilles and other heroes in the *Iliad*, the problem of how a hero can survive a situation in which the honor through which he is identified to himself and to the world is not steadily available to him.[10] This victory

---

[10] Thus, while Bruno Snell's claim that "In Homer, a . . . separation between

shows why the conflict embedded in the epic tradition[11] between reliance on *biē*, "force," represented by Achilles, and reliance on *mētis*, "guile," represented by Odysseus, is resolved in the *Odyssey* in favor of *mētis*. The capacity for thinking one thing and saying another that goes with *mētis*, allows the hero to tolerate and even to manipulate disjunctions between his own ongoing sense of merit and outer appearances. For a hero like Odysseus, who is characterized by the epithet "πολύτροπος," which includes among its connotations "versatility" and "adaptability," such disjunctions are not misfortunes but part of a plot that reflects Odysseus' ability to control not only himself but his fortunes.[12]

The *Odyssey*'s solution in favor of *mētis* is aided by the way Odysseus' disguise casts the suspension of recognition in the broader sense in terms of the suspension of identity in the most literal sense. The genuine conflict between past and present valuations that is involved when a hero, for whatever reason, cannot live up to his reputation becomes differently weighted when it is cast in terms of whether or not a hero's identity is known. Whatever his fortunes, a person has something that can be called a stable identity, which derives from the circumstances of his birth, his appearance (which is of course a reflection of his parentage), and his history. As the Phaeacian king Alcinous

---

external and internal values is never made" (*The Discovery of the Mind*, 49) is certainly overstated, the *Odyssey*'s stress on disguise does not, as Joseph Russo has argued ("The Inner Man in Archilochus and the *Odyssey*," 145–146), exemplify a distinction between inner and outer values so much as an attempt to cope with fluctuations of external circumstances in the absence of such a distinction.

[11] For a recent discussion of this conflict, see Gregory Nagy, *The Best of the Achaeans*, 45–49.

[12] On *mētis* as a quality that protects against the vicissitudes of time, see Marcel Detienne and Jean-Pierre Vernant, *Cunning Intelligence in Greek Culture and Society*, esp. 13–14, 20. As Detienne and Vernant point out, the nature of the man who is *polutropos* can be apprehended in the way he resembles the man who is *ephēmeros*, who represents the extreme of susceptibility to fortune and change, but with the crucial difference that the one who is *polutropos* actively controls his mutability. "The *polutropos* one, on the other hand, is distinguished by the control he possesses: subtle and shifting as he is, he is always master of himself and is only unstable in appearance" (40).

points out to his disguised guest, "*οὐ μὲν γάρ τις πάμπαν ἀνώνυμός ἐστ' ἀνθρώπων*," "No one of men is entirely anonymous" (*Od.* 8.552).[13] While the connection between identity and status may, in moments of crisis, such as those dramatized in the *Iliad*, become subject to question, the actual possession of identity—what is expressed in the claim to be a certain person who was given a certain name by certain parents—is not a matter of opinion. Thus any suspension of identity represents not an open question but an obscuring of the truth, and it is impossible to regard it without a degree of detachment or irony that applies to the dishonor involved as well.

The representation of dishonor as disguise circumvents the connection between performance and truth embodied in the heroic conception of identity, a connection that is prevalent in archaic Greek thought generally.[14] Conversely, the equation, as the hero's disguise is shed, of heroic performance with the establishment of an unchanging truth gives that performance a definitive, conclusive character it otherwise lacks. What a hero in the *Iliad* proves by defeating another in battle is true only until his next encounter, but what Odysseus proves by stringing the bow and shooting through the axes is always true.[15]

The superiority over circumstances allowed by Odysseus' disguise can be related to the fact that disguise is typically not a human but a divine strategy. As has been increasingly noted, the *Odyssey's* account of Odysseus' homecoming is cast in the form of a kind of story that is regularly told about the gods. Greek mythology provides many examples of gods who disguise

[13] Alcinous' statement alludes even more forcefully than he realizes to the notion that everyone has a claim on some place in the world that can never quite be taken away from him. For it contains a punning reference to "*Outis*," "No one," the disguise that Odysseus uses against the Cyclops (as is noted by Jenny Strauss Clay, *The Wrath of Athena*, 28, n41). Thus the statement suggests that the conditions that enforce anonymity may be seen not only as inessential but as a deliberately manipulated screen.

[14] For a thorough account of this connection in archaic thought, see Marcel Detienne, *Les maîtres de vérité dans la Grèce archaïque*.

[15] Thus his action is compared with song, of which one function is to tell the truth, in the simile at *Od.* 21.406–410.

11

themselves as mortals, go among men, usually for the purpose of testing them, and ultimately disclose themselves.[16] Gods often disguise themselves in the Homeric epics: Aphrodite in *Iliad* 3 appears to Helen as an old serving woman, and Athena in the *Odyssey* appears to Telemachus disguised first as "Mentes" and then as Mentor. And stories of disguised gods engaging with mortals are a prominent feature of the Homeric Hymns, for example Demeter's visit to the house of Celeus, Dionysus' encounter with the pirates, and Aphrodite's seduction of Anchises.

The *Odyssey* is pervaded by an underlying analogy between stories of this kind and the events of Odysseus' return. At one point this analogy is drawn explicit, although unwittingly, for the speakers do not realize that it is Odysseus they are speaking of—when the rest of the suitors warn Antinous of the danger of mistreating the stranger:

Ἀντίνο᾽, οὐ μὲν κάλ᾽ ἔβαλες δύστηνον ἀλήτην,
οὐλόμεν᾽, εἰ δή πού τις ἐπουράνιος θεός ἐστι.
καί τε θεοὶ ξείνοισιν ἐοικότες ἀλλοδαποῖσι,
παντοῖοι τελέθοντες, ἐπιστρωφῶσι πόληας,
ἀνθρώπων ὕβριν τε καὶ εὐνομίην ἐφορῶντες.

Antinous, you did not do well to hit this wretched wanderer.
A curse on you—he might be a god from heaven.
For the gods do liken themselves to strangers from abroad,
taking on all sorts of forms, and they roam through our cities,
observing the violence and the orderliness of men.
(*Od.* 17.483–487)

This analogy is also expressed in the similarity between the scenes in which Odysseus sheds his disguise and reveals himself

---

[16] For an extensive list of references to stories in classical mythology of gods going among mortals in disguise, see Anne Pippin Burnett, "Pentheus and Dionysos: Host and Guest," 24–25, n8. On the parallels between this kind of myth and the *Odyssey*, see Emily Kearns, "The Return of Odysseus: A Homeric Theoxeny"; Cora Sowa, *Traditional Themes and the Homeric Hymns*, 250–261.

and scenes of divine epiphany.[17] The words with which he introduces himself to the Phaeacians, "εἴμ᾽ Ὀδυσεὺς Λαερτιάδης, ὅς πᾶσι δόλοισιν / ἀνθρώποισι μέλω, καί μευ κλέος οὐρανὸν ἵκει," "I am Odysseus son of Laertes, known for my deceits / to all men, and my fame goes up to heaven," (*Od.* 9.19–20), are strikingly similar to those with which disguised gods reveal themselves in several of the Homeric Hymns.[18] Other moments of self-disclosure involve other typical features of divine epiphanies: sudden transformation[19] (often accompanied by increased stature), the manifestation of special powers, and the announcement of punishments and rewards. In particular, Odysseus' self-disclosure to the suitors closely parallels a god's self-revelation to punish the unworthy.[20]

[17] For the typical features of divine epiphanies, see F. Pfister, *RE*, suppl. 4: 277–323; N. J. Richardson, *The Homeric Hymn to Demeter*, esp. 188–191; H. J. Rose, "Divine Disguisings."

[18] Cf. *Hymn to Demeter*, 268–269: "εἰμὶ δὲ Δημήτηρ τιμάοχος, ἥ τε μέγιστον / ἀθανάτοις θνητοῖσί τ᾽ ὄνεαρ καὶ χάρμα τέτυκται," "I am Demeter the honored, the greatest / benefit and joy to immortals and to mortals." *Hymn to Apollo*, 480; *Hymn to Dionysus*, 56–57. Nausicaa's identification of herself at *Od.* 6.196–197 also takes this form, but she does not identify herself by her own name and attributes but rather those of her more powerful father, from whom her social prestige derives.

[19] The suddenness of Odysseus' self-revelations is especially stressed in the hypothetical account of his return with which he tests Eumaeus and Philoetius (*Od.* 21.195–196) and in Amphimedon's retrospective account (*Od.* 24.160).

[20] He suddenly changes his appearance by throwing off his rags (*Od.* 22.1). He stands on the threshold to reveal himself (*Od.* 22.2), a gesture that is related to a number of thematic strands in the poem but clearly resembles Demeter's partial epiphany on the threshold of Celeus' house in the *Hymn to Demeter*. (On the significance of the motif of the threshold in the *Odyssey*, see Charles P. Segal, "Transition and Ritual in Odysseus' Return," 337–340. For its more general connotations, see N. J. Richardson, *The Homeric Hymn to Demeter*, 189.) He displays his extraordinary powers by performing a feat only he can do, dispatching Antinous with the bow only Odysseus can wield (*Od.* 22.8–12). Like a newly revealed god, he reproaches the mortals who have displeased him and metes out swift punishment. He points to the suitors' specific transgressions, their desire for his wife and his possessions that has blinded them to the possibility of his return and made them overlook the operation both of divine justice and of human vengeance (*Od.* 22.35–41).

13

In the case of the gods, it is clear that the conditions that make up their disguises are alien to their true nature. When they pretend to be mortals, they are concealing the characteristics that define them as gods. This is underscored by the way they tend to disguise themselves as mortals who, like the disguised Odysseus, are old and dispossessed, who show outward signs of the susceptibility to fortune and the passage of time, that all mortals share and that sets mortals apart from the gods.[21] Odysseus' participation in this divine scenario defines his superiority to other mortals. It is an elaboration, on a grand scale, of the characterization of heroes as comparable to gods that is common in the Homeric epics and is reflected in a number of familiar epithets, such as "θεοειδής" and "θεοείκελος," which mean "godlike." Through his adoption of a disguise, Odysseus is portrayed as capable of transcending normal human limits, as being like the gods for whom the experience of mortal limitation is a form of playacting.

The disguise that is strategically essential to Odysseus' return also by its nature expresses what that return signifies—the conquest of normal mortal constraints.[22] Odysseus' return is only made possible by repeated evasions of death. He survives a set of experiences that comprises many forms of engagement with death: the risky life of a warrior at Troy, encounters with deadly monsters, the oblivion of life with Calypso, a journey to the underworld, solitary confrontation of the elements.[23] Along with

[21] For examples of goddesses disguising themselves as old women, see N. J. Richardson, *The Homeric Hymn to Demeter*, 101. For the conception of old age as something that can be sloughed off, ibid. 276.

[22] The link between disguise and the disabilities of low social status, weakness and mortality is beautifully illustrated by a detail: the disguised Odysseus always sits on a δίφρος, the kind of chair used by women, slaves, and those who are about to die, but once he has revealed himself, he sits on a θρόνος, the proper seat of aristocratic men. See George W. Houston, "Θρόνος, Δίφρος, and Odysseus' Change from Beggar to Avenger."

[23] Odysseus' survival of these experiences represents the specifically Homeric version of what folklorists see as fundamental to every story of return and recognition: return from death, and rebirth. See, for example, Barry Powell, *Composition by Theme in the Odyssey*, 4–5, esp. the statement, "But concealment is

Odysseus' ability to evade death goes freedom from the effects of time. The very notion of Odysseus' return involves a denial of the normal human restriction to a single linear lifetime. Odysseus is able to experience both of the lives that Achilles in the *Iliad* is forced to choose between, returning from a life devoted to seeking *kleos* away from home to start over and live out a quiet life at home.

The challenges Odysseus faces when he reaches Ithaca are consequences of the passage of time. The suitors represent a new generation that has arisen in his absence, and it is clear that he can only hope to defeat them if he is still as he was before he left for the Trojan War. Thus, the hopes of Odysseus' old friends for his return are explicitly tied to the idea that he will be as he was on some remembered occasion before his departure for Troy.[24] When Odysseus does encounter the suitors, the question of whether he is still as he was in the past becomes an explicit issue of their contest: he formulates his desire to have a chance with the bow as a wish to test this question (*Od.* 21.281–284); when he succeeds in stringing the bow, he points out that this is confirmation that he has retained his strength (*Od.* 21.426–427).

Odysseus conceals himself from the suitors by a disguise that mimics what the normal effects of the past twenty years could be expected to be. This is dramatized at the suspenseful point in Book 19 when Penelope seems, for a moment, to have recognized him prematurely. Ordering Eurycleia to give the stranger a bath, she says,

---

typologically equivalent to death and disclosure to birth." For return from death as the underlying connotation of diction associated with return home in the *Odyssey*, see Douglas Frame, *The Myth of Return in Early Greek Epic*, esp. 9–18.

[24] E.g., "Mentes" at *Od.* 1.255–266; Menelaus at *Od.* 4.341–346. An interesting parallel to these reminiscences is found at *Il.* 4.317–325 where Nestor expresses a similar wish to be as he was during a specific exploit of his youth, but then adds that it does not matter that he is not because there are others younger to do the fighting. In Odysseus' case it does matter because he must do his own fighting, and it is the presence of younger people that he is fighting against.

νίψον σοῖο ἄνακτος ὁμήλικα. καί που Ὀδυσσεὺς
ἤδη τοιόσδ᾽ ἐστὶ πόδας τοιόσδε τε χεῖρας·
αἶψα γὰρ ἐν κακότητι βροτοὶ καταγηράσκουσιν.

Wash your master's agemate. For Odysseus
must by now have just such feet and hands.
In misfortune men grow old quickly.
(*Od.* 19.358–360)

When he reveals himself, he does so as a god often does, by becoming suddenly younger, recovering what is understood to be
his true appearance as someone in his prime.[25] This element of
sudden rejuvenation is particularly marked in the recognitions
with Telemachus, in which Telemachus comments on it directly
(*Od.* 16.194–200), and with Penelope, in which Penelope does
not recognize Odysseus until he recovers the appearance he had
when he left for Troy (*Od.* 23.175–176).[26]

Thus, the recognition scenes of the *Odyssey*, in which Odysseus' return is announced and his continued capacity to claim
the status that constitutes his identity is confirmed, express this
exceptional hero's transcendence of the fluctuations of fortune
and of mortality. The meaning of these scenes is, therefore, very
different from that often attributed to episodes of recognition
or (to use Aristotle's term) *anagnōrisis*, especially when they are
found in tragedy: the confrontation of those harsh truths that
people generally try to ignore. Thus it is significant that, of the
two Homeric epics, the *Iliad*, which stresses the painful awareness of human limitation that is often labeled tragic, contains no
scenes of recognition, while the *Odyssey*, which offers a counter
to that vision, is, as Aristotle put it, "ἀναγνώρισις . . . διόλου,"
"recognition throughout" (*Poetics* 1459b15).[27]

---

[25] Cf. Odysseus' companions, who appear younger on their "return" from
their transformation into swine (*Od.* 10.395–396).

[26] Cf. *Od.* 19.165–250, where as the stranger Odysseus convinces Penelope
he is speaking reliably of having met Odysseus by describing the clothes he wore
and the followers who accompanied him at that time.

[27] Thus the application of this "tragic" conception of recognition to epic goes
hand-in-hand with a greater respect for the courageously reduced vision of the
Iliad than for the more romantic, optimistic vision of the *Odyssey*. See, for ex-

INTRODUCTION

The notion that recognizing and being recognized are activities that mark the conquest of mortality not only underlies the construction of the *Odyssey*'s plot as a series of recognition scenes, but also surfaces throughout the Homeric epics in less dramatically significant episodes in which forms of the verb for recognizing someone, "γιγνώσκω," are used apart from the motif of disguise. For example, in *Iliad* 15 Apollo goes to look for Hector, who has fallen into a swoon after being hit by a rock thrown by Ajax, and finds him sitting up, regaining his strength, and recognizing his companions, "ἀμφὶ ἓ γιγνώσκων ἑτάρους" (*Il.* 15.241–242). Hector's recognition of his companions expresses the recovery of consciousness that marks his evasion of death.[28] The connection between recognition and the conquest of death is even clearer in the account of Odysseus' visit to the underworld. There Odysseus is disturbed to find that his mother does not acknowledge his presence; but once, following the instructions of Teiresias, he allows her to drink the blood of the sheep he has sacrificed, she is reanimated and recognizes him at once (*Od.* 11.153).[29] In the *Iliad* death makes those who fall in battle and lie unburied hard to recognize (*Il.* 7.424). Significantly, the term *sēma*, "sign," designates both the token by which a living person is recognized and the tomb by which the memory of a dead person is kept alive—if he is sufficiently honored to be accorded the recognition of a glorious burial.[30]

---

ample, Thomas Greene's comment that "The most important recognition scenes in epic are not between two people but between the hero and his mortality." *The Descent from Heaven*, 15.

[28] Hector himself says that he expected to die (*Il.* 15.251–252), and when he next returns to the battlefield, the Greek hero Thoas expresses surprise and disappointment that Hector has eluded death (*Il.* 15.286–289).

[29] Similarly, Odysseus' conversations with Agamemnon (*Od.* 11.390), Achilles (*Od.* 11.471), and Heracles (*Od.* 11.615) all begin with their recognition of him. Only Heracles recognizes Odysseus on sight without drinking the blood, presumably because Odysseus is meeting with an *eidōlon*, or phantom, of Heracles, a stand-in for the real Heracles, who has not died but has joined the immortal gods, an *eidōlon* that shares the real Heracles' immortality.

[30] It should be noted that the Trojans who have become hard to recognize at

Odysseus, for all his evasion of mortality, is not an immortal god but the most godlike of mortals. His mortality is reaffirmed when he deliberately chooses the goal of returning to Ithaca over the chance to become immortal. His success in achieving that goal is only meaningful if it is acknowledged by others, and it can only be acknowledged if he sheds his disguise and is recognized as his mortal self by other mortal characters. This need to be known as his true mortal self is dramatized in his recognition scene with Telemachus. Odysseus is frustrated when Telemachus is convinced, because of his sudden transformation, that he must be one of the gods (*Od.* 16.194–200). He responds rather sharply that he is not a god, that his changed appearance is due to Athena (*Od.* 16.201–212). He insists on recognition not as a god but as a hero, a mortal who resembles the gods and enjoys special divine favor.[31]

To be recognized as himself Odysseus must win the assent of Telemachus and others to a two-sided notion, a definition of himself that is based on a simile—the comparison of a man to a god—and that therefore involves both a divine and a human term; they must agree to a conception of Odysseus that preserves rather than resolves the ambiguity inherent in his disguise. He must reassert an identity that, while it may be conditioned by divine favor, is rooted in a social position conferred on him by other mortals. Thus, he must negotiate the world of those for whom the conditions represented by his disguise are not an illusion but a reality. For a disguise is not simply false: its success depends on its resemblance to the truth. At the same time that the falseness of a disguise suggests that it is not to be

---

Il. 7.424 receive only a mass burning with no mourning (*Il.* 7.427) and no tomb. On these two meanings of *sēma*, see Dale S. Sinos, *Achilles, Patroklos and the Meaning of Philos*, 48–49, and Gregory Nagy, "Sēma and Noēsis: Some Illustrations," 45–50. Nagy also points out the connection between the possession of *noos*, the mental faculty employed in recognition, and the return from death.

[31] When Odysseus is mistaken for a god earlier by Alcinous, it is at a time when he is not ready to reveal his identity. So he responds by insisting that he bears no resemblance to the gods and receives only misery from them (*Od.* 7.208–241).

taken seriously, its capacity to seem true, to command belief, demands that it be taken seriously. The mortal disguises that the gods take on are accurate descriptions of the conditions in which mortal men must live, and Odysseus' disguise describes conditions to which he, too, might have been subject.

Alcinous' blandly reassuring statement that no one is anonymous is only true within the world of human civilization that his protected island exemplifies. Only the society that men construct for themselves to mitigate their difference from the gods can counter the real threat of annihilation that lies outside the borders of the civilized world—or within the confines of a civilized world in decline, such as the Ithaca of Book 1. Thus, the realization of Odysseus' return depends on his negotiation of the human social world, as well as on his construction of a master plot with Athena. He must reconstruct the relationships with members of his family and household that articulate his place in the world, and he must do so by defining himself in relation to the institutions of human society. The second half of the *Odyssey* tells two parallel stories: the story of Odysseus' reliance on Athena and his divine connections, and the story of his reliance on other mortals and the resources of the human social world. The narrative in which these two stories unfold becomes an exploration of how they relate to one another and finally of how they unite to bring about Odysseus' triumphant recognition. The chapters that follow trace that interrelation, focusing on the central institutions of peacetime Homeric society: the household, in Chapters 1 and 2; hospitality, in Chapter 3; marriage, in Chapter 4; and heroic song, in Chapter 5.

ONE

Recognition and
the Return of Odysseus

DURING their meeting in Book 13, Athena and Odysseus sit
down together at the base of an olive tree and concoct the plot
through which, imitating the story of a disguised god, he will
defeat his enemies. This then becomes the plot, in a literary
sense, of the second half of the poem, a plot shaped by the de-
ployment of a divine strategy to make possible a story of mortal
revenge. Its climactic moment is Odysseus' imitation of a divine
epiphany when, having strung the bow, he reveals himself to
the suitors with bewildering suddenness and proceeds to punish them for their transgressions against him.

But while Odysseus' moment of triumph over the suitors resembles a divine epiphany, it also differs from one in that it is
only possible with the aid of certain human accomplices, whose
help is secured in a series of private scenes of recognition that
structure the second half of the poem.[1] As he advances geographically towards the center of his house, where he will confront and defeat the suitors, Odysseus also advances strategically. He accumulates a group of supporters who will make his
success possible in a series of reunions that take the form of recognition scenes: with Athena when he arrives on the shore of
Ithaca; with Telemachus when he has arrived at the hut of the
swineherd Eumaeus at the edge of his own holdings; with the

---

[1] On recognition by a future accomplice as a standard feature of South Slavic
return songs, see Albert B. Lord, *The Singer of Tales*, 103. That Odysseus' return
takes the form of a series of reunions means that it is an especially elaborate and
dramatic version of the narrative pattern through which return is regularly expressed in Homeric epic. Cf. Nausicaa's return to the house of Alcinous (*Od.*
7.1–13), Telemachus' return to the house (*Od.* 17.26–43), Priam's return to
Troy with Hector's body (*Il.* 24.697ff).

dog Argus when he arrives at the threshold of his house; with his nurse Eurycleia at the hearth; with Eumaeus and Philoetius in the courtyard outside the megaron as he embarks on his action against the suitors.

When the decisive moment of the contest of the bow is at hand, Odysseus is able to rely on the aid of all those to whom his true identity is known, and they act as a kind of team to bring about his success. Penelope—who, uniquely, acts as his accomplice without knowing who he is—proposes the contest and insists that Odysseus be allowed to take part. Telemachus orders that the bow be placed in Odysseus' hands and urges Eumaeus on when he falters. Eumaeus hands Odysseus the bow and tells Eurycleia, in Telemachus' name, to close the doors. Similarly, when Odysseus has moved from his recovery of the house to his recovery of the estate as a whole and has been recognized by Laertes and by Dolius and his sons, he forms from them, and Telemachus, a band of followers with whom to face the attack of the suitors' relatives. These encounters diminish the success of the suitors' challenge, both in the sense that they reduce the number of people from whom Odysseus' return is concealed, of whose recognition he is deprived as a result of the suitors' presence, and in the sense that they give him the allies he will need to remove the suitors from his house.

Odysseus' time-defying defeat of the suitors requires this acquisition of accomplices and thus depends on the conquest of time in another, more ordinary way as well: it depends on the reanimation of past relationships. The permanence of Odysseus' claim to his position may mimic the timeless power of the gods, but it actually rests on the durability of his domestic relationships, his capacity to recover a series of roles defined by his relations with others: father, son, husband, and master.[2] The success of his return is dependent on the qualities that make such relationships last, the close identification of interests that makes the association beneficial to both participants. The suc-

[2] On the second half of the *Odyssey* as expressing Odysseus' self-definition through the recovery of social roles, see Cedric H. Whitman, *Homer and the Heroic Tradition*, 301–305.

cessive scenes of recognition in which Odysseus' base of support in Ithaca is reconstructed articulate the *Odyssey*'s account of his return in two senses: through their sequence, these scenes provide the structure of the plot; and through their internal form, they express the interdependence of the relationships that make it possible for Odysseus to come back.

In their typical form, the *Odyssey*'s recognition scenes act out the essential mutuality of the relationships that are being revived.[3] They involve a process of identification and testing leading to emotionally-charged reunions, which are experienced in gestures of physical union such as embracing, kissing, or in the case of Odysseus and Penelope, making love.[4] Within these episodes there is often a progression from expressions of solitary, one-sided emotion, which often evoke the pain of the separation that is now to be cured, to the shared emotion of reunion.[5] These reunions are achieved through a two-sided process consisting of disclosure of identity on one side and recognition of identity on the other, gestures which are not neutral but have the broader connotations of mutual acknowledgment or praise, implying a willing concession of honor or service on both sides.[6]

[3] For a more detailed account of the *Odyssey*'s recognition scenes as versions of a narrative type, see Sheila H. Murnaghan, "*Anagnōrisis* in the *Odyssey*," Chapter 2.

[4] *Od.* 16.213–219; 21.222–225; 23.205–246, 288–296 (cf. 10.347); 24.345–348. Cf. *Od.* 13.353–360, where Odysseus kisses the shore of Ithaca when he has recognized his home. During the tense recognition with Eurycleia in 19, this element of physical contact recurs in a hostile form: *Od.* 19.479–481, cf. 4.259. At *Od.* 23.32–34, where for a moment Penelope accepts the news of Odysseus' return, this embrace is displaced from Odysseus to his messenger Eurycleia.

[5] These expressions of one-sided emotion, which give way to the shared joy of reunion, may take the form of pleasure in a reunion the other person does not yet realize is taking place (e.g. *Od.* 16.190–191); or sorrow at the absence of someone who, while present, is still unrecognized (e.g., *Od.* 19.361–362; 24.315–317); or pity at the sorrow of someone who mourns someone who is present but unrecognized (e.g., *Od.* 24.234).

[6] This connotation is reflected in the use of diction associated with honor to describe recognition of identity. For example, when Odysseus explains to Te-

When, under the dangerous, necessarily clandestine conditions of Odysseus' return, he identifies himself to one of his loyal supporters, that gesture of self-disclosure is also a gesture of acknowledgment; it acknowledges, sometimes after a considerable period of testing, the demonstrated reliability and loyalty that make him willing to risk disclosing himself. At the same time, when Odysseus identifies himself, he stakes a claim to a certain status, and those who recognize him acquiesce in that claim.[7] Their recognition of his identity is not unlike the modern idea of political recognition, acknowledgment of legitimacy in a position of power. Penelope's suitors, who withhold this acknowledgment from Odysseus, prove to be incapable of recognizing his identity, while each of his loyal supporters acts out his acquiescence to Odysseus' claims by recognizing him. The importance of mutual loyalty to the meaning of recognition scenes is underscored by the way these scenes regularly end with the two figures who have been reunited plotting together against their shared enemies.[8]

The account of Odysseus' self-disclosure to Eumaeus and Philoetius illustrates well how these episodes of recognition of identity also act out an identification of interests that is based on mutual recognition in a broader sense and outweighs in importance the immediate occasion of the removal of one figure's dis-

---

lemachus that Penelope cannot recognize him because of his beggar's disguise, he says "that is why she dishonors [ἀτιμάζει] me and does not say that I am her husband" (*Od.* 2.116).

[7] Gregory Nagy has shown that in Homeric poetry recognition entails knowledge of the code or system in which a *sēma*, "sign," participates. "Sēma and Noēsis: Some Illustrations," 38–39. Recognition of identity, then, entails appreciation of the system of social relations according to which people are at once connected to one another and ranked in relation to one another.

[8] *Od.* 4.253–256; 13.361–428; 16.235–320, where this element of plotting seems to be present largely in order to complete the recognition scene, since the plans made are impractical and are never fulfilled. (On this problem, see Hartmut Erbse, *Beiträge zum Verständnis der Odyssee*, 3–41; Bernard Fenik, *Studies in the Odyssey*, 111–117; W. J. Woodhouse, *The Composition of Homer's Odyssey* 158–168); *Od.* 19.495–498; 21.228–241; 23.350–365; 24.351–360. Cf. also *Od.* 19.570–587, where this element occurs in the absence of actual recognition.

guise.[9] First, Odysseus asks for a hypothetical show of loyalty by asking what Eumaeus and Philoetius would do if Odysseus were to return. When Eumaeus responds by praying to all the gods for Odysseus' return, then Odysseus discloses himself.

αὐτὰρ ἐπεὶ δὴ τῶν γε νόον νημερτέ᾽ ἀνέγνω,
ἐξαῦτίς σφε ἔπεσσιν ἀμειβόμενος προσέειπεν·
"Ἔνδον μὲν δὴ ὅδ᾽ αὐτὸς ἐγώ, κακὰ πολλὰ μογήσας,
ἤλυθον εἰκοστῷ ἔτεϊ ἐς πατρίδα γαῖαν.
γιγνώσκω δ᾽ ὡς σφῶϊν ἐελδομένοισιν ἱκάνω
οἴοισι δμώων . . ."

But, when he had recognized their unswerving mind,
he spoke to them again, answering them with words,
"Here I am, myself, within the house, having struggled much;
I have returned in the twentieth year to the land of my fathers.
I recognize that I come wished for by you
alone of my servants . . ."
(*Od.* 21.205-210)

Here the language of recognition (ἀνέγνω, 205; γιγνώσκω, 209) is applied to Odysseus' apprehension of Eumaeus and Philoetius' loyalty, their willingness to recognize him,[10] which he acknowledges through his self-disclosure. The words with which Odysseus discloses himself are at once the announcement of a prayed-for benefit and a boast containing a bid for acknowledgment of his achievement in returning home and for aid in his

---

[9] Cf. *Od.* 22.501, where, in the account of Odysseus' reunion with his faithful serving women, what is stressed is Odysseus' recognition of them, even though he is the one who has been in disguise. Similarly, Odysseus' companions recognize him after they have been turned back from swine into men (*Od.* 10.397). And in the episode from *Iliad* 15 discussed in the Introduction, Hector recognizes his companions even though he is the one who has nearly died (*Il.* 15.252). In those examples, the characters who have, in some sense, returned to life experience that return by acknowledging other people who play some role in making it possible.

[10] Specifically, he recognizes their *noos*, "mind," which is precisely the mental faculty involved in recognition. See Gregory Nagy, "Sēma and Noēsis: Some Illustrations."

further struggle.[11] An action consisting of the revelation and recognition of identity becomes the occasion for a dialogue articulating a series of mutual claims and obligations, a dialogue involving expressions of praise that are verbal tokens of a mutual commitment to material aid.

The mutuality and interdependence of Odysseus' relationships with members of his household is, then, represented formally in the structure of the scenes of recognition in which, as his identity becomes more and more widely known, his disguise is gradually dispelled. But the mutuality of experience between Odysseus and the loyal members of his household is more complex and pervasive. As his dependents, these characters derive their identities and capacities from their place in the *oikos*, "household," of which he is the head. In his absence, Laertes, Telemachus, Eumaeus, and Penelope cling to their literal identities as father, son, loyal servant, and wife of Odysseus. But Odysseus' absence and the presence of the suitors make it difficult for them to enjoy the status, to exercise the power, that ought to be inextricable from those roles. Like Odysseus when he lands on the shore of Ithaca, they experience a disjunction between their nominal identities and the places they ought to occupy in the social world. And that disjunction is similarly represented in their cases as a kind of disguise. Theirs is not the deliberately contrived and willfully assumed disguise that Odysseus takes on, but rather genuine experience of the unimpressive appearance, powerlessness, subjugation to time, foreignness to the house of Odysseus, and lowered social status that are elements in his disguise. But these experiences nonetheless take on the character of disguises because they prove reversible, and like Odysseus' more literal disguise, are removed with the revelation of his return.

Thus the reunions of these characters with Odysseus involve these characters' own shedding of disguise and recognition as well as his. And Odysseus, in the course of repossessing his

[11] Odysseus' words of self-revelation typically contain this element of boasting: *Od.* 9.19–21; 16.205–206; 24.321–322.

25

house, imitates Athena not only by revealing himself but also by bringing out of disguise those on whom his recovery of Ithaca depends, much as she uncovers Ithaca from its obscuring mist. In different ways, depending on the nature of their relationships to Odysseus, the members of Odysseus' household rehearse their own versions of return and recognition. The way in which each recognition scene functions as a climactic moment in both of two intersecting stories of recovery and recognition conditions, in each case, its particular timing and construction; in responding to these factors, these episodes become precise depictions of how the distinct but interdependent characters involved are related to one another.

That the effects of Odysseus' absence create a kind of disguise is most apparent in the case of the last of the figures by whom Odysseus is recognized, his father Laertes. The condition into which Laertes has fallen is described to Odysseus by his mother Anticleia when he meets her in the underworld.

πατὴρ δὲ σὸς αὐτόθι μίμνει
ἀγρῷ, οὐδὲ πόλινδε κατέρχεται· οὐδέ οἱ εὐναὶ
δέμνια καὶ χλαῖναι καὶ ῥήγεα σιγαλόεντα,
ἀλλ᾽ ὅ γε χεῖμα μὲν εὕδει ὅθι δμῶες ἐνὶ οἴκῳ
ἐν κόνι ἄγχι πυρός, κακὰ δὲ χροῒ εἵματα εἶται·
αὐτὰρ ἐπὴν ἔλθῃσι θέρος τεθαλυῖά τ᾽ ὀπώρη,
πάντῃ οἱ κατὰ γουνὸν ἀλωῆς οἰνοπέδοιο
φύλλων κεκλιμένων χθαμαλαὶ βεβλήαται εὐναί·
ἔνθ᾽ ὅ γε κεῖτ᾽ ἀχέων, μέγα δὲ φρεσὶ πένθος ἀέξει
σὸν νόστον ποθέων· χαλεπὸν δ᾽ ἐπὶ γῆρας ἱκάνει.

       Your father stays there
on the farm, and does not go to town. He has no bed
or bed clothes or blankets or shining coverings,
but in the winter he sleeps in the house where the servants do
in the dust near the fire, and wears vile clothing;
but when summer comes and the fruitful harvest-time,
everywhere along the slope of his vineyard,
he throws together his bed of fallen leaves.

And there he lies grieving, and a great sorrow grows in his
  mind
as he longs for your homecoming. And harsh old age comes
  over him.

(*Od.* 11.187–196)

In response to Odysseus' absence, Laertes himself has withdrawn from both home and society. He has fallen into a state of
grief that combines elements of Odysseus' anonymous persona
on Phaeacia and his deliberate disguise on Ithaca.[12] Like Odysseus when he arrives on the Phaeacian shore, Laertes is barely

[12] The way Laertes' response to Odysseus' absence both mimics the effects of
that absence on Odysseus himself and has the temporary and inessential qualities of disguise reflects the conception of mourning as sympathetic imitation
that is found throughout Homeric poetry. As James Redfield puts it, "The dead
person is going on a journey and the impulse of the mourners is to go with him;
the most perfect mourning would be suicide, and this is treated as a real possibility ([*Il.*] 18.34). Short of this the mourner may suspend his life, as Achilles
abstains from food, sleep, washing, and the act of love ([*Il.*] 24.129–131)"
(*Nature and Culture in the Iliad*, 181). This conception involves the same kind
of ambiguity inherent in literal disguises: the mourner's seeming death expresses the degree to which his own efficacy and identity are threatened by the
loss, while the affinity of his behavior to playacting expresses the intrinsic tran-
sitoriness of mourning. In the *Odyssey* one character, Anticleia, does respond to
Odysseus' absence with mourning so intense that it leads to her own death, but
for the other characters, mourning remains a different experience from the one
it imitates. The close connection between the themes of mourning, disguise,
and the imitation of death also underlies the myth told in the *Homeric Hymn to
Demeter*. Like Laertes, Demeter disfigures herself in grief for the loss of a child,
with the result that she is unrecognizable (94–95). Similarly, when she first
misses Persephone, she refuses to bathe (50), an action that regularly leads to
recognition, and when she enters the house of Celeus, she holds a veil in front
of her face (197), a gesture of mourning that is also, like Odysseus' similar attempts in Phaeacia, designed to conceal her identity. Demeter's mourning and
disguise also involve a kind of mimicking of death (and, because she is a goddess, the idea that any involvement with death is only playacting is a given of
the story). She takes on the appearance of an old woman and withdraws from
Olympus to involve herself with mortals—an action that parallels Persephone's
removal to the realm of death. Cf. *Hymn to Aphrodite*, 241–246, where Aphrodite says she is enveloped by ἄχος, "grief," because of her involvement with the
mortal Anchises who will be enveloped (the verb used in each case is ἀμφικα-

alive and barely participating in civilized life. In both cases this virtually uncivilized state is represented through sleeping, not indoors in a bed or at least in a fixed place, but outdoors on the ground in a random pile of leaves. In fact, Laertes is dressed in an anomalous costume[13] that seems to suggest a kind of animal suit, as if he were no longer fully human (*Od.* 24.229–231).[14] Like Odysseus when he disguises himself both on his return to Ithaca and during the spying mission to Troy (as is recounted to Telemachus by Helen in *Odyssey* 4), Laertes has taken on the rags and activities of a poor servant and the outward signs of old age.

When Odysseus meets Laertes in *Odyssey* 24, Laertes is much more conspicuously disguised than Odysseus is.[15] When Odysseus first addresses his father, he comments on his appearance, saying to him, in essence, "You seem to be in disguise."

ὦ γέρον, οὐκ ἀδαημονίη σ᾽ ἔχει ἀμφιπολεύειν
ὄρχατον, ἀλλ᾽ εὖ τοι κομιδὴ ἔχει, οὐδέ τι πάμπαν,
οὐ φυτόν, οὐ συκέη, οὐκ ἄμπελος, οὐ μὲν ἐλαίη,
οὐκ ὄγχνη, οὐ πρασιή τοι ἄνευ κομιδῆς κατὰ κῆπον.
ἄλλο δέ τοι ἐρέω, σὺ δὲ μὴ χόλον ἔνθεο θυμῷ·

λύπτω) by γῆρας, "old age." On the many parallels between the plots of the *Homeric Hymn to Demeter* and the Homeric epics, see Mary-Louise Lord, "Withdrawal and Return"; Howard W. Clarke, *The Art of the Odyssey*, 70–71.

[13] Cf. Stanford's commentary on *Od.* 24.229–230.

[14] Cf. the way Menelaus and his men are disguised as seals in order to surprise Proteus (*Od.* 4.435–440) and the way Odysseus disguises himself as a ram to outwit the Cyclops (*Od.* 9.431–435). The capacity to adopt an animal disguise is clearly a sign of the ability to survive; the capacity actually to become an animal, as in the case of Odysseus' companions who are transformed by Circe, is an indication of the opposite.

[15] That Laertes is essentially in disguise is noted by M. E. Heatherington, "Chaos, Order, and Cunning in the *Odyssey*," 233 n19. Barry Powell comments on the formally reciprocal character of this recognition scene: "Thematic elements in this final recognition are curiously transferred back and forth between father and son." *Composition by Theme in the Odyssey*, 49. It is possible that a very slight indication of disguise for Odysseus is given when he puts aside his armor (*Od.* 24.219). It will be seen in Chapter 3 that during Odysseus' visit to Eumaeus, Odysseus' lack of a cloak constitutes part of his disguise.

αὐτόν σ' οὐκ ἀγαθὴ κομιδὴ ἔχει, ἀλλ᾽ ἅμα γῆρας
λυγρὸν ἔχεις αὐχμεῖς τε κακῶς καὶ ἀεικέα ἕσσαι.
οὐ μὲν ἀεργίης γε ἄναξ ἕνεκ᾽ οὔ σε κομίζει,
οὐδέ τί τοι δούλειον ἐπιπρέπει εἰσοράασθαι
εἶδος καὶ μέγεθος· βασιλῆι γὰρ ἀνδρὶ ἔοικας.
τοιούτῳ δὲ ἔοικας, ἐπεὶ λούσαιτο φάγοι τε,
εὐδέμεναι μαλακῶς· ἡ γὰρ δίκη ἐστὶ γερόντων.

Old man, you show no lack of skill in tending
the orchard. It is well cared for, and there is no
tree, no fig, no vine, nor any olive,
no pear, and no bed of greens uncared for in your garden.
But I will tell you something else, and you must not be angry:
you yourself are not well cared for. For you are wretchedly old
and miserably dirty and you wear shabby clothes.
It is not on account of laziness that your lord neglects you,
and nothing about you suggests a slave,
neither your form nor your size, for you seem like a king.
You seem like the kind who, when he has bathed and eaten,
sleeps comfortably. That is the way of the elders.

(*Od.* 24.244–255)

In this speech Odysseus contrasts Laertes' current appearance
with what appears to be his proper role,[16] and he does so in a
way that associates Laertes' proper role with qualities and gestures that are, in the *Odyssey*, specifically associated with the removal of disguise or the establishment of identity. He contrasts
Laertes' shabby appearance to his careful tending of the orchard; when he proves his own identity to Laertes, it is by recalling how he learned to tend that very orchard. Then he goes
on to say that Laertes looks as if he could be altered by a bath

---

[16] One element of this contrast, the difference between the condition of the
farm and that of Laertes himself, has been cited as a problematic inconsistency
by some critics of the end of the poem (cf. G. S. Kirk, *The Songs of Homer*, 250;
M. I. Finley, *The World of Odysseus*, 87). But that difference can be understood
as an account of the disjunction between Laertes' true and apparent states that
makes his condition similar to a disguise. Cf. Dorothea Wender, *The Last Scenes
of the Odyssey*, 52–53.

and that he might end up by sleeping more comfortably, presumably in a bed. In the *Odyssey* a bath is often the occasion of the removal of disguise, and sleeping in a bed is often its result—most notably, of course, in the recognition scene between Odysseus and Penelope in which Odysseus proves his identity and regains his marriage bed all at once.

Odysseus counters this disguise by bringing himself to his father's attention; first he evokes an absent, fictitious version of himself in the false tale that he tells, and then he identifies himself openly and announces that he has defeated the suitors. The sequel to this revelation is the removal of Laertes' disguise. When Laertes returns to his house, he has a bath, through which both his rags and his old age are cast aside, and he emerges looking like the gods (*Od.* 24.365–370). When Odysseus comments on this change, he is, in a sense, recognizing his father. Laertes answers with a wish: that he could have been as he was during one of the great victories of his youth and could have joined in the previous day's battle against the suitors (*Od.* 24.376–382). This wish is reminiscent of the wishes of Odysseus' friends that Odysseus would return as he was on some past occasion. Odysseus' success in fulfilling those wishes is here transferred to Laertes, who, by recognizing Odysseus, also puts aside the effects of time and then goes on to play a leading role in the battle with the suitors' relatives, which reenacts the battle with the suitors themselves.

The reunion of Odysseus and Laertes, then, combines a graphic reversal of the effects of time with a demonstration of reciprocity: Odysseus brings Laertes out of the state of weakness and grief that oppresses him and obscures his identity, and Laertes helps Odysseus ward off the final threat to his own recovery of his proper position and identity. This reciprocity is reinforced by the effective leveling of their ages that occurs as Laertes is restored to his prime. The reversal of the effects of time involved in Laertes' reanimation not only signals the return of the past but also removes the imbalance inherent in the chronologically unequal relationship of father and son, an imbalance which, at this time in their lives, makes the son

30

more powerful than his aged father. This imbalance is also countered by the proof that Odysseus is obliged to offer his father. Odysseus may be a more powerful figure in this encounter, confronting a father who is his dependent and controlling his own self-disclosure, but he cannot win Laertes' recognition without satisfying his demand for proof. In meeting this demand he recalls times in their lives when the balance of their relationship was different. He shows him the scar, which evokes the time when he was only just entering manhood and underwent a kind of initiation; and he recalls an even earlier time when Laertes showed him the orchard, taught him the names of the trees, and gave him some of them—a time when he was Laertes' dependent and received only a token portion of his inheritance (*Od.* 24.330–344).

But at the same time that this episode, in one way, plays down the imbalance in their relationship (by making it clear that the imbalance stems only from this particular point in their history), it also, in other ways, draws attention to that imbalance. It does so especially through two related features: the extremity of Laertes' destitution, which is expressed in the transfer of the motifs of disguise to him, and the placement of the episode late in the narrative, which gives it a belated or tacked-on quality. Laertes' condition of extreme dependency means that Odysseus can only appear to him late in the story when his return is virtually complete. Only then is Odysseus' presence sufficiently powerful to bring Laertes out of the decline that has been his response to the suitors' presence. Simply the prospect or likelihood of Odysseus' return is insufficient to revive Laertes, as is clear when he responds to Odysseus' false tale by nearly dying. Thus Odysseus appears to Laertes virtually undisguised himself and couples the revelation of his identity with the announcement that he has destroyed the suitors. The confrontation with the suitors' relatives, which still remains and with which Laertes does help, is not as essential to Odysseus' recovery as the defeat of the suitors themselves. That this confrontation lies before him is not as great a challenge to his identity as the presence of the suitors has been, and the help that

Laertes gives him is not as decisive as the help he has received from other supporters within the house.

This depiction of the imbalance between father and son, even in an encounter which also does away with it, is partly a reflection of the *Odyssey*'s partiality for its hero, which causes him to be portrayed to best advantage, and thus at that time in his life when his glory cannot be rightly challenged, even by his own father. It also expresses a constant feature of the relationships between fathers and sons as they are affected by the passage of time. It is always the case that, while the father is the chief source of the son's identity, his continued presence is not necessary for the continuation of that identity. The father is likely to die while the son is still alive, but the son must be able to continue on without him and thus must not depend on him to retain the position he inherits. Odysseus can, and must, remain the son of Laertes with all that that means, even after Laertes is no longer alive. On the other hand, it is only through his son's possession of this heritage that the father's identity can, in any sense, continue after his death, as the loss of selfhood with which Laertes responds to Odysseus' absence attests.[17] The sense of many readers from antiquity on that the recognition between Odysseus and Laertes is an inessential appendage is appropriate,[18] but that does not mean that our *Odyssey* has been added to; rather it gives in this way an accurate account of the relationship of father and son.[19] The *Odyssey* would be present-

[17] Notably, Laertes' condition intensifies when he learns that his grandson may be lost as well (*Od.* 16.141–145).

[18] This issue is, of course, inseparable from the larger issue of the authenticity of the entire ending from *Od.* 23.297 on. For a forceful statement of the arguments against authenticity, see Denys Page, *The Homeric Odyssey*, 101–136; for rebuttal of those arguments see Hartmut Erbse, *Beiträge zum Verständnis der Odyssee*, 166–244; Carroll Moulton, "The End of the *Odyssey*"; Dorothea Wender, *The Last Scenes of the Odyssey*. Of particular relevence to this discussion is the recurrent sense that the recognition scene with Laertes is misplaced because Odysseus' continued self-concealment is, at this point in the story, gratuitously cruel. This point is stressed by Page (112), but also acknowledged by critics who are less certain that the scene is inauthentic, e.g., Bernard Fenik, *Studies in the Odyssey*, 47–50.

[19] That many features of this scene, including its placement, stem from uni-

ing a less true picture if it made it seem indispensable that Odysseus be reunited with his father in order to resume his place in his home. At the same time, the poem recognizes that Odysseus' place derives above all from his relationship to his father and acknowledges this in its final episode.[20]

The same features of the relationship of father and son that cause Odysseus' reunion with his father to be the last in the series that makes up the account of his return cause his reunion with his son Telemachus to be the first (or first with an actual member of his household). Odysseus encounters Laertes only after his victory over the suitors is complete because Laertes' recovery is so thoroughly dependent on his return and because he does not need Laertes' help very much. He encounters Telemachus when he has still made very little progress towards the achievement of his return and because Telemachus needs the assurance of his presence relatively little and is more in a position to help his father than to be helped by him.

Like Laertes, Telemachus is not fully himself when the story opens but becomes so by the end; the way in which, by the poem's conclusion, events have brought both of them into a similar state of paramount vigor is expressed in the final tableau in which they both fight at Odysseus' side in his battle against the suitors' relatives. But while Telemachus' distance from his proper state also manifests itself in powerlessness in the face of the suitors' presence and mournful longing for Odysseus' return, what keeps him from asserting himself is not his father's absence but his own immaturity. The change in him that comes to be recognized in his encounter with his father is not the recovery of a previous state but growth into a new state of maturity, and the role played in this change by Odysseus is consequently different.

---

versal features of the relationship of parent and child is suggested by Albert Lord's observation that the *Odyssey* conforms to a pattern common in Yugoslav return songs in which the hero's recognition by a parent comes after his recognition by his wife. *The Singer of Tales*, 178.

[20] On the necessity for this episode, see Dorothea Wender, *The Last Scenes of the Odyssey*, 57–59.

Laertes has become Odysseus' permanent dependent whose survival depends absolutely on his return. But it is Telemachus' role to stop being Odysseus' dependent eventually and to become his successor. When that happens, Telemachus must be able to survive even if Odysseus is not present, even if, as will sooner or later be the case, Odysseus is dead. Furthermore, he must be capable of succeeding his father on the basis of his own comparable merits. It is essential to the poem's celebration of inherited excellence that Telemachus be able to take his father's place even if his father does not return to hand it to him personally. Therefore Telemachus must be seen not to need his father's direct influence in order to attain to a state in which he can take hold of what is rightfully his.[21]

When the poem opens, Telemachus is in a state of unreadiness to assert himself that is reminiscent of Odysseus' reticence on Phaeacia. This is a less extreme version of disguise than that displayed by Laertes, which depends on Odysseus' miraculous presence for its reversal; Telemachus' state is not a debilitating decline but an indication of still-unfulfilled potential. Much as Odysseus holds back his identity unnecessarily on Phaeacia, Telemachus refuses the recognition spontaneously offered him by "Mentes." When "Mentes" suggests to Telemachus that he must be the son of Odysseus, Telemachus gives a noncommittal answer: his mother says that he is, but he is not sure; no one knows for sure who his father is, and he would rather have been the son of someone more fortunate, someone who died at home among his possessions (*Od.* 1.214–220).

While Telemachus believes that his father's absence is his problem and dreams of his father's return as the solution (*Od.* 1.113–117), his discernable resemblance to Odysseus suggests that the capacity to heal the Ithacan situation is also present in him. As it turns out, he does not overcome this uncertainty about himself by being exposed to Odysseus and recognizing him. At the prompting of Athena, he adopts another, more sat-

[21] On Telemachus' recognition in the *Odyssey* as the assertion of the inheritability of *aretē*, "excellence," as the basis of hereditary monarchy, see Peter W. Rose, "Class Ambivalence in the *Odyssey*," 138.

isfactory and realistic solution: rather than simply waiting for his father to return, he grows up independently. He asserts himself against the suitors and takes a voyage to Pylos and Sparta, where he comes to know his father from others' memories of him. He undertakes an independent voyage that is in its structure and import parallel to the return of Odysseus.[22] Like Laertes, he responds to Odysseus' absence with an absence of his own, but his absence takes the form of an autonomous voyage from which he can make a more forceful return.

Telemachus' voyage, like Odysseus' return, takes the form of a series of encounters; in each of these encounters Telemachus is recognized as his father's son and heir: by "Mentes," by Nestor, by Helen and Menelaus—an episode in which the discovery of his identity is a central element—by Theoclymenus,[23] and finally by Odysseus himself in a reunion that marks simultaneously the return of Odysseus and the return of Telemachus. In these encounters Telemachus meets people who both recognize him as Odysseus' son and tell him stories that reveal Odysseus' greatness. As a result, he learns both that he actually resembles Odysseus—that his connection to Odysseus is inherent and apparent and not simply something his mother asserts—and that Odysseus is someone whose son he would want to be, a great hero whether he succeeds in returning to Ithaca or not. By the last of these encounters, the meeting with the stranger in Eumaeus' hut, Telemachus identifies himself unhesitatingly not only as the son of Odysseus but also as part of a line that includes Arcesius and Laertes (*Od.* 16.117–120).

The story of Telemachus' journey is an adaptation of the disguise-and-recognition plot structure that shapes the story of Odysseus' return to the particular dimensions of Telemachus' situation. Although elements in Telemachus' story—most no-

---

[22] On the structural and thematic parallels between the *Telemachy* and the story of Odysseus, see Bernard Fenik, *Studies in the Odyssey*, 21–28.

[23] Cf. Howard Clarke's comment on Theoclymenus' speech at 15.533–534, "... it is not a prophecy; it is an accolade, a ceremony to complete the *Telemacheia* by marking Telemachus' attainment to true manhood." *The Art of the Odyssey*, 39.

tably his recognition by Menelaus and Helen because of his secret weeping at the mention of Odysseus—are reminiscent of Odysseus' visit to Phaeacia, Telemachus has a much easier time establishing his identity than Odysseus does in that episode. Telemachus is able to benefit from some of the privileges of his position as Odysseus' son; his discovery of his identity is paralleled by his learning to take advantage of that legacy. While he arrives at Pylos and Sparta in the anonymous condition of all strangers, Telemachus is also traveling with the proper trappings of his station, especially a ship full of companions. He goes among people who have a connection to his father, and who are prepared to recognize him and welcome him because of that connection. Telemachus also inherits the help of his father's supporters, in particular his father's divine patron Athena, who helps him in the guise of old friends of his father. Because of his father's connection with Nestor, Telemachus gains his own companion, Peisistratus, whose capacity to help him be recognized is seen when he speaks up to confirm Menelaus' and Helen's spontaneous identification (*Od.* 4.155–167).

The way Telemachus discovers his identity reflects the degree of dependence that a son has on his father at Telemachus' stage of life. His father must be in his background—the son must inherit some advantages from him and must have access to memories of him—but he no longer needs to be an actual presence in his life. Telemachus' journey is not at all an attempt to bring Odysseus back: it is an attempt to bring about his own emergence as the son of Odysseus so that he can take control of his household in his father's absence.[24] When "Mentes" tells Telemachus to go on the journey, he does not tell him to look for Odysseus but to look for information about him (*Od.* 1.279–283).

[24] This way of dramatizing a son's relationship to his father is not unique to the *Odyssey*. As David E. Bynum has shown in his study of analogous narratives of initiatory journeys undertaken by young heroes, the young hero's failure to recover his father, even when it is his ostensible purpose to do so, is a standard feature of such stories. "Themes of the Young Hero in Serbocroatian Oral Epic Tradition," 1300–1301.

Telemachus' reunion with Odysseus is the culminating moment of Telemachus' growth to a point where he no longer needs Odysseus' return. Thus, the scene is placed at the beginning of Odysseus' homecoming, when Odysseus can offer little support and needs a good deal of help. At the same time, Telemachus' attainment of this condition is made premature by Odysseus' return, and his new prominence must be suspended as long as Odysseus is still alive. This suspension is dramatized during the contest of the bow, when Telemachus nearly succeeds in stringing the bow himself but steps aside at a signal from Odysseus (*Od.* 21.101–135). Thus, although the placement of their recognition acknowledges Telemachus' newfound maturity, other aspects of the subsequent scene are designed to play down this maturity or to counter it in the light of Odysseus' return.

While still disguised, Odysseus as the stranger suggests that the situation on Ithaca could be remedied either by a son of Odysseus or by Odysseus himself (*Od.* 16.100–101). But he does not recognize at first that Telemachus is ready for recognition; he has to be told by Athena not to wait any longer before disclosing himself to him. The words Odysseus uses to impress his identity on Telemachus also emphasize Telemachus' dependence on him.

οὔ τίς τοι θεός εἰμι· τί μ᾽ ἀθανάτοισιν ἐΐσκεις;
ἀλλὰ πατὴρ τεός εἰμι, τοῦ εἵνεκα σὺ στεναχίζων
πάσχεις ἄλγεα πολλά, βίας ὑποδέγμενος ἀνδρῶν.

I am no god. Why do you compare me to the immortals?
But I am your father, the one for whom you have been
    grieving
as you suffer many hardships, receiving the insults of men.
(*Od.* 16.187–189)

As they make his own presence known, Odysseus' words return Telemachus to the helpless condition he was in when the poem opened, when Athena came upon him, grieving and dreaming of his father's return (*Od.* 1.113–117). They serve to deny the effects of his intervening voyage on Telemachus, effects that must, for the time being, be suspended.

These two recognition scenes, the one between Odysseus and Telemachus and the one between Odysseus and Laertes, frame the story of Odysseus' return, but are segregated from the central action and central arena of the narrative, Odysseus' defeat of the suitors in his own house. The recognition scenes that cluster around the defeat of the suitors involve the recreation of more difficult relationships with people to whom Odysseus is not related by blood: his loyal servants, Eurycleia, Eumaeus, and Philoetius, and his wife Penelope. Because these relationships are not based on any natural tie but are artificial social constructs, their continuity over time is genuinely subject to question as the continuity of the indissoluble kinship of father and son is not. Thus the aspects of Odysseus' identity affirmed by his relations with these figures are more seriously threatened by his absence than is his identity as son of Laertes or father of Telemachus. This great threat is registered in the narrative by the way in which reunions with those figures take place close to the center of his home and of the story of his recovery and, especially in the cases of Eumaeus and Penelope, only after a long period of testing and renegotiation.

Odysseus' ties to his servants are even more vulnerable to the effects of his absence than is his tie to his wife. While a marriage begins without any kinship between husband and wife, it creates kinship between them through their children. But the relationship of master and servant is permanently unequal in status and, on the part of the servants, or more properly slaves, originally involuntary. Although the poem refers to the acts of generosity with which masters win the loyalty of their servants, it also acknowledges that slaves are won by force (for example, *Od.* 1.398). And it shows, especially in its portrayal of the majority of Odysseus' servants who have not remained loyal to him, that such gracious acts are not sufficient to create ties that automatically endure when the master is not present.

The *Odyssey* registers the inherent difficulty of such relationships by making their revival important and far from routine prerequisites to the hero's triumphant self-revelation. It has often seemed to interpreters of the poem that the placement of the recognitions involving Eumaeus and Eurycleia is determined by considerations having to do with the treatment of other, more important characters. A recognition with Eumaeus in his hut seems to have been postponed to make way for the reunion with Telemachus;[25] the recognition by Eurycleia seems to have been inserted to avert a premature recognition with Penelope. In other words, these characters' subordinate, servile status has seemed to be recapitulated in the way in which their allotment of narrative attention is designed to serve the presentation of other, more socially elevated characters. But it is possible to read the distribution of Odysseus' recognitions in another way, to see it as a means of highlighting his dependence on the loyalty of his social subordinates, a loyalty that is far from automatic. The tense moment of real danger to Odysseus' whole project created by Eurycleia's recognition of him dramatizes how much he needs to be able to rely on her and on others like her. The recognition by Eumaeus comes as a crucial prelude to Odysseus' participation in the contest of the bow and is given weight both by the long account of Odysseus' preceding encounter with Eumaeus and by the way Eumaeus' role is duplicated in the figure of Philoetius.[26]

In addition, the *Odyssey* makes sense of the continued voluntary submission of unrelated subordinates by assimilating these relationships to the socially equal and involuntary relationships of kinship. As they recognize Odysseus and are recognized by him, the poem suggests that Eurycleia and Eumaeus are more

[25] For this view, see W. J. Woodhouse, *The Composition of Homer's Odyssey*, 151–152. Cf. also Karl Reinhardt's remarks on Eumaeus' role, "Homer und die Telemachie," 45.

[26] Cf. Helene P. Foley, " 'Reverse Similes' and Sex Roles in the *Odyssey*," especially the observations that "Through Eumaeus, Odysseus symbolically recovers an understanding with those men, often originally strangers, who maintain the external economies of the household" (15), and, commenting on the recognition with Laertes, ". . . its late appearance in the poem makes clear that the success of Odysseus' homecoming does not depend on his father. Odysseus renegotiates his social, not his natural relationships" (25 n21).

like relatives than like servants. The capacity of mutual recognition to bring to light kinship where none has been apparent is here used to imply a metaphorical kinship where none actually exists. Odysseus' retainers lose their social inferiority as if it were, like his, a disguise. As their similar names suggest, Eurycleia is, in many ways, a doublet for Odysseus' mother, Anticleia. Her role of nurse is naturally very close to that of mother. The account of her history given at *Odyssey* 1.429–433 makes it clear that she is Anticleia's equal in social status and nearly her equal in position in the household of Laertes.[27] Although she is now a slave, she was originally an aristocrat, as the provision of her father's and grandfather's names at 1.429 attests, and has received as much honor as his wife from Laertes, who has only refrained from sharing his bed with her out of fear of his wife's anger (*Od.* 1.432–433). In the account of how Odysseus got his scar that evokes their past relationship, Eurycleia is virtually identified with Odysseus' mother.

Αὐτόλυκος δ᾽ ἐλθὼν Ἰθάκης ἐς πίονα δῆμον
παῖδα νέον γεγαῶτα κιχήσατο θυγατέρος ἧς·
τόν ῥά οἱ Εὐρύκλεια φίλοις ἐπὶ γούνασι θῆκε
παυομένῳ δόρποιο, ἔπος τ᾽ ἔφατ᾽ ἔκ τ᾽ ὀνόμαζεν·
"Αὐτόλυκ᾽, αὐτὸς νῦν ὄνομ᾽ εὕρεο ὅττι κε θῆαι
παιδὸς παιδὶ φίλῳ· πολυάρητος δέ τοί ἐστι."
    Τὴν δ᾽ αὖτ᾽ Αὐτόλυκος ἀπαμείβετο φώνησέν τε·
"γαμβρὸς ἐμὸς θυγάτηρ τε, τίθεσθ᾽ ὄνομ᾽ ὅττι κεν εἴπω . . ."

Autolycus came to the rich land of Ithaca
and there found a child newly born to his daughter;
this child Eurycleia laid on his knees
as he finished his dinner, and called him by name and said to
    him,
"Autolycus, you yourself find a name to be given
to this child of your child. You have prayed much for him."
Then Autolycus spoke and gave her an answer,

---

[27] On Eurycleia's position, see Jean-Pierre Vernant, *Mythe et société*, 67.

"My son-in-law and daughter, give him the name I tell
you . . ."

(*Od.* 19.399–406)

The child of his daughter whom Autolycus has come to see is
presented to him by Eurycleia, and she poses a question to
which the answer is addressed to Odysseus' father and mother.
Any reader of these lines who did not know otherwise would
assume that Eurycleia was Odysseus' mother.

Eumaeus has a history similar both to the history that goes
with Odysseus' disguise and to Eurycleia's history. He, too, is
originally of noble birth and has occupied a place in the house
of Laertes comparable to that of a member of the family. He has
been raised almost as if he were Odysseus' brother, only a little
less honored than Odysseus' sister Ctimene (*Od.* 15.363–
365).[28] Only on reaching adulthood has he been relegated to a
farm on the periphery of the estate and to the status of a servant
(*Od.* 15.370). And only with the advent of the suitors has he
been truly confined to that place and role.

Odysseus' recognition of Eumaeus repairs Eumaeus' social
subordination. As they are recognized by Odysseus, Eumaeus
and Philoetius are absorbed into Odysseus' family as brothers to
Telemachus. Between his declaration and his show of proof,
Odysseus promises,

εἴ χ᾽ ὑπ᾽ ἐμοί γε θεὸς δαμάσῃ μνηστῆρας ἀγαυούς,
ἄξομαι ἀμφοτέροις ἀλόχους καὶ κτήματ᾽ ὀπάσσω
οἰκία τ᾽ ἐγγὺς ἐμεῖο τετυγμένα· καί μοι ἔπειτα
Τηλεμάχου ἑτάρω τε κασιγνήτω τε ἔσεσθον.

If by my hand a god destroys the arrogant suitors,
then I will get you both wives, and allot you possessions
and houses built next to mine. And then
you both will be companions and brothers of Telemachus.

(*Od.* 21.213–216)

---

[28] See the comments of Barry Powell, *Composition by Theme in the Odyssey*, 53.
At 14.147 Eumaeus refers to Odysseus as "ἠθεῖον" instead of naming him; see

41

The assimilation that is implicit in the recognition scene with Eurycleia is here made explicit.

Eumaeus' recognition comes not at a hut at the edge of the estate but in the courtyard of the house, only a small distance from the center of Odysseus' power. Similarly, Eumaeus' relationship to Odysseus is revealed to be not that of a distant inferior but one that involves only a relatively minor degree of subordination. Eumaeus' subordination is that of a son to his father (which is, after all, only temporary) or that of a great hero's companion, neither of which involves social inferiority.[29] Eumaeus' servile status, like Laertes' old age and peasant's rags, is not an inescapable condition but a form of disguise that Odysseus' return, rather than reaffirming their unequal relationship, removes.

Like his reunion with Eumaeus, Odysseus' reunion with Penelope comes only after a long period of testing and negotiation and involves a more complex interrelation of two separate stories of recovery and recognition than do his reunions with Laertes and Telemachus. The recognition of Penelope and Odysseus occurs only after a series of meetings that are difficult to interpret and that are intertwined with Odysseus' other interactions with his household. This greater complexity is a reflection of the nature of Odysseus and Penelope's relationship, which is more definitive, more nearly balanced, and less intrinsically secure than Odysseus' relationships with his father and with his son. As husband and wife Odysseus and Penelope are closer in age and are involved in a more nearly equal relationship than fathers and sons usually are. While Laertes may have been the source of Odysseus' identity in the past, and Telemachus may represent the greatest prospect of its continuation into the future, Penelope is the figure on whom the recovery of

---

W. B. Stanford's discussion of that line in his commentary, which includes his report of a scholiast's observation that this is the proper term for an older brother or close friend.

[29] This transaction recreates a relationship that Eumaeus has compared favorably to his relationship to his parents in his original, princely home (*Od.* 14.140–141).

his power to assert it in the present most depends. In the middle of his life, Odysseus is most decisively defined by his role as her husband. At the same time, that role, because it is created through an artificial and reversible social tie rather than through an unalterable bond of blood kinship, is vulnerable in a way that his identity as Laertes' son and Telemachus' father is not. Odysseus is not naturally Penelope's husband, as he is naturally Laertes' son; that role could have been played by any of a number of men and now that he is absent could be taken over by someone else. Consequently, the most serious challenge to Odysseus' identity comes from Penelope's suitors, rivals who would like to replace him in that role.

The inherent instability of the roles of husband and wife as expressions of identity can only be countered by the willingness of the partners to see it as inviolable, as having the irreversible quality of a tie of blood. A successful marriage comes to resemble kinship both because husband and wife come to be related through their children and because they invest their relationship with the particularity and permanence of kinship. But this kinship always remains metaphorical, the product not of biology but of an attitude of mind. This notion of mental kinship is expressed in the idea of *homophrosynē*, "likeness of mind," which is identified by Odysseus in his speech to Nausicaa as the central quality of a successful marriage (*Od.* 6.180–185). Because the form of kinship represented by marriage is in this way entirely voluntary, its recognition—expressed in this poem by Penelope's recognition of Odysseus as her husband and by Odysseus' recognition of Penelope as his wife—signals not the effects of heredity but the virtue of marital fidelity.

Odysseus' definitive yet inherently difficult relationship to Penelope is expressed in the plot of the *Odyssey* in Penelope's decisive role in the suitors' defeat through her setting of the contest of the bow, and in the placement of their recognition scene. Because the status of this relationship is so profoundly affected by the suitors' presence, the relationship is reinstated immediately after, but only after, the suitors have been eliminated. Thus, Odysseus can neither wait to be reunited with Penelope, as he can with Laertes, nor reveal himself at once and plot openly with her, as he does with Telemachus. And because Penelope's continued identity as Odysseus' wife is dependent on his actual return in a way that Telemachus' identity as his son is not, that identity can appropriately be resumed only when Odysseus' homecoming is truly secure.

Penelope's dependence on Odysseus' presence for her identity is reflected in her response to his absence, which, like Laertes', combines elements of mourning and disguise. It involves partly physical withdrawal to the inner portion of the house, from which she emerges only rarely, but primarily emotional withdrawal into grief, despair, and inactivity. Furthermore, she is in a state of physical decline that resembles a disguise. She describes this condition to the stranger during their meeting in Book 19. When he compliments her by saying that she has been able to take Odysseus' place in his absence, she quite correctly denies it.

ξεῖν', ἦ τοι μὲν ἐμὴν ἀρετὴν εἶδός τε δέμας τε
ὤλεσαν ἀθάνατοι, ὅτε Ἴλιον εἰσανέβαινον
Ἀργεῖοι, μετὰ τοῖσι δ' ἐμὸς πόσις ἦεν Ὀδυσσεύς.
εἰ κεῖνός γ' ἐλθὼν τὸν ἐμὸν βίον ἀμφιπολεύοι,
μεῖζόν κε κλέος εἴη ἐμὸν καὶ κάλλιον οὕτω.

Stranger, all my excellence, my form and appearance,
were destroyed by the immortals, when the Argives
embarked for Ilium and my husband Odysseus went with
    them.
If he were to come back and take care of my life,
my glory would be greater and so more beautiful.
(Od. 19.124–128)

As in the case of Laertes, the outward effects of time and unhappy experience are here given the obscuring and reversible qualities of a disguise, but a disguise that can only be lifted with Odysseus' return.

Penelope's recognition of Odysseus, then, represents for her, as it does for him, emergence from a debilitating state of eclipse.

Like the reunion of Odysseus and Telemachus, the reunion of Odysseus and Penelope marks a double return. But Penelope's return is emotional rather than physical, and so resembles Odysseus' only metaphorically.[30] This metaphorical resemblance is delineated in the simile describing the embrace which marks their reunion.

κλαῖε δ᾽ ἔχων ἄλοχον θυμαρέα, κεδνὰ ἰδυῖαν.
ὡς δ᾽ ὅτ᾽ ἂν ἀσπάσιος γῆ νηχομένοισι φανήῃ,
ὧν τε Ποσειδάων εὐεργέα νῆ᾽ ἐνὶ πόντῳ
ῥαίσῃ, ἐπειγομένην ἀνέμῳ καὶ κύματι πηγῷ·
παῦροι δ᾽ ἐξέφυγον πολιῆς ἁλὸς ἤπειρόνδε
νηχόμενοι, πολλὴ δὲ περὶ χροῒ τέτροφεν ἅλμη,
ἀσπάσιοι δ᾽ ἐπέβαν γαίης, κακότητα φυγόντες·
ὣς ἄρα τῇ ἀσπαστὸς ἔην πόσις εἰσοροώσῃ,
δειρῆς δ᾽ οὔ πω πάμπαν ἀφίετο πήχεε λευκώ.

He wept holding his beloved wife, whose thoughts were
    sound.
And as the land appears welcome to men who are swimming,
whose well-built ship Poseidon has smashed
on the sea, driven on with winds and big swells.
A few escape from the gray sea to dry land
swimming, with sea-salt coating their skin,
and rejoicing they step on shore, escaping evil,
so welcome was her husband to her as she saw him before her,
and she clung to his neck with her white arms.
                    (*Od.* 23.232–240)

The way this simile identifies Odysseus and Penelope's experiences is enhanced by its construction: a reader or listener first

---

[30] This parallelism is well described by John Finley, who writes that, "Each of the three main characters dominates a part of the *Odyssey*, and each makes a journey, son and father outward journeys on sea and land, Penelope an inner journey from the sad fixity of her twenty-year isolation." *Homer's Odyssey*, 2. Grief and the loss of the desire to live such as Penelope and Laertes manifest are explicitly opposed to return in the *Iliad* when Achilles expresses his grief at the death of Patroclus (*Il.* 18.89 ff). See Douglas Frame, *The Myth of Return in Early Greek Epic*, 122–124.

assumes that the simile applies to Odysseus and realizes only at line 239 that it applies to Penelope. This poetic relocation of experiences like Odysseus' in Penelope's emotional life not only suggests an internalized version of the withdrawal and return plot that is basic to heroic narrative[31] but also evokes the necessarily imaginary or notional kinship on which their marriage is based: Penelope's ability to experience Odysseus' trials in her imagination is a sign of their *homophrosynē*, their "likeness of mind."

Not only does the recognition scene of Odysseus and Penelope mark Penelope's return as well as Odysseus', but there is also a notable similarity between her experiences in the second half of the poem and his. Just as Odysseus undergoes a series of preliminary, clandestine recognitions that lead up to his open self-disclosure and general acknowledgment, so Penelope undergoes a series of experiences that in important ways resemble recognition scenes, in which she somehow acknowledges Odysseus' presence and is recognized by him and through which important steps are taken towards securing Odysseus' reinstatement: her appearance in the hall in Book 18, her meeting with the stranger in Book 19, and her institution of the contest of the bow in Book 21. But while Odysseus' recognitions remain generally unacknowledged, in the sense that they are kept secret by the participants, Penelope's recognitions remain unacknowledged in a further sense. They are not perceived as

---

[31] On Penelope's experience as a realization of that plot type, see Cora W. Sowa, *Traditional Themes and the Homeric Hymns*, 107. While Penelope's story represents a striking example of the internalization of this plot, it is also true that the stories of Achilles' and Odysseus' withdrawals and returns are not told in the Homeric epics solely in terms of physical presence and absence, but have a component that might variously be labeled mental, ideological, or psychological. Achilles' physical withdrawal from the Achaean army, which is geographically rather slight, is the outward expression of a more considerable sense of ideological alienation from the Achaean leaders, which, like Penelope's emotional withdrawal, stems from a lack of appropriate recognition. And Odysseus' attempt to overcome the very great distances that separate him from his family and home depend as much on what might be called presence of mind as on physical accomplishments.

recognition scenes by the characters involved; they are recognition scenes only at the level of their thematic and structural affinities.

The ambiguous status of these episodes as both recognition scenes and not recognition scenes can be understood as the narrative accommodation of a certain necessary paradox. On the one hand, Penelope must not know that Odysseus is back until the end of her gradual recovery because her recognition of him actually signals its completion; on the other hand, she must know that Odysseus is back from the beginning because she cannot begin to recover until she does know. Only as she recovers does she become capable of helping Odysseus in his operations against the suitors, and thereby of bringing about the circumstances under which her actual recognition of Odysseus can take place. This means that, for most of the narrative, she must somehow know and acknowledge that Odysseus is back but still not recognize him.

These paradoxical conditions are met through a narrative characterized by ambiguity and indirection. Odysseus remains disguised from Penelope but makes his presence known to her in indirect ways. He impresses himself upon her in two distinct forms—as her absent, remembered husband and as the present stranger—while refraining from the crucial revelation that would collapse these two figures into one. He evokes his absent self by making predictions of his own return, by introducing himself as a character into his own false tales, and by encouraging the hopes that still linger in Penelope's dreams and private thoughts. As the stranger, he stirs up the household, reenacts their courtship,[32] and—in a process to be discussed in some detail in a later chapter—reawakens her interest in performing the duties of a host. In response to these gestures, Penelope acts out a kind of recognition of Odysseus but does not actually recognize him. Thus, like Odysseus after each episode of recognition,

---

[32] On Odysseus' behavior towards Penelope as a form of courtship, see Norman Austin, *Archery at the Dark of the Moon*, 211; Alice J. Mariani, "The Forged Feature," 146 ff.

she, after each of these encounters, firmly disavows what has just occurred. But while Odysseus denies his own return by reassuming his beggar's disguise, she denies it by asserting her certainty that Odysseus will never return (for example, *Od.* 19.568–569).

Perhaps the best illustration of the kind of scene of self–revelation that Odysseus' presence causes Penelope to stage is her appearance before the suitors in Book 18.[33] While this scene does not involve actual revelation of identity, it is very much an episode of recognition in the broader sense. Athena implants in Penelope a desire to appear before the suitors,

> . . . ὅπως πετάσειε μάλιστα
> θυμὸν μνηστήρων ἰδὲ τιμήεσσα γένοιτο
> μᾶλλον πρὸς πόσιός τε καὶ υἱέος ἢ πάρος ἦεν.

> . . . so that she might open as much as possible
> the hearts of the suitors and become even more honored
> in the eyes of her husband and son than she was before.
> (*Od.* 18.160–162)

Penelope's appearance is an opportunity for her to display before a gathering of those best suited to acknowledge them her most glorious attributes, the combination of sexual attractiveness and chastity that makes her at once desired by the suitors and valued by her husband and son. In the course of her appearance, she wins praise from the suitors (*Od.* 18.244–249) and then insists that that be followed with material recognition in the form of gifts. In addition, she earns Odysseus' admiration for the way she uses trickery to elicit the suitors' gifts (*Od.* 18.281–283).

The timing of this episode is like that of Odysseus' self-disclosures, for it marks a significant moment in Penelope's psychological return. It is her first response to a cluster of events that have brought Odysseus to her notice: Telemachus' report of what he has learned on his journey, Theoclymenus' "prophecy"

[33] For references to the main discussions of this scene, see Thomas Van Nortwick, "Penelope and Nausicaa," 267 n1.

that Odysseus has already returned, Odysseus' actual entrance into the house in disguise, and Eumaeus' praise of his guest of the night before.

While Penelope's behavior in this episode is inspired by Odysseus' presence, the workings of this inspiration are obscured in the narrative both by what she doesn't know and by what she won't admit. No indication is given of precisely how the impulse to descend to the hall, which Athena sends her, presents itself to Penelope's mind. As she expresses it to her nurse, she seems to be openly puzzled by her wish to show herself to the suitors, but to have already formulated a justification for acting on it based on her maternal duty to Telemachus.

ἀχρεῖον δ᾽ ἐγέλασσεν ἔπος τ᾽ ἔφατ᾽ ἔκ τ᾽ ὀνόμαζεν·
"Εὐρυνόμη, θυμός μοι ἐέλδεται, οὔ τι πάρος γε,
μνηστήρεσσι φανῆναι, ἀπεχθομένοισί περ ἔμπης·
παιδὶ δέ κεν εἴποιμι ἔπος, τό κε κέρδιον εἴη,
μὴ πάντα μνηστῆρσιν ὑπερφιάλοισιν ὁμιλεῖν,
οἵ τ᾽ εὖ μὲν βάζουσι, κακῶς δ᾽ ὄπιθεν φρονέουσι."

She laughed in an idle way and called her by name and
    addressed her.
"Eurynome, my heart desires, although before it did not,
to appear to the suitors, although they are still hateful to me.
I would speak a word to my son, for it would be more to his
    advantage
not always to go among the arrogant suitors,
who speak nicely, but have evil intentions."
                    (*Od.* 18.164–168)

Penelope's own words point to the way in which this desire represents a change in her and thus reveal that, however unaware of it she may be, her action is a response to the changes that have occured in the household, of which the most important is Odysseus' entrance into it as the stranger.

During her appearance, Penelope effectively acknowledges that Odysseus is somehow behind her actions, although she does not know that that is literally the case and she does so in statements whose sincerity is impossible to assess. When she confronts Telemachus, she does not warn him against the suitors as she has suggested she would; rather, she scolds him for the mistreatment that the disguised Odysseus has suffered (*Od.* 18.215–225). When she turns to her other purpose of extracting gifts from the suitors, she says she has finally reached the point when she must marry again and claims that this decision is in accord with instructions given her by Odysseus when he left for the Trojan War (*Od.* 18.251–280). Her gesture of acting more like a potential bride so that the suitors will act more like proper suitors is, in this way, tied to an evocation of Odysseus as he was when she last saw him, the point at which his image was left in her memory and from which she herself dates her decline. Odysseus' role in motivating Penelope's behavior is thus expressed, but indirectly and in a sense inaccurately in speeches that are far from straightforward. She alludes to him as he presents himself, in disguised or distanced forms, as either the present beggar or the long-absent Odysseus of the past.

Penelope's self-revelation in this scene is further allied to more narrowly defined scenes of recognition by the element of physical transformation. As Odysseus' disguise often is, Penelope's careworn appearance is suspended temporarily for a preliminary scene of recognition. With Athena's aid, she is suddenly transformed so that she looks more beautiful and resembles the gods (*Od.* 18.190–196). In this case, though, she is herself unaware of her transformation and denies that it has taken place, responding to Eurymachus' praise in the same words with which she denies the stranger's praise in the passage quoted above (*Od.* 18.251–255). In fact, when this transformation occurs, she actively resists it. When she tells Eurynome that she would like to show herself to the suitors, Eurynome suggests that she should wash and anoint herself, that is, that she should willfully change her appearance, and links the cessation of mourning that this would signal to Telemachus' maturity (*Od.* 18.171–176). Penelope responds by saying, in effect, that Telemachus' maturity is not sufficient to rouse her from her present condition; she must remain disguised as long as Odysseus is absent.

Εὐρυνόμη, μὴ ταῦτα παραύδα, κηδομένη περ,
χρῶτ᾽ ἀπονίπτεσθαι καὶ ἐπιχρίεσθαι ἀλοιφῇ·
ἀγλαΐην γὰρ ἐμοί γε θεοί, τοὶ Ὄλυμπον ἔχουσιν,
ὤλεσαν, ἐξ οὗ κεῖνος ἔβη κοίλης ἐνὶ νηυσίν.

Eurynome, don't suggest such things, much as you care for
    me,
as washing my body and anointing myself with oil.
For the gods who live on Olympus destroyed my beauty
since the day when that man embarked in the hollow ships.

(*Od.* 18.178–181)

From her perspective, the event that is necessary for her deliverance has not occurred. Not knowing that Odysseus has returned (however much she may be acknowledging Odysseus' return in her behavior) Penelope cannot cooperate with Athena in bringing about the transformation that precedes her descent into the hall. Instead, Athena must first make her unconscious by putting her to sleep in order to accomplish it.

The way in which, throughout this episode, Penelope persistently denies and resists those aspects of her own behavior that make it most like the combination of revelation of oneself and recognition of another of which episodes of recognition consist, highlights the paradoxical or ambiguous character of her preliminary encounters with Odysseus. In many of their formal characteristics, these encounters are episodes of recognition, but they are not acknowledged as such by any of the participants. This is particularly apparent during their meeting in Book 19 where the growing psychological sympathy that precedes recognition is achieved through a series of displaced gestures of recognition. In the early part of the episode Penelope recognizes, not the stranger, but the absent figure of Odysseus whom the stranger claims to have met,[34] in a process that shares the formal features of actual recognition scenes: the expression of solitary emotion (*Od.* 19.209–212); a demand for proof (*Od.* 19.215–219); the presentation of tokens (*Od.* 19.220–

---

[34] On the present stranger and the absent Odysseus as two distinct figures in this scene, see H. Vester, "Das 19. Buch der Odyssee."

248); even the formula describing recognition, "σήματ᾽ ἀνα-γνούσῃ τά οἱ ἔμπεδα πέφραδ᾽ Ὀδυσσεύς," "as she recognized the sure signs that Odysseus had pointed out" (*Od.* 19.250, cf. *Od.* 23.206, *Od.* 24.346).[35] Later, Odysseus' recognition is evoked obliquely through Penelope's account of her dream and the stranger's response to it. But again the recognition does not actually occur. Yet, this interchange leads directly to the typical conclusion of a recognition scene, the construction of a plot (*Od.* 19.570–587), a plot that so strongly suggests the sequel to recognition that it is interpreted as a sure sign that a recognition has taken place by at least one of the suitors (*Od.* 24.167–169) and by many readers of the poem.[36]

At the surface level of the plot, Odysseus does not reveal himself to Penelope and she does not recognize him until after the suitors have been dealt with. But in terms of the patterns their actions fulfill, Odysseus and Penelope participate in a series of encounters in which they go through the motions of recognition, each acknowledging the other, which anticipate and lead up to their openly-avowed reunion in Book 23. These encounters are, in a sense, recognition scenes that have gone underground: they resemble the moment of open recognition that they anticipate, but do not share its openness; they are recognitions on the level of the underlying import of the actions that make them up but not in the consciousness of the characters. In the case of Penelope, the meaning that her actions derive from their formal and thematic associations assumes special importance as a guide for interpreting them, because the poem is silent about her thoughts and feelings at crucial junctures in the narrative. (The implications of Penelope's reticence and the interpretive problems it causes will be discussed in a later chapter.)

The plot of Odysseus' return to Ithaca is thus complicated by

---

[35] See also the similar discussion of this episode by Chris Emlyn-Jones, "The Reunion of Penelope and Odysseus," 8.

[36] This problem will be discussed at greater length in Chapter 4. It should, however, be noted here that this episode's resemblance to a recognition scene between Odysseus and Penelope may well spring in part from the influence of an earlier version of the story in which such a scene did take place at this point.

the intertwined stories of the loyal supporters who recognize him, stories that, in various ways, resemble his own. The differences between these stories and the ways in which they intersect delineate the important distinction that always remains between Odysseus, as the dominant heroic figure on whom the poem centers, and his followers. Just as Odysseus' extraordinary voyage remains different from Telemachus' tame trip to the mainland and from Penelope's difficulties at home, so there is finally a significant difference between the literal disguises that Odysseus assumes and discards at will and the metaphorical disguises of Laertes, Telemachus, Penelope, and Eumaeus. These characters' oppressive conditions take on the reversible quality of disguise only because of Odysseus' return against all odds and against all expectations. In various ways, the encounters discussed above all delineate relationships that, while reciprocal, also involve dependence on Odysseus. Odysseus' single-handed self-restoration in Phaeacia and his resort to literal disguise on Ithaca set him apart as a hero who is not subject to these limitations, a hero who is so thoroughly in control of his situation that he can adopt and abandon these limitations at will, and who can serve as the agent of their transcendence by others. With these characters Odysseus is able to play the role of a god, to act towards them as Athena acts towards him.

Odysseus' disguise is an artificial device that allows him to structure the plot of his return by controlling the timing of his self-revelations so that he can, at the proper moment, disclose himself like a disguised god instead of running headlong into destruction like that ordinary mortal Agamemnon. Similarly, the *Odyssey*'s plot of the hero's return in disguise and recognition is an artificial device through which the poem organizes and controls the celebration of its hero Odysseus. And just as the success of Odysseus' strategies and of the divine scheme into which they are subsumed depends on proper timing, so the poem's success in presenting Odysseus playing this godlike role with the various dependent members of his household also depends on timing, on the story being set at a particular point in Odysseus' life.

The importance of the story's timing is suggested most urgently by the mounting pressures on Penelope to marry again, to cast someone else in the role of her husband. It is also seen in relation to the two members of Odysseus' own family who recognize him: his father, who was once a more powerful figure than he, and his son, who someday will be. The challenge to Odysseus' preeminence that these figures represent is implicit in the poem's nearly final image of Odysseus fighting the suitors' relatives with Laertes and Telemachus, both in a state of paramount vigor, at his side. Only because the poem is set at the time when Telemachus is still too young and Laertes is already too old to assert himself effectively can Odysseus remain the dominant figure in this tableau.

The significance of timing is further reflected in the way Odysseus times the self-revelations that animate the heroism of his father and son. Telemachus is encountered soon after Odysseus' arrival and is consigned to the role of his father's lieutenant. Laertes does not realize his wish of recovering his youth in time to fight against the suitors. Odysseus' delay in revealing himself to Laertes assures that his father is not able to share the limelight when Odysseus performs his most glorious feat. Only in the context of what is represented as a secondary challenge, the battle with the suitors' relatives, does the poem directly represent the competition between the generations.[37] And then this generational competition is depicted as a welcome rivalry: Odysseus reminds Telemachus of the tradition of heroism he must live up to (*Od.* 24.506–509); Telemachus responds that he will do his best (*Od.* 24.511–512); and Laertes rejoices that his son and his grandson are vying in *aretē*, "excellence" (*Od.* 24.514–515). This final vision, which stresses the family's figurative conquest of time through the continuity of the line, cannot outweigh the singularity of Odysseus' achievements as revealed in the actions that lead up to it.

Finally, the poem's success in depicting Odysseus as extraordinary is aided by its geographical as well as its temporal setting.

---

[37] Although W. B. Stanford finds latent antagonism between father and son in the recognition scene earlier in Book 24. *The Ulysses Theme*, 60.

For it is only at home in Ithaca that Odysseus can find people with whom he has relations of mutual support capable of being revived after many years in which he plays this dominant role. Only there can he defeat his enemies by putting together a band of followers consisting solely of family members and personal retainers. Outside his own home he must cooperate with others who are not naturally subordinated to him by virtue of their age, gender, or social status. Only at home can he count on being able to play the central part in a godlike scenario. The setting and the action that occurs in it are entirely interdependent, and what is in one sense the goal of the story is in another its precondition. The apparent conquest of limitation implied in the hero's achievements is inextricable from an acceptance of limitation, the limitation of his sphere of action to his own home. What appears to be a story of godlike transcendence is in fact bounded by the restricted conditions of ordinary human life.

TWO

Odysseus and the Suitors

THE EPISODE, spanning Books 21 and 22 of the *Odyssey*, in which Odysseus makes himself publicly known as he strings the bow, shoots through the axes, and turns on the suitors is at once the central recognition scene of the poem and the most anomalous. It lacks the essential characteristics of the scenes analyzed in the previous chapter, for it contains no element of reciprocity or mutuality. While its central action is the removal of disguise, it is devoid of recognition. Odysseus neither seeks the suitors' recognition nor receives it, and he offers the suitors no acknowledgment in return. Although Odysseus' self-revelation in this episode has many of the features of a divine epiphany, it lacks the ringing announcement of his name that occurs in most of the other recognition scenes of the *Odyssey*. He does not enter into negotiations with the suitors but begins to attack them at once; it is only after he has killed Antinous that he tells the suitors who he is, and even then he does so indirectly in a speech of relentless hostility. "ὦ κύνες, οὔ μ᾽ ἔτ᾽ ἐφάσκεθ᾽ ὑπότροπον οἴκαδ᾽ ἱκέσθαι / δήμου ἄπο Τρώων, ὅτι μοι κατακείρετε οἶκον," "You dogs, you didn't believe I would still come back / home again from Troy, and so you lay waste my household. . . ." (*Od.* 22.35–36). He makes no attempt to distinguish among them but addresses them collectively as "*kunes*," "dogs," less than humans.

Nor do the suitors acknowledge the claim to be Odysseus that is implicit in his speech and actions. Eurymachus, even in a speech designed to placate Odysseus and to deny that any of them but Antinous has really ignored Odysseus' rights, betrays his insincerity by refusing to concede absolutely that this is Odysseus. "εἰ μὲν δὴ Ὀδυσεὺς Ἰθακήσιος εἰλήλουθας, / ταῦτα μὲν αἴσιμα εἶπας, ὅσα ῥέζεσκον Ἀχαιοί," "If you

56

really are Odysseus of Ithaca, having returned, / then what you have said is fair about what the Achaeans have done to you. . . ." (*Od.* 22.45–46).¹ When this speech is unsuccessful, and the hostility between them has become open and violent, Euryma-chus, calling the rest of the suitors to arms, refers to Odysseus as "οὗτος ἀνήρ," "this man," attributing to him the anonymity appropriate to an enemy. As the public announcement of his re-turn, Odysseus' self-revelation in the hall does lead to his gen-eral recognition, but the recognition comes not from the suitors but from the faithful maidservants, with whom he celebrates a reunion after the battle is over (*Od.* 22.497–501).

Odysseus reveals himself to the suitors not to cure their ig-norance but to punish it, so that, instead of bringing them to life, their encounter with him leads to their death. The suitors learn his identity too late and only acknowledge it when they are dead. It is only in retrospect, when Amphimedon in the under-world gives his account of Odysseus' return, that the suitors can recognize Odysseus. In Amphimedon's version Odysseus is identified by name as soon as he arrives on Ithaca, and his return is attributed to the activity of a god at his side. "καὶ τότε δή ῥ' Ὀδυσῆα κακός ποθεν ἤγαγε δαίμων / ἀγροῦ ἐπ' ἐσχατιήν," "Just then an evil divinity brought Odysseus back from somewhere / to the edge of his estate. . . ." (*Od.* 24.149–150). Again, when his definitive act of self–revelation, his stringing the bow, is re-lated, he is given his name, although none of the suitors was willing to concede it at the time. "αὐτὰρ ὁ δέξατο χειρὶ πολύ-τλας δῖος Ὀδυσσεύς, / ῥηϊδίως δ' ἐτάνυσσε βιόν, διὰ δ' ἧκε σιδήρου," "Then much-enduring Odysseus took the bow in his hand / and easily strung it and shot an arrow through the iron" (*Od.* 24.176–177).² Odysseus' association with the gods is ac-

---

¹ The use here of εἰ with the indicative is of the type that Chantraine cate-gorizes as serving "pour poser une hypothèse comme realisée" (*Grammaire homérique*, II, 416, p. 283) and thus expresses well that Eurymachus regards Odysseus' identification as a hypothesis, not a fact. Cf. the closely parallel state-ments made by Penelope and Laertes before they are willing to recognize Odys-seus at *Od.* 23.107–109 and 24.328–329.

² It is significant that Amphimedon here acknowledges Odysseus' heroic

knowledged when Amphimedon says that Zeus inspired him to hide the armor (*Od.* 24.164), and the recognition of that association is actually included in the narrative of the battle "γνωτὸν δ᾽ ἦν ὅ ῥά τίς σφι θεῶν ἐπιτάρροθος ἦεν," "It could be seen that one of the gods was his helper" (*Od.* 24.182)—although this wasn't seen by any of the suitors at the time. Finally, the suitors' inferiority to Odysseus is linked to their inability to recognize him as the same formula, "οὐδέ τις ἡμείων δύνατο," "not one of us was able," introduces both a report of the suitors' key physical inadequacy, their inability to string Odysseus' bow, and, just before, a statement that they were unable to recognize him (*Od.* 24.159, 170).[3]

This very different version of a recognition scene defines the very different relationship Odysseus has with the suitors than with the loyal members of his household, a relationship that is competitive and one-sided rather than cooperative and mutually supportive. Through his refusal to recognize the suitors and his ability to make their recognition of him coincide with their death, Odysseus shows himself to be irremediably hostile and unquestionably superior to them. His ability to make this decisive and final show of superiority depends on the disguise through which he blinds them to his presence until the bow is in his hands. Thus Odysseus' superiority is closely related to the exceptional assurance of divine favor and the exceptional similarity to a god expressed by his assumption of a disguise. And, like those qualities, it is tied to his homecoming.

---

character through his use of the epithet "πολύτλας," "much-enduring." Usually when the suitors refer to Odysseus, they do not use those epithets that characterize him as intelligent or enduring. See Norman Austin, *Archery at the Dark of the Moon*, 51.

[3] Amphimedon's account occurs in a context in which recognition in a variety of forms is a dominant motif: when the suitors' shades arrive, Achilles is hearing an account of the funeral with which the Achaeans honored him after his death; the encounter begins when Agamemnon recognizes Amphimedon (*Od.* 24.102) and they revive their old relationship of guest-friendship; after Amphimedon's narrative, Agamemnon offers a speech of praise for Odysseus and, especially, Penelope, in which he prophesies that Penelope will win undying *kleos* for her fidelity.

Odysseus' ability to disguise himself from the suitors indicates a godlike superiority over a group of men who represent his competitors, a superiority that a hero normally doesn't have. The series of recognition scenes analyzed in the previous chapter shows that, within the extended family that constitutes his household, the hero can depend on acknowledgment of his claims to a heroic preeminence that is as secure and permanent as his identity. This acknowledgment represents a form of recognition, in which the broader and narrower senses of that English term are inextricable, that is intrinsic to familial and certain quasi-familial relations. The way the loyalty over time of Odysseus' supporters within his immediate household is rooted in permanent relations of kinship assures him an acknowledgment as continuous as that which the gods can command. But the breadth of a hero's aspirations is such that he wants the recognition of a much wider audience than his immediate household; his ambition is to be known throughout his society and eventually to be remembered by people he has never met, living in places where he has never been and in times he has not survived into. Thus he hopes, by playing a leading role in the joint enterprises of his society, either by fighting especially hard and well or by taking on some institutional role that automatically guarantees recognition, to earn from his fellow men a degree of honor like that accorded to the gods—an honor that is continuous and lasting[4] and sets him apart from the community, the undifferentiated group of people from whom this honor comes, as a whole.[5]

---

[4] This notion of honor that is not only permanent but also uninterrupted is expressed in the adjective *aphthiton*, "unfailing," which is regularly applied to *kleos*. As Gregory Nagy has shown, the basic association of this adjective is with a continuous or unfailing stream of liquid. *Comparative Studies in Greek and Indic Meter*, 244.

[5] In the *Iliad* Hector twice formulates a fantasy of being immortal or the child of a god as a desire to be honored just as Athena and Apollo are honored (*Il.* 8.540; 13.827). While this aspiration may be fulfilled outside epic in the institution of the hero cult, within epic, as Gregory Nagy points out (*The Best of the Achaeans*, esp. 148–150), it is impossible and heroes are obliged to act within the constraints of mortality, searching for honor that simulates that of the gods.

But this unfailing recognition is much more difficult to achieve in a wider society populated by non-kin than it is within the family. The hero must try to earn recognition from others who have no automatic obligation to recognize him and are not "naturally" subordinated to him by virtue of their youth, age, gender, or social status. He seeks the recognition of his contemporaries and social equals, who may possess similar heroic capabilities. Thus, a hero is always seeking acknowledgment from others who are also his competitors, who are always prepared to challenge his claims and to demand recognition for themselves, and thus who resist classification into an undifferentiated category of people among whom the hero stands out. Furthermore, because mortals' powers are not unfailing, as gods' are, they must be continuously displayed if they are to be continuously recognized. Thus the evaluations that prevail within a society are always subject to challenge and revision. This instability is tempered by the existence of institutionalized arrangements regularizing acknowledgment, such as the political institution of kingship, but even they do not guarantee stability, as Agamemnon's problems in the *Iliad* make clear. In the wartime setting that the *Iliad* depicts, this insecurity is especially acute for all heroes because they are called on to prove themselves constantly, and the chances of failure are very high. And because the expedition against Troy is a pan-Hellenic enterprise, it provides

---

Thus Sarpedon includes in the list of honors that heroes fight for that "πάντες δὲ θεοὺς ὣς εἰσορόωσι," "all men look on us as if we were gods" (*Il.* 12.312); the members of Agamemnon's embassy promise Achilles that if he returns to them the Achaeans will honor him like a god (*Il.* 9.302, 603); and heroes are frequently said to be honored by their communities as if they were gods if they hold an office that routinely confers honor, either the political office of king (*Il.* 9.155, 297; 10.33; 11.58; 13.218; cf. Hesiod *Theogony* 91) or the religious office of priest (*Il.* 5.78; 16.605). While these expressions may contain latent references to cult worship, as Nagy has recently argued ("On the Death of Sarpedon," 197–203), their recurrent formulation as a comparison maintains the distinction between men and gods that the worship of heroes blurs. The focus of the epics remains on the glory men win as men and through human institutions (note the emphasis in these expressions on the *dēmos*, the people, as the source of honor).

individual heroes, each of whom may be preeminent wherever he comes from, with the opportunity to win wider recognition from a larger and more far-flung group of people but also with a corresponding need to face greater danger and sharper competition.[6]

The *Odyssey*'s story of its hero's *nostos* is an account of his return to a place, his own home, where he should no longer need to compete with a group of peers to win recognition. Although the conditions of this setting limit the sphere in which he is recognized, they also eliminate the need to acknowledge and compete with the society of peers with whom he has constantly to come to terms during an enterprise undertaken jointly with other heroes away from home, such as the expedition against Troy. The great but also circumscribed advantages of operating within this sphere are well illustrated in the final episode of the *Odyssey*, where they are seen pursued to their limits. Odysseus is able to defend his house up to the boundary created by the edge of his holdings with a band of warriors composed of family members and dependents—his father, his son, and his family retainers—whose ability to help him is sufficient but falls short of threatening his own position of preeminence.[7] He does not,

---

[6] A good example of a hero who is greatly honored at home but eclipsed by others when he comes to Troy is Thoas, who is not a particularly prominent hero in the *Iliad* but is said to be "the best of the Aetolians" (*Il.* 15.282) and to be honored like a god by the *dēmos* (*Il.* 13.218).

[7] Not only can Odysseus rely only on family members, but he can rely only on family members whose relationship to him is notably unequal, for he has no brothers. In other words, he lacks the kind of relative with whom he would have a relationship most similar to the one between fellow warriors who are not related by blood. This may seem to be a disadvantage, because it means that he cannot put together even a rudimentary army to confront the suitors. But it can also be seen as an advantage: it requires Odysseus to adopt the kind of clandestine strategy at which he excells and for which he can get all the glory. The underlying advantage of brotherlessness is indicated obliquely during the encounter between Odysseus and Telemachus in Book 16: Odysseus asks Telemachus if it is because his brothers are inadequate to help him that he is oppressed by the suitors (*Od.* 16.95–98), and Telemachus explains that he has no brothers by citing his genealogy, thus pointing to the source of his and Odysseus' power (*Od.* 16.118–120).

therefore, have to reach any accommodation with the unrelated contemporaries and social equals who shared both the burden and the glory during the expedition to Troy. All figures of that kind now appear as the enemy; the entire adult male population of Ithaca, with whom Odysseus must compete for any recognition outside his own household, is represented as a body of people with whom Odysseus is overtly and understandably in conflict.

Odysseus' near destruction of the last remaining Ithacans from the vantage of his own house illustrates, as does Achilles' near destruction of the Achaeans through his withdrawal from the Achaean cause, the way the hero's desire for preeminence makes him potentially hostile to the whole of the community of his peers that lies beyond his own family and household. If he can arrive at a position in which he no longer needs the cooperation of outsiders, then the hero can afford to become their enemy. This is something Achilles seems to achieve through the favor that Thetis obtains for him from Zeus, but the achievement proves illusory since Achilles cannot detach himself wholly from the Achaean cause. Odysseus attains a much truer state of self-sufficiency as he recovers his home, and would gladly dispense with the rest of Ithacan society if Athena did not finally intervene to preserve the larger community and to indicate the limits of his undisputed power. Odysseus achieves something similar to Achilles' impossible wish that he could forget the rest of the Achaeans and take the citadel of Troy, aided only by Patroclus, the one member of the Achaean army with whom he has a noncompetitive, quasi-familial relationship (*Il.* 16.97–100). Odysseus is actually able to win a war with the help only of those with whom he has the kind of relationship that Achilles has with Patroclus.[8]

[8] Not only does the *Odyssey* focus on Odysseus' actions in the context in which he can be solely triumphant, but in it Odysseus describes the taking of Troy in terms that surpass even Achilles' wish, claiming to have destroyed the city in partnership only with Athena (*Od.* 13.388). See Pietro Pucci, "The Proem of the *Odyssey*," 44–45. On the other hand, when he conceals his identity from the Cyclops, Odysseus must suppress that claim and so gives all the credit for the taking of Troy to Agamemnon (*Od.* 9.264–266).

As Odysseus achieves the genuine distance from the world of combat that Achilles only simulates, he becomes progressively less dependent on, and progressively more hostile towards, the various groups of men who, in successive settings, represent a society of his peers: the other Achaean warriors, his own companions on the homeward journey, the suitors, and finally the suitors' kinsmen. In its presentation of Odysseus' separation and distinction from his peers, the poem is able to find justification for their increasing treatment as his enemies. This justification is closely allied both to Odysseus' acquisition of continuous divine aid in the figure of Athena, who is regularly at his side, and to his own assimilation to the role of a god.

It is with the suitors that Odysseus succeeds best in doing what every hero would like to do: he asserts an unqualified superiority over his rivals as he removes them forever. Furthermore, he does so in a setting in which this action represents the restoration of order and the execution of justice. The suitors define themselves as transgressors by choosing to compete with Odysseus in the one realm in which he ought not to have to compete with his peers, the household, in which he is entitled to a position of uncontested eminence created through a network of relationships with subordinates and dependents. This fundamental fact of human social organization is endorsed and charged with moral significance in the Homeric epics by the way a hero's claims are upheld systematically by the gods in this setting, as they are not in the less stable and highly competitive environment of the wartime camp. It is in relation to the rights and obligations of the individual household that the Homeric gods act according to principles that are sufficiently consistent to be identified with justice. They support heroes who are avenging offenses against the integrity of their households and impose certain obligations, associated with the institution of hospitality, on the household in its relations with the outside world.[9]

[9] On the inconsistency between the view of the gods as just that is associated with the account of Odysseus' return to Ithaca and the view of them as arbitrary and capricious that is associated with the account of Odysseus' adventures, see

Odysseus acquires the undivided sponsorship of one of the gods only for that part of his story that is concerned with his repossession of his house. Although, as Nestor recalls (*Od.* 3.218–222), Athena has always shown favor to Odysseus, at Troy as well as elsewhere, in the *Iliad* she helps other heroes, such as Diomedes, as well, and in the *Odyssey* she is Odysseus' constant patron only during the time he is specifically engaged in regaining his house.[10] She actively helps him only from the moment he is destined to make his solitary journey from Calypso's island and shows open support for him only from the time he actually reaches the shores of Ithaca. As long as he is in the wider world beyond Ithaca, he is still in the realm where other heroes, with other gods helping them, have conflicting claims, which makes Athena's partisanship neither possible nor appropriate.

During the time of his wanderings, Odysseus is subject to the wrath that Athena turns against all of the returning Achaeans (*Od.* 5.105–109).[11] In Homer, divine wrath, whatever its often inscrutable cause, expresses itself at the point of mortal limitation; it is evoked against mortals as they experience the limits of their knowledge, cleverness, strength, or luck. Athena's gener-

---

Bernard Fenik, *Studies in the Odyssey*, 209–227; Jenny Strauss Clay, *The Wrath of Athena*, 213–239. Awareness of this opposition within the *Odyssey* must qualify any attempt to distinguish between the morality of the *Odyssey* and the morality of the *Iliad* along the lines suggested by Werner Jaeger ("Solons Eunomie") and Felix Jacoby ("Die geistige Physiognomie der Odyssee"). On the way the *Odyssey* contrasts settings in which human institutions, such as agriculture and sacrifice, are operative with settings in which they are not, see Pierre Vidal-Naquet, "Valeurs religieuses et mythiques de la terre et du sacrifice dans l'*Odyssée*."

[10] Cf. Jenny Strauss Clay's explanation of Athena's resumption of support for Odysseus: "It is not so much Odysseus himself, but the pressure of events on Ithaca that compels Athena to release Odysseus and to bring him home to set things right." *The Wrath of Athena*, 234.

[11] Odysseus' exposure to Athena's wrath is discussed at length by Jenny Strauss Clay, who argues that Odysseus does not simply suffer from Athena's wrath by virtue of being one of the returning Achaeans, but that he provokes her wrath through his nearly godlike cleverness. *The Wrath of Athena*, 43–53, 209.

alized anger against the Achaeans corresponds to their time at sea, the time when they are outside the limited realm in which human society mitigates the violence and precariousness of human existence. Then Athena's help is unavailable to Odysseus, and Zeus sides with Polyphemus and Helios against him, despite Odysseus' claims to justice.[12]

Athena's aid to Odysseus becomes open only as his return progresses. First she works only behind the scenes, persuading Zeus to send Hermes to secure Odysseus' release from Calypso; in Phaeacia she herself acts to help him but, out of deference to Poseidon, appears only in disguise (*Od.* 6.328–331). It is only when he reaches Ithaca and is no longer subject to Poseidon's wrath that Athena appears to him openly and offers him unlimited support (*Od.* 13.341–343). And at the end of the poem, when Odysseus begins to move outside his household again, stepping beyond the boundaries of his farm to attack a segment of the Ithacan population that has not invaded his house, Athena no longer is automatically on his side; rather, she forces him to reach an accommodation with his rivals. He is now in a situation like that of the Achaean camp, in which he must acknowledge the claims of others who are his peers, and so her final epiphany is not, like earlier ones, a sign of unqualified support for his assertion of himself. It is, rather, like her appearance to Achilles at the beginning of the *Iliad*. Achilles interprets the appearance as a sign of partisanship, asking her if she has come to witness Agamemnon's misdeeds. But Athena's appearance is actually inspired by Hera's equal love for Achilles and Agamemnon and is intended to stop Achilles from destroying his rival (*Il.* 1.193–218).

The values of the poem, then, are such that the suitors, by virtue of the setting they have chosen for themselves, condemn themselves to the role of the poem's villains and eventually to being the victims of a divine plot. The poem at once develops

[12] When Odysseus is in transit between this world and his home, Zeus plays a role that could be called transitional, siding partly with Poseidon and partly with Odysseus as he negotiates a reduced punishment for the Phaeacians.

this characterization, portraying the suitors as murderous and uncivilized, and allows it to be seen that this characterization is a function of setting. Odysseus' role as just avenger is successfully established but not left entirely unquestioned.

In particular, Odysseus' treatment of the suitors as an undifferentiated group is shown to be questionable. He asserts an undiscriminating superiority to all of them and makes no attempt to recognize their individual merits or degrees of culpability. But, on the basis of the evidence presented by the *Odyssey*, it is, in fact, impossible to arrive at any stable collective characterization or moral assessment of the suitors. After Odysseus has decisively revealed both his identity and his intentions towards the suitors by killing Antinous, Eurymachus tries to save the others by claiming that only Antinous was to blame for the suitors' transgressions (*Od.* 22.45–59). Coming from Eurymachus, the speech is hypocritical, and the claim is false, but the underlying contention that not all the suitors are equally culpable has a merit that Odysseus chooses to ignore. Certainly the ringleaders, notably Eurymachus and Antinous, are more blameworthy than the others. Furthermore, the portrayal of the relationship between individual suitors and the suitors as a group, a relationship that is often expressed in the alternation between speeches attributed to the suitors as a whole and speeches attributed to individuals, tends to shift. For example, when Antinous throws a footstool at the disguised Odysseus in Book 17, the rest of the suitors collectively reproach him, reminding him of the possibility that the stranger could be a god (*Od.* 17.483–487). But when this episode is replayed in Book 18, and Eurymachus throws a footstool at the beggar, the suitors respond collectively by wishing the stranger had never come to ruin their feast (*Od.* 18.400–404), and only Amphinomus speaks up in favor of the stranger's rights (*Od.* 18.414–421).

Odysseus, however, absolves himself of any obligation to discriminate among the suitors. In the explanation he gives for his refusal to pardon the seer Leodes, he insists that if Leodes associated with the suitors he must have shared their unforgivable desire that he, Odysseus, never return to recover his house, and thus Leodes cannot escape their fate (*Od.* 22.322–325). That Odysseus' undiscriminating hostility to the suitors is a function of their situation in the house is most clear in the similarly unsettling episode in which Odysseus urges Amphinomus to leave, but Athena binds him there to be killed eventually by Telemachus (*Od.* 18.119–157). Athena looks out for Odysseus' interests in this episode by keeping even this sympathetic and upright rival in the one place where Odysseus' hostility has the unwavering support of the gods.[13]

The unqualified superiority that Odysseus asserts against the suitors is dramatized by his success in concealing his identity from them and taking them by surprise. The gap between the truth of their situation and their understanding of it defines a distance between them and him comparable to that between mortals and the gods whose epiphanies his self-revelation mim-

---

[13] In these respects the treatment of the suitors should be compared to that of Odysseus' companions. They too are presented as an undifferentiated group, and the fact that they die while Odysseus survives (which is an essential element of his return—cf. *Od.* 13.340) is attributed to their own reckless actions. This is especially true in the prologue, in which the justification of Odysseus' return without his companions is made virtually the first business of the poem. (Cf. especially the characterization of their behavior as "*atasthalia*," "reckless actions," a term that, as Jenny Strauss Clay has recently shown, is used "to place the blame for a destructive act on one party while absolving another." *The Wrath of Athena* 37.) The actual narrative of the homeward journey, like the overall portrayal of the suitors, shows, however, that Odysseus' companions cannot be so easily lumped together or blamed for their own destruction. They are not all lost under the same circumstances, and the loss of those who survive the encounters with the Ciconians, the Cyclops, and Scylla is doubly motivated, stemming both from Odysseus' refusal to forego identifying himself to the Cyclops (*Od.* 9.533–535) and from the companions' own inability to resist the temptation to eat the cattle of the sun (*Od.* 11.114–115). In accord with their situation in the story of the homeward journey rather than in the hero's house, the case against Odysseus' companions is made much more mildly than that against the suitors; it has an ambiguous quality that corresponds to their intermediate position between Odysseus' highly esteemed fellow warriors in the Achaean camp and his deadly enemies, the suitors. Odysseus' refusal to accept any of the companions as a legitimate rival is dramatized when he overreacts to Eurylochus' challenge to his leadership (*Od.* 10.428–448). Eurylochus' claim to compete with Odysseus is reinforced by the fact that he is Odysseus' close kinsman (*Od.* 10.441).

ics. The failure of mortals to recognize a disguised god, which is a prominent feature of accounts of divine disguise in the Homeric epics and the Homeric Hymns, is echoed in the suitors' failure to recognize Odysseus. The significance of failed recognition in those parallel stories, especially as it relates to setting, can illuminate the role of similar failures in the *Odyssey*'s depiction of the suitors' just subordination to Odysseus.

Both in the Homeric epics and in the Homeric Hymns, failure to recognize a disguised god often brings mortals to disaster, and this disaster is frequently accompanied by a display of divine anger, as in the case of the sailors in the *Hymn to Dionysus* or of Metaneira in the *Hymn to Demeter*. And yet the gods are so good at disguising themselves that mortals can hardly be expected to recognize them. As Odysseus says to Athena when she has disguised herself from him, "ἀργαλέον σε, θεά, γνῶναι βροτῷ ἀντιάσαντι, / καὶ μάλ' ἐπισταμένῳ· σὲ γὰρ αὐτὴν παντὶ ἐίσκεις," "It is hard, goddess, for a mortal who meets you to recognize you / even if he is very intelligent. For you can disguise yourself as anything" (*Od.* 13.312–313). To recognize gods with ease is characteristic of gods, not of men, as the poet comments while describing Hermes' visit to Calypso (*Od.* 5.77–80).[14]

[14] For this very reason, however, it is a particularly heroic trait. This is well illustrated in the *Iliad* when Athena shows her favor towards Diomedes by giving him the power to recognize gods in battle and thus to avoid fruitless confrontations with them (*Il.* 5.127–128). In accord with the circular way in which the causes and results of divine favor are inextricably linked, a hero may recognize that a god is on his side and fight better as a result (e.g., *Il.* 13.43–80). Cf. *Od.* 1.323–324, where Telemachus is said, in one line, to recognize Athena and in the next to join the suitors, "ἰσόθεος φώς," "a man comparable to a god." In the *Odyssey*, the distinguished hero Nestor is the one to recognize Athena as she leaves his palace (*Od.* 3.375–384) and, in the retrospective account of the burial of Athena in Book 24, he alone is able to identify the terrible mourning cry of Thetis (*Od.* 24.46–57). Noemon, the man who lends Telemachus his ship, perhaps represents more ordinary humanity; he recognizes the goddess in Mentor, not through a flash of heroic insight but through the process of deduction (*Od.* 4.653–656). Telemachus' near, but still incomplete, attainment of his father's maturity and stature is measured in relation to this ability in the episode that opens Book 19. He is alert to the signs of Athena's presence, but Odysseus must interpret them for him and must guide his reaction (*Od.* 19.33–46). In

The inability to see beyond the immediately present, to penetrate beyond the disguises that characterize the world of transitory appearances, is one of the limitations that distinguishes men from gods. Thus, in the *Hymn to Demeter* Demeter expresses her wrath at Metaneira for not recognizing her by berating her for her lack of divine foresight.

Νήϊδες ἄνθρωποι καὶ ἀφράδμονες οὔτ᾽ ἀγαθοῖο
αἶσαν ἐπερχομένου προγνώμεναι οὔτε κακοῖο·
καὶ σὺ γὰρ ἀφραδίῃσι τεῆς νήκεστον ἀάσθης.
ἴστω γὰρ θεῶν ὅρκος ἀμείλικτον Στυγὸς ὕδωρ
ἀθάνατόν κέν τοι καὶ ἀγήραον ἤματα πάντα
παῖδα φίλον ποίησα καὶ ἄφθιτον ὤπασα τιμήν·
νῦν δ᾽ οὐκ ἔσθ᾽ ὥς κεν θάνατον καὶ κῆρας ἀλύξαι.
τιμὴ δ᾽ ἄφθιτος αἰὲν ἐπέσσεται οὕνεκα γούνων
ἡμετέρων ἐπέβη καὶ ἐν ἀγκοίνῃσιν ἴαυσεν.

Men are too ignorant and foolish to know ahead of time
the portion of good which is coming to them, or of evil.
You too were incurably blinded by your foolishness.
Let the relentless water of the Styx by which the gods swear
be my witness: immortal and ageless for all days
I would have made your beloved son, and I would have
  granted him unfailing honor;
but now there is no way that he can escape death and its
  spirits.
But unfailing honor will always be his because
he climbed on my knees and slept in my arms.
(256–264)[15]

---

the encounter of Odysseus and Athena in Book 13, in which Odysseus' exceptional and godlike heroism is dramatized, his failure to recognize Athena then and his claim to have recognized her on a previous occasion combine to define his abilities as close to those of the gods, but still falling short of them. See the discussion by Jenny Strauss Clay, *The Wrath of Athena*, 198–202. On the distinction between those who can recognize gods in disguise and those who cannot, see Marcel Detienne, *Les maîtres de vérité*, 75.

[15] At *Hymn to Demeter* 258, I follow Richardson in reading Voss' νήκεστον instead of the manuscript reading μήκιστον. For references to other instances of gods reproaching mortals for not knowing as much as they do, see N. J. Richardson, *The Homeric Hymn to Demeter*, 243–244.

The punishment for this failing is simply another expression of what it itself represents: being mortal. Demophon's restriction to a mortal life is the inevitable consequence of having a mortal mother, and this story of his lost chance at immortality is a means of expressing what was always already true. As the son of a mortal woman, Demophon cannot be a god, but only a mortal who has "τιμὴ ἄφθιτος," "unfailing honor" because of his association with a god.

On the battlefield in the *Iliad*, for a hero to be able to recognize a god fighting on the other side is essential to survival;[16] it allows him to retreat from a confrontation that he would be bound to lose (for example, *Il.* 16.118–124; 16.657–658). Failure to recognize a god fighting against him is a signal that a hero is destined to survive no longer. It means that he has reached the limit, which exists for every mortal hero, of the number of times he can risk his life in battle without being killed. This failure to recognize a god represents the point at which, for reasons he cannot know and which may have nothing to do with him, a hero has lost the gods' support. Thus Patroclus' inevitable fate is heralded by the entry of Apollo into battle against him, of which Patroclus himself is oblivious (*Il.* 16.783–792). And when, during the final confrontation of Hector and Achilles, Zeus has weighed their fates in the balance and Hector's death has been decided upon, this situation is at once expressed in the behavior of the gods on the battlefield: Apollo abandons Hector, while Athena appears openly to Achilles to assure him of her support, but she disguises herself from Hector in order to defeat him. She appears to Hector in the guise of his brother Deiphobus and tricks him into relying on her so that he turns to face Achilles. His failure to see through her disguise leads directly to his death.

What prevents these heroes from recognizing the gods who oppose them is the decision of the gods to destroy them. In each case this failure of recognition represents the hero's disadvantage at the moment when he is destined to fall at the hands of

---

[16] On this point, see James M. Redfield, *Nature and Culture in the Iliad*, 130–131.

another hero who is even greater and even more favored by the gods. This failure to recognize a god may correspond to a broader failure in perception, an error in judgment brought on by a surge of confidence and zeal for battle; it may even, as in the account of Patroclus' death, accompany a fatally provocative attempt to be "δαίμονι ἶσος," "equal to a divinity" (*Il.* 16.786), but it does not represent a moral failing that would make a hero culpable in human terms. Rather, it is a sign of the inevitable frailty and impotence of even the greatest mortals in a universe controlled by the gods, a condition that is often labelled tragic. It is a form of ignorance of the true nature of the situation in which one is operating comparable to tragic *hamartia*, which often takes the form of misperception of identity. These heroes' subsequent realization that they have been engaged in a vain attempt to fight a god is closely reminiscent of the late learning often experienced by characters in tragedy. Hector does eventually recognize, when he turns to ask him for the spear he promised to hold and finds him gone, that the figure he thought was Deiphobus was actually Athena. But that means only that he is painfully aware of his imminent and unavoidable death (*Il.* 22.296–305). Similarly, Helen's recognition that the old woman who calls her to Paris' bed is really Aphrodite means that, for all her anger and reluctance, she has no choice but to go (*Il.* 3.383–420).

But the inability of humans to see through divine disguises is not always given so thoroughly tragic a treatment as it receives in the *Iliad*. While human ignorance may be irremediable, it can be mitigated; and some narratives, such as the Homeric Hymns, which address the possibilities of mediation between men and gods, draw attention to this possibility. In the *Hymn to Dionysus* the helmsman distinguishes himself from the other pirates by his awareness when their captive resists binding that he must be one of the gods, even though he doesn't know which one and suggests several identifications—Zeus, Apollo, Poseidon—all of them wrong.[17] Thus he urges them to put the stran-

---

[17] Cf. Anchises in the *Hymn to Aphrodite* who at once recognizes that Aphrodite is some goddess, but also tries out a series of different specific identifications: Artemis, Leto, Aphrodite, Themis, Athena, one of the Graces, one of the

ger ashore for fear that he might raise a storm against them. He is rewarded for this when Dionysus stops him from jumping overboard and becoming a dolphin like his shipmates, making him instead "πανόλβιος," "extremely fortunate," and revealing his true identity to him.

The helmsman's recognition of Dionysus' divinity stems from an awareness of the immanence of the divine in the world that compensates for his inability to penetrate the god's disguise. He is set apart from his companions because he can understand the import of an indirect display of power, the stranger's evasion of binding, and can connect it with the potential for that power to be displayed in more direct and painful ways through the manipulation of natural forces. Thus he acknowledges the power of the gods even when it manifests itself only partially or is perceived only as a potentiality. Furthermore, the general piety displayed by the helmsman in this hymn can be formalized in religious rituals, whose observation does not even demand the degree of perspicuity he reveals. For example, the story of Demeter's encounter with the household of Celeus concludes with an institutionalized solution to the problem of divine obscurity. Demeter gives instructions for the establishment of a cult through which the family can regularly recognize her power and secure her favor.[18] Routinized piety thereafter compensates for mortal inability to recognize the goddess' disguised and unpredictable appearances. The *Hymn to Dionysus* and the *Hymn to Demeter* each suggests that there are ways in which human inferiority to the gods can be tempered and that the gods honor them.[19]

Nymphs (92–99). Cf. Ove Jörgenson's observation that there is a recurrent distinction in the Homeric epics between our knowledge (transmitted by the poet, who is inspired by the all-seeing Muses) of the activity of a specific divinity and the characters' awareness simply of "θεός," or "δαίμων," "some god" at work. "Das Auftreten der Götter in den Büchern ι-μ der Odyssee," 363–367.

[18] On the combination of the epiphany of a god and the institution of rites as a traditional thematic cluster, see Cora Sowa, *Traditional Themes and the Homeric Hymns*, 241–250.

[19] Cf. *Hymn to Aphrodite*, 102–106, where these themes occur in a highly compressed form. Recognizing Aphrodite as some goddess but not knowing

The gods also honor the expedients men devise among themselves for countering the precariousness and unpredictability of mortal life. In his speech at the beginning of the *Odyssey*, Zeus berates mortals for suffering more than they have to, "ὑπὲρ μό-ρον," "beyond their share" (*Od.* 1.34). It is through the institutions of society, in particular through the rules and customs centering on the household, that men attempt to mimimize the effects of human subjectedness to time, strife, and changes of fortune. Within a properly functioning household, each person has an uncontestable right to a certain place, a place that is always his. As a medium of inheritance, the household provides for the orderly transfer of property and allows its members to participate in something that has the quality of permanence of which they are in their own lives deprived. And as the focus of hospitality, the household offers a counter to the hunger and exposure to the elements that face those who are temporarily or permanently away from home; the household mediates the good fortune of those who have a home, with all that means, and the bad fortune of those who do not.[20]

The gods endorse these efforts to reduce systematically the difficulties of human life by themselves supporting these efforts regularly and predictably as they do not the sporadic adventures of individuals. Thus Aegisthus, whose example prompts Zeus' general observation on human folly, is actually warned by Hermes of the consequences of his transgression. As has been seen, Athena consistently and reliably supports Odysseus when

---

which one she is, Anchises immediately offers her an altar and, at the same time, asks for the gifts through which humans can achieve an approximation of immortality: fame, long life, and flourishing descendants. On the partial communion between men and gods delineated in the Homeric Hymns, see William G. Thalmann, *Conventions of Form and Thought in Early Greek Epic Poetry*, 92–96.

[20] Recent treatments of the institution of hospitality in the Homeric epics, to which this discussion is indebted, include: M. I. Finley, *The World of Odysseus*; David E. Belmont, "Early Greek Guest-Friendship and Its Role in Homer's *Odyssey*"; Hélène J. Kakridis, *La notion de l'amitié et de l'hospitalité chez Homère*; Douglas Stewart, *The Disguised Guest*, passim, esp. 17 ff; Agathe Thornton, *People and Themes in Homer's Odyssey*, 38–46. For the typical forms of scenes of guest welcome, see Walter Arend, *Die typischen Szenen bei Homer*, 39–51.

he is engaged in reasserting his right to his home. And when the gods go among mortals in disguise, they test them for their hospitality as well as for their piety.[21]

As a result, when Athena and Odysseus arrive in disguise to reclaim Odysseus' house, the suitors' failure to recognize them is not simply a sign of a shared and irremediable frailty in relation to the gods, although that is there. The suitors' fallibility is felt particularly in the poet's rhetorical question as he describes Antinous' death,

> φόνος δέ οἱ οὐκ ἐνὶ θυμῷ
> μέμβλετο· τίς κ᾽ οἴοιτο μετ᾽ ἀνδράσι δαιτυμόνεσσι
> μοῦνον ἐνὶ πλεόνεσσι, καὶ εἰ μάλα καρτερὸς εἴη,
> οἷ τεύξειν θάνατόν τε κακὸν καὶ κῆρα μέλαιναν;

> Slaughter was far from
> his mind. For who would think that, in a company of men
>   feasting,
> one man among the many, even if he were very strong,
> would contrive for him evil death and a black fate?
> (*Od.* 22.11–14)

But because they are met within the household, where they can be expected to recognize certain customs and usages, the suitors, in failing to recognize Odysseus and the god who stands beside him, are more like the pirates of the *Hymn to Dionysus*[22] than like Patroclus and Hector in the *Iliad*.

No one on Ithaca can be expected to recognize Odysseus as long as he maintains his disguise, and no one does (with the exception of his dog, whose instincts even a disguise cannot baffle). But the nonrecognition of the suitors takes on an entirely different quality from that of Odysseus' loyal supporters; it can

[21] On the parallels between stories in which gods test the hospitality of mortals and the plot of the *Odyssey*, see Emily Kearns, "The Return of Odysseus: A Homeric Theoxeny."

[22] The suitors suffer a metaphorical transformation into animals that is reminiscent of the literal transformation suffered by the pirates in the *Hymn to Dionysus*: as Odysseus gives the suitors a last glance to make sure they are all dead, they are compared to a pile of dead fish (*Od.* 23.384–399).

be related to broader failures of recognition of which they are also guilty. Odysseus' supporters are sometimes dull to the possibility, which always exists, that the gods could work a miracle, the fact of which Athena, as Mentor, reminds Telemachus that, "ῥεῖα θεός γ᾽ ἐθέλων καὶ τηλόθεν ἄνδρα σαώσαι," "A god, if he wished, could easily bring back a man, even from far away" (*Od.* 3.231), and this causes them to lose hope when they ought not to. When they express their despair in the presence of the disguised Odysseus, the resulting irony makes it clear that they are suffering beyond what is necessary. But Penelope's suitors not only are blind to the possibility of miracles but also fail to recognize the ordinary principles of human behavior that the gods routinely uphold.[23] The suitors ignore the alignment of the gods with the proper functioning of the household, an alignment that constitutes a pattern of divine behavior that ought to be recognizable even to mortals too shortsighted to identify a god when they see one. Thus, while the suitors cannot be expected to perceive Odysseus' presence, their failure to do so is bound up in their cases with their failure to recognize him in ways they can be expected to.

The suitors can be expected in a certain way to recognize Odysseus even when he is absent: they ought to recognize his right to his household even when he is not there to assert it or when it resides in a legitimate representative who is too weak to assert it. (Which of these possibilities actually describes the situation on Ithaca remains, in the absence of information about Odysseus' fate, unclear.) Thus the suitors can be expected to acknowledge Telemachus' right to the house even if he cannot yet defend it. Odysseus' entitlement to his household entitles him, in that one sphere, to the kind of recognition of his power, even when it is not manifested, that the gods can always claim.

The suitors can also be expected, in another way, to recognize Odysseus in the form in which he is present to them, the form

[23] For a detailed account of the suitors' transgressions against the laws of human society and of the importation of the bestial into the realm of civilization, see Suzanne Saïd, "Les crimes des prétendants, la maison d'Ulysse et les festins de l'*Odyssée*."

of a homeless beggar. Whether or not they know who he is, they ought to receive him with hospitality and thereby to confer on him a measure of recognition. In the Homeric world, hospitality is a social institution that provides outsiders, who are by nature without status, with that place in society that constitutes an identity. As James Redfield puts it, "the household is obligated through household ceremonies to convert the stranger from a nonentity to a person with a status."[24]

On Ithaca, Odysseus' friends and enemies differ—not in their ability to see through his disguise, but in their willingness to accord him the kind of recognition entailed by hospitality. His supporters offer him an hospitable reception that (as we will see in the next chapter) both substitutes for and results in the recognition of his identity. In contrast, the suitors and their allies repeatedly reject him. And in doing so they are not simply failing to see his particular heroism as expressed by Athena's steady protection; they are failing to recognize the generalized association with divine protection that he enjoys as a stranger and suppliant. The suitors disregard an alliance between strangers and Zeus that anyone could be expected to recognize because it is expressed in a general principle—the principle that "πρὸς γὰρ Διός εἰσιν ἅπαντες / ξεῖνοί τε πτωχοί τε," "all strangers and beggars are under the protection of Zeus" (*Od.* 6.207–208)—rather than in a momentary and veiled encounter with a god.

---

[24] James Redfield, *Nature and Culture in the Iliad*, 197–198. To be another person's guest is to be someone. When being someone's guest is institutionalized in the relationship of guest-friendship, that simple recognition can become a permanent and impressive mark of identity. "Mentes," for example, identifies himself to Telemachus in part by saying that he and Odysseus claim one another as guest-friends (*Od.* 1.187–188). Like other aspects of identity, guest-friendship is not only permanent but also inheritable. Telemachus, as he both discovers and discloses his heritage as son of Odysseus, inherits his father's relations of guest-friendship with Nestor and Menelaus. As a way of institutionalizing mutual recognition between people who are usually absent from one another, guest-friendship is an important example of a social institution that systematically assures for mortals the continuous recognition that the gods enjoy. Very good hosts, such as the Phaeacians, are said to honor their guest as if he were a god (*Od.* 5.36; 19.280; 23.339).

Concern for strangers is not an isolated event but a regular attribute of Zeus, who is referred to as "Ζεύς Ξείνιος," "Zeus, Protector of Strangers," or "Ζεύς· Ἱκετήσιος," "Zeus, Protector of Suppliants." In addition, the suitors are blind to the universal precariousness of human fortune, the possibility that anyone might someday be a homeless wanderer, that makes Zeus' protection of strangers so necessary and so highly valued. The suitors miss the hints embedded in the stranger's fictional autobiography and lack the sense of potential similarity between Odysseus and the stranger that is, for Penelope (*Od.* 19.358–360) and for Eumaeus and Philoetius (*Od.* 21.204–207), a significant step towards recognition.

Odysseus' entrance into his household in a beggar's disguise broadens the significance of his return so that his personal triumph over his enemies becomes also an exemplary vindication of the laws of hospitality. Odysseus' achievement of recognition for his exceptional heroism simultaneously enforces the principle of social life that demands recognition even for those without status. As each interprets the meaning of the suitors' death, both Odysseus and Penelope point out that the suitors have inverted this principle: instead of honoring even poor beggars, they have honored no one, "οὔ τινα γὰρ τίεσκον ἐπιχθονίων ἀνθρώπων, / οὐ κακὸν οὐδὲ μὲν ἐσθλόν, ὅτις σφέας εἰσαφίκοιτο," "they honored no one of all earthly men / whether base or noble, who came to them" (*Od.* 22.414–415; 23.65–66). In other words, the suitors entirely misunderstand the nature of τιμή, "recognition": they honor only "οὔτις," "no one"—a contradiction in terms because to honor someone is to make him someone other than "οὔτις." Like the Cyclops, whose encounter with Odysseus this line recalls, the suitors help to create the disguise that enables Odysseus to defeat them. By making him "οὔτις," by keeping him unrecognized, they make themselves vulnerable to his surprise attack. Further, unlike the Cyclops, they are situated in the realm of human civilization so that they are expected to know better. Here Odysseus' claim to be acting in consort with Zeus and the other gods is not a hollow boast, as it is when he makes it to Polyphemus.

The suitors' understandable failure to recognize Odysseus as he is present before them is contaminated by their refusal in this broader sense to recognize the rights either of Odysseus while absent or of the beggar whose form conceals him while present. The suitors express their nonrecognition of Odysseus and Athena in terms that are always entwined with their disregard for Telemachus or for the beggar or for both. The result is a series of speeches, particularly those of the suitors' ringleader Eurymachus, which reflect a subtle relationship between perceptual errors and moral failings.

An early example of such a speech occurs towards the end of Book 1 when Telemachus is distinguished from the suitors by his ability to recognize, from the nature of her departure, that "Mentes" is really Athena. After Athena has left, Telemachus displays a new confidence by asserting himself in a number of ways: he speaks sharply to Penelope when she asks Phemius to sing another song; he announces the following day's assembly; and when Antinous taunts him by saying he hopes he will never become king, Telemachus answers that he may not ever be king, although he would like to be, but he does intend to take control of the household. To this Eurymachus replies:

Τηλέμαχ᾽, ἦ τοι ταῦτα θεῶν ἐν γούνασι κεῖται,
ὅς τις ἐν ἀμφιάλῳ Ἰθάκῃ βασιλεύσει Ἀχαιῶν·
κτήματα δ᾽ αὐτὸς ἔχοις καὶ δώμασι σοῖσιν ἀνάσσοις.
μὴ γὰρ ὅ γ᾽ ἔλθοι ἀνὴρ ὅς τίς σ᾽ ἀέκοντα βίηφι
κτήματ᾽ ἀπορραίσει᾽, Ἰθάκης ἔτι ναιεταούσης.
ἀλλ᾽ ἐθέλω σε, φέριστε, περὶ ξείνοιο ἐρέσθαι,
ὁππόθεν οὗτος ἀνήρ, ποίης δ᾽ ἐξ εὔχεται εἶναι
γαίης, ποῦ δέ νύ οἱ γενεὴ καὶ πατρὶς ἄρουρα·
ἠέ τιν᾽ ἀγγελίην πατρὸς φέρει ἐρχομένοιο,
ἦ ἑὸν αὐτοῦ χρεῖος ἐελδόμενος τόδ᾽ ἱκάνει;
οἷον ἀναΐξας ἄφαρ οἴχεται, οὐδ᾽ ὑπέμεινε
γνώμεναι· οὐ μὲν γάρ τι κακῷ εἰς ὦπα ἐῴκει.

Telemachus, this question is in the hands of the gods:
who of the Achaeans will be king in sea-washed Ithaca.
But may you yourself hold your possessions and rule over your
household.

And may no man come who, against your will, would take
    away
your possessions by force, as long as Ithaca is inhabited.
But I want, best of men, to ask you about the stranger,
where this man came from, what sort of land he claimed to
    belong to,
where his family and his ancestral fields are.
Did he bring you some message about your returning father?
Or did he come pursuing some business of his own?
How suddenly, rushing away, he disappeared. He didn't wait
to be known. He was no insignificant man, from the looks of
    him.

(Od. 1.400–411)

The falseness of Eurymachus' perception that "Mentes" was a
person (conveyed pointedly as Eurymachus mentions the very
feature of Athena's visit that should have alerted him to her true
identity, her rapid departure) is linked to the deliberate and sinister falseness of his claim to consider Telemachus "φέριστε,"
"best of men" and to wish him well. His speech modulates from
a designedly hypocritical statement acknowledging Telemachus' claims (a specific manifestation of the bad faith that generally underlies his claim to be present in the house as Penelope's suitor) to an unintended travesty of a statement
acknowledging a divine epiphany. Furthermore, the speech is
based in another way on a false assumption, the assumption tht
Telemachus has not changed, even though his behavior has become so different that Eurymachus should see that he has.

    All of these forms of falseness have the same source: failure to
recognize Telemachus' claim to his house. Telemachus' divinely
protected claim to his house means that Eurymachus is wrong
to think he can deprive him of it, to trust that the wish he expresses insincerely will go unfulfilled. That claim also means
that Telemachus has the support of Athena against the suitors,
support that is manifested in her visit and in the changes in him
that her visit inspires. What in Eurymachus' speech he thinks is
true is actually false, and what he thinks is false is actually true.
And this persistently crossed relationship to the truth is recapit-

ulated when Telemachus exercises his newfound ability to contend with Eurymachus and to protect his rights by deceiving Eurymachus. He repeats Athena's deceptive tale of being "Mentes," although "φρεσὶ δ᾽ ἀθανάτην θεὸν ἔγνω," "in his mind he recognized the immortal goddess" (Od. 1.420). The same qualities that make the suitors unable to recognize the presence of a god lead them to reject the omens and prophecies through which the gods communicate with men.[25] This is especially marked in an episode in Book 2 in which Telemachus, stymied in his attempt to stand up to the suitors, appeals to Zeus for help, and Zeus responds with an omen. Halitherses correctly interprets this omen as a sign of Odysseus' imminent return and of the coming defeat of the suitors, while Eurymachus rejects it, denying altogether that it is an omen. Halitherses further links this omen to his own prophecy, made when Odysseus left for Troy,

φῆν κακὰ πολλὰ παθόντ᾽, ὀλέσαντ᾽ ἄπο πάντας ἑταίρους,
ἄγνωστον πάντεσσιν ἐεικοστῷ ἐνιαυτῷ
οἴκαδ᾽ ἐλεύσεσθαι· τὰ δὲ δὴ νῦν πάντα τελεῖται.

I said that, having suffered much and lost all his companions,
unrecognized by anyone, in the twentieth year,
he would come back home again. And now all this is being
accomplished.

(Od. 2.174–176)

This refinement of the omen's meaning turns it into an advance representation of Odysseus' return, focusing in the word "ἄγνωστον," "unrecognized" on the issue of Odysseus' recognition. Halitherses' words test hypothetically the suitors' ability to recognize Odysseus, an ability that will be tested directly when Odysseus returns. Presented with the idea of Odysseus returning in disguise, they reject it just as they will later reject him himself.

[25] On the role of omens in Odysseus' return, see A. J. Podlecki, "Omens in the *Odyssey*"; Anne Amory, "The Reunion of Odysseus and Penelope," esp. 119, where she notes that the term *sēma* means both omen and recognition token.

Eurymachus' first response to this speech is to threaten Halitherses and his children. His rejection of the prophecy is thus linked to a demonstration of the suitors' tendency to bully the weak, a quality which is reflected in the suitors' central transgression of taking advantage of Telemachus' helplessness in order to consume his household. Eurymachus' indifference to divination is linked directly to his lack of respect for Telemachus. He dismisses Telemachus' defense of his rights and Halitherses' prophecy in a single breath.

οὐ γὰρ πρὶν παύσεσθαι ὀίομαι υἷας Ἀχαιῶν
μνηστύος ἀργαλέης, ἐπεὶ οὔ τινα δείδιμεν ἔμπης,
οὔτ᾽ οὖν Τηλέμαχον, μάλα περ πολύμυθον ἐόντα·
οὔτε θεοπροπίης ἐμπαζόμεθ᾽, ἣν σύ, γεραιέ,
μυθέαι ἀκράαντον, ἀπεχθάνεαι δ᾽ ἔτι μᾶλλον.

I do not think the sons of the Achaeans will cease from
their harsh courtship, for we certainly do not fear anyone,
not even Telemachus, even though he is so eloquent.
Nor do we care for any prophecy, which you, old man,
may tell us, which will not happen, and will make you even
    more hated.

                                (*Od.* 2.198–202)

Eurymachus also offers his own counterinterpretation of the omen.

ταῦτα δ᾽ ἐγὼ σέο πολλὸν ἀμείνων μαντεύεσθαι.
ὄρνιθες δέ τε πολλοὶ ὑπ᾽ αὐγὰς ἠελίοιο
φοιτῶσ᾽, οὐδέ τε πάντες ἐναίσιμοι· αὐτὰρ Ὀδυσσεὺς
ὤλετο τῆλ᾽, ὡς καὶ σὺ καταφθίσθαι σὺν ἐκείνῳ
ὤφελες.

I can interpret these matters much better than you can.
Many birds fly here and there under the
rays of the sun, and not all are significant. But Odysseus
died far away, as you too should have died
with him.

                                (*Od.* 2.180–184)

81

Eurymachus is not the only one to conclude from Odysseus' absence that he is dead; similar statements are made by Telemachus and often by Penelope. But to Eurymachus that conclusion becomes a warrant for seizing control of Odysseus' house; in other words, Eurymachus' failure to recognize Odysseus' power of survival, his extraordinary heroism, so long as it remains unproven translates itself into a refusal to recognize Telemachus' rights so long as Telemachus is unable to defend them by force. Eurymachus' dismissal of the omen recalls the episode in *Iliad* 12 in which Poulydamas interprets an omen to mean that the Trojans should retreat from battle, but Hector rejects the omen. Hector denies the omen's validity and speaks harshly to Poulydamas (*Il.* 12.195–250). But while Hector's obtuseness leads him to behave in ways that are disturbing, it does not detract from his stature or brand him as a villain. Unlike Eurymachus' blindness, Hector's represents an unavoidable conflict built into the heroic system: the search for glory in battle requires disregard of the risks of fighting, risks whose reality is here emphasized by the authority of the omen.

When the suitors are finally confronted with the actual figure of the disguised Odysseus, they give repeated demonstrations of their inability to recognize him and of the reckless disregard for his rights—both as Odysseus and as the stranger—that lies behind their failure. Odysseus tests them with veiled, hypothetical, or incomplete disclosures of his identity like the hints of his presence with which he animates Penelope. These disclosures may consist of the display of a godlike attribute or of victory in a contest or of a recognition that does not happen but is talked about, prophesied, or threatened. They correspond structurally and conceptually to the partial epiphanies with which disguised gods test mortals, such as Demeter's sudden transformation on the threshold of Celeus' house or Dionysus' evasion of his fetters. In these episodes the god's disguise slips a bit—indeed no mortal could recognize a god who wished to conceal his identity entirely—and mortals are tested by their reaction to or interpretation of this event.[26]

[26] Cf. the remarks on Odysseus' repeated rejection by the suitors of Albert

ODYSSEUS AND THE SUITORS

Odysseus' prolonged interaction with the suitors while he is
in disguise becomes a protracted verbal battle over the interpretation of such episodes. The issue of their meaning becomes the
focus of a growing hostility between them and the stranger that
is the surface expression of the latent enmity between them and
Odysseus. Their original refusal to recognize Odysseus' claims
to his house, which has occurred in the past and in his absence,
is recapitulated in their active inability to recognize his identity
in the present and in his presence; their inability to recognize
his identity is similarly recapitulated in their refusal to respond
to him with hospitality.

While the issue of whether the suitors will suffer for these offenses is, in one sense, a matter of suspense and depends on the
outcome of the trial of the bow, that contest is repeatedly antic-
ipated—not for the poem's characters but for its audience—and
repeatedly won by Odysseus in these preliminary verbal skir-
mishes. The suitors and Odysseus encounter each other in an
arena of mutual deception in which the contest, as in the dialogue of Eurymachus and Telemachus at the end of Book 1 discussed above, is between forms of duplicity. Both Odysseus and
the suitors often speak falsely, and both think that they understand and control the relationship between what they are saying
and the actual truth. But only Odysseus knows the central, un-
revealed fact on which their contest implicitly centers: his own
return. For the audience of the poem the issue between Odysseus and the suitors becomes the question of who is in control
of the meaning of his own words, of who controls the ironies
that pervade their dialogue. And the issue of who controls the
meaning of the dialogue comes to stand for the larger issue of
who controls the territory in which the dialogue takes place, of
who controls the house of Odysseus. In this poem, based on the
premise that he who should control it will do so (for that is the
meaning of the gods' support for Odysseus), the possession of

Lord, who writes, "These incidents are multiforms of a single theme . . . whose
meaning, deeply imbedded in the myth underlying the story, is that the resur-
rected god in disguise is rejected by the unworthy, who cannot recognize him."
The Singer of Tales, 175.

83

the truth becomes equated with the right to possess the house. The narrative weight given to Odysseus' encounters with the suitors when he is still in disguise causes the question that is settled through action when he reveals himself, the question of who is stronger, to be recast and prejudged in another form, the question of who the stranger is. Odysseus' identity becomes the reference point for all the poem's evaluations, and the advantage to Odysseus of this shift is one more expression of the advantage that he gains from his disguise.

Odysseus' victory in his fight with the beggar Irus in Book 18 is one of the most overt of his partial epiphanies, and it generates a revealing debate about its meaning.[27] Odysseus conceals its significance, modifying the spectacular feat of which he might be capable to prevent the suitors from recognizing him (*Od.* 18.94). But the suitors still condemn themselves through their misinterpretation of Odysseus' victory. They thank Odysseus for ridding them of Irus, whom they will now ship off to the mainland, and they say that they hope Zeus and the other gods will grant Odysseus whatever he desires most. Odysseus, we are told, "$\chi\alpha\hat{\iota}\rho\epsilon\nu$ $\delta\grave{\epsilon}$ $\kappa\lambda\epsilon\eta\delta\acute{o}\nu\iota$," "was pleased at the omen" (*Od.* 18.117). The suitors, having seen only a display of power sufficient to defeat Irus, interpret it as only that and respond with a cheerful generosity they would never extend to someone they considered competition for themselves. But the redefini-

---

[27] As Albert Lord puts it, this episode is "a frustrated, a vestigial recognition scene brought about by accomplishing a feat of strength possible only to the returned hero" that is closely parallel to the trial of the bow. *The Singer of Tales*, 175. Before fighting Irus, Odysseus is transformed physically by Athena, and as in other recognition scenes, there is the suggestion of rejuvenation. The battle is, several times, treated as a contest of young against old (*Od.* 18.21, 31, 52–53); thus, this contest is, like the final one (cf. *Od.* 21.282–284), a test of whether Odysseus' strength is what it was in his youth. Odysseus puts aside his rags in much the same gesture as accompanies his ultimate self-disclosure during the contest of the bow (*Od.* 18.67, cf. 22.1). The response is that which usually follows an act of self-revelation or a divine epiphany: amazement (*Od.* 18.71). When the contest is over, Odysseus takes up his wallet once again, effectively reassuming his entire disguise (*Od.* 18.108–109). For further parallels between this episode and the contest of the bow, see Daniel Levine, "*Odyssey* 18: Iros as Paradigm for the Suitors."

tion of their speech as an omen, in which poet and hero conspire in the construction of line 117 (and have already conspired in the presentation of Odysseus in disguise), takes its meaning out of their hands and turns it against them. The susceptibility of their words to this treatment is itself a sign of the inevitable defeat those words now invoke; the suitors' inadvertent irony causes them, in effect, to work towards their own defeat.

As a verbal battle develops between Odysseus and his supporters, and the suitors and their supporters, over the significance of this and other such events, the unacknowledged conflict over who is speaking the truth becomes a purposeful and explicit conflict over who is capable of perceiving the truth, a conflict in which the suitors actively betray their ignorance. Shortly after the battle with Irus, Odysseus gives a more subtle hint of his power by offering to tend the lamps in the hall.[28] This partial epiphany is instantly rejected in an abusive speech by the suitors' accomplice, Melantho. She treats Odysseus' offer as a form of madness, which she attributes either to drunkenness or to overconfidence after his victory over Irus, and she goes on to warn him against meeting a better man than Irus. Thus, she equates what we know to be an accurate response to his victory with madness (*Od.* 18.327–336).

Shortly afterwards Eurymachus refers to Odysseus with what he thinks is a parody of a speech acknowledging a divine epiphany.

οὐκ ἀθεεὶ ὅδ᾽ ἀνὴρ Ὀδυσήϊον ἐς δόμον ἵκεν·
ἔμπης μοι δοκέει δαΐδων σέλας ἔμμεναι αὐτοῦ
κὰκ κεφαλῆς, ἐπεὶ οὔ οἱ ἔνι τρίχες οὐδ᾽ ἠβαιαί.

---

[28] Odysseus' offer suggests the sudden bright light which is one of the most common features of a divine epiphany. See N. J. Richardson, *The Homeric Hymn to Demeter*, 189. For radiance as a sign of the hero, see Michael Nagler, *Spontaneity and Tradition*, 117–118; Cedric H. Whitman, *Homer and the Heroic Tradition*, 128–153. Cf. also *Od.* 4.71–75, where Telemachus thinks Menelaus' palace must be like Zeus' because everything is gleaming, and *Od.* 19.34, where Athena reveals herself to Odysseus and Telemachus by providing a light for them as they remove the armor from the hall.

Not without divine providence has this man come to the
   house of Odysseus.
It certainly seems to me that he can provide torchlight
from his head, since there aren't any hairs on it, not even a few.
                                                           (*Od.* 18.353–355)

Not only is Eurymachus unwittingly speaking the truth about
Odysseus' association with the gods, but his speech precisely indicates that his mistake is due to Odysseus' disguise. The feature
of Odysseus' appearance that he makes fun of by pretending to
claim that it makes him godlike—Odysseus' baldness—is actually part of his disguise; in that sense it does make him godlike.

Odysseus responds, in essence, by suggesting a recognition
scene. In response to Eurymachus' taunting offer of work on his
estate, Odysseus proposes a contest between the two of them
and claims that he would win it (*Od.* 18.365–380). He then
turns against Eurymachus the kind of accusation he himself has
already had from Melantho. He impugns Eurymachus' mental
faculties, claiming that his opponent is incapable of accurate
judgment, and then goes on to warn Eurymachus of a more for-
midable enemy—in this case, Odysseus.

ἀλλὰ μάλ᾽ ὑβρίζεις καί τοι νόος ἐστὶν ἀπηνής·
καί πού τις δοκέεις μέγας ἔμμεναι ἠδὲ κραταιός,
οὕνεκα πὰρ παύροισι καὶ οὐκ ἀγαθοῖσιν ὁμιλεῖς.
εἰ δ᾽ Ὀδυσεὺς ἔλθοι καὶ ἵκοιτ᾽ ἐς πατρίδα γαῖαν,
αἶψά κέ τοι τὰ θύρετρα, καὶ εὐρέα περ μάλ᾽ ἐόντα,
φεύγοντι στείνοιτο διὲκ προθύροιο θύραζε.

But now you insult me and your spirit is harsh,
and doubtless you think of yourself as someone tall and
      powerful
because you associate with few men and ones who aren't
      brave.
But if Odysseus should return and reach his fatherland,
suddenly the gates of the house, although they are very broad,
would hem you in as you fled out through the door.
                                                           (*Od.* 18.381–386)

The last three lines of this speech vividly express the idea that this whole series of episodes illustrates, the idea that the recognition of Odysseus that will eventually be forced upon the suitors will involve a sudden and dramatic reversal of their perceptions.

Eurymachus responds in the same words used by Melantho: he suggests that Odysseus must be drunk, deranged, or overly elated by his victory (*Od.* 18.389–393). While Odysseus' speech may represent a veiled self-revelation, to Eurymachus it is simply an act of insolence by someone he refuses to accept as a guest. When he converts words into action by throwing the pitcher, his blindness to Odysseus' presence takes the form of an inhospitable act, and the debate over who is sane is expanded to serve as a test of hospitality, as well. The suitors respond by rejecting the guest who has proved an irritant rather than the boorishness of Eurymachus: they wish the guest had never come and complain that the quarrel he has provoked is ruining the feast (*Od.* 18.401–404). This complaint is countered by two speeches in favor of Odysseus that, taken together, reinforce the links between receptivity to the stranger's outlook, sanity, and hospitality. Telemachus, knowing the stranger's identity, identifies his own view with sanity, and accuses the suitors of being mad or drunk themselves; he also, in effect, corrects their identification of the stranger, suggesting that it is a god, not a beggar, who has stirred them up (*Od.* 18.406–409). His speech is seconded by Amphinomus who, dissociating himself from the rest of the suitors, proposes that Telemachus has spoken justly and should be allowed to treat the stranger as his guest (*Od.* 18.414–421).

The conflict between Odysseus and the suitors, which is, at base, a conflict over whether they have to acknowledge his authority when he is not there to enforce it, has become a conflict over whose perceptions are reliable. In this conflict each accuses the other of distorted vision, but it is Odysseus and his supporters who possess the truth. This conflict continues right up until the moment of Odysseus' disclosure. Theoclymenus' fantastic vision is yet another intimation of Odysseus' presence and elicits another accusation of insanity from Eurymachus (*Od.*

20.360–362). Here, too, the contrast in perceptions is identified with a contrast in attitudes towards hospitality. Eurymachus associates Theoclymenus' madness with his foreignness (*Od.* 20.360), and when Theoclymenus goes off to be received properly by Peiraeus, the suitors taunt Telemachus about his two guests and suggest they should be sold into slavery (*Od.* 20.376–384).

On the day of the trial, each move Odysseus makes as he comes closer to actually revealing his identity is wildly misinterpreted by the suitors. When Odysseus asks to take the bow, Antinous, like Melantho and Eurymachus in Book 18, assumes he must be deranged (*Od.* 21.288–292). He accuses him of being drunk and goes on to cite the highly inappropriate parallel of the centaur Eurytium—an exemplum that applies far better to the suitors than to Odysseus[29]—and to make an inaccurate prediction about what will happen if Odysseus should succeed in stringing the bow (*Od.* 21.305–310). When Odysseus takes the bow and examines it in a proprietary fashion, the suitors contemptuously decide that he must be either a craftsman or a thief. This failure of recognition is followed by another unintentionally ominous statement (*Od.* 21.397–403). Odysseus' success in stringing the bow and shooting through the axes should tell the suitors who he is, especially since that success is confirmed by *sēmata*, "signs," from Zeus. Yet it does not, although Odysseus himself points out that his feat has discredited their perceptions: "ἔτι μοι μένος ἔμπεδον ἐστιν, / οὐκ ὥς με μνηστῆρες ἀτιμάζοντες ὄνονται," "My strength is still steady, / not as the suitors scornfully claimed, doing me no honor" (*Od.* 21.426–427). When he directs his next arrow at Antinous, his victim is taken completely by surprise, not understanding that the situation has changed, that this is no longer a normal feast. Nor do the the rest of the suitors realize even then. They believe, as they have often before, that Odysseus could not have acted as he did intentionally, misinterpreting entirely the situation and its consequences for them.

[29] See the discussion of this passage by W. Büchner, "Die Penelopeszenen in der Odyssee," 161.

Ἴσκεν ἕκαστος ἀνήρ, ἐπεὶ ἦ φάσαν οὐκ ἐθέλοντα
ἄνδρα κατακτεῖναι· τὸ δὲ νήπιοι οὐκ ἐνόησαν,
ὡς δή σφιν καὶ πᾶσιν ὀλέθρου πείρατ᾽ ἐφῆπτο.

Each one was speculating, for they really thought he had not
  intended
to kill the man. The fools did not realize
that upon every one of them the bonds of death had been
  fastened.

(*Od.* 22.31–33)

The suitors, particularly when viewed as group and not as represented chiefly by Eurymachus, often seem to be the victims of a divine plot that they can hardly be expected to discern; thus they seem to represent the perpetual disadvantage of all mortals in a world controlled by gods capable of deceiving them. But in the *Odyssey* that divine plot is paralleled by a human plot that is not a secret conspiracy but a public network of benefits and obligations binding people together in a more-or-less orderly society; the *Odyssey*'s world is such that those who observe that human plot do not have to uncover the divine one. A final example of an episode in which the suitors' blindness is contrasted to Odysseus' knowledge will illustrate how these two plots can parallel each other.

During the battle between Odysseus and the suitors, Athena makes an appearance disguised as Mentor. Odysseus recognizes her but does not show that he does, addressing her as if she were Mentor.

"Μέντορ, ἄμυνον ἀρήν, μνῆσαι δ᾽ ἑτάροιο φίλοιο,
ὅς σ᾽ ἀγαθὰ ῥέζεσκον· ὁμηλικίη δέ μοί ἐσσι."
ὣς φάτ᾽, ὀϊόμενος λαοσσόον ἔμμεν᾽ Ἀθήνην.

"Mentor, come to my aid, remember me, your beloved
  companion,
I who have done you many favors. For you grew up with me."
Thus he spoke, but he thought it was Athena, rouser of
  armies.

(*Od.* 22.208–210)

One of the suitors, Agelaus, failing to recognize the goddess, also addresses her as if she were Mentor: he warns Mentor against joining with Odysseus, saying that when Odysseus is defeated, as he surely will be, the suitors will kill Mentor and deprive his wife and children of their house (*Od.* 22.213–223). The issue of recognition is, in a sense, irrelevant to the significance of this exchange: the critical difference between Odysseus and the suitors is made clear in terms of human morality, in the difference between the respect with which Odysseus addresses Mentor and the boorish disregard with which Agelaus tries to bully him. The overt content of Odysseus' speech is an adequate substitute for the recognition it conceals; it replaces direct acknowledgment of Athena's divinity with a gesture towards the kind of recognition that occurs between men, an attempt to revive a long-standing and reciprocally beneficial relationship.

The substitution that Odysseus makes here deliberately and slyly can also be made unwittingly. By following the scenarios written for them by society, especially scenarios for the reception of strangers (one of the most ritualized activities in the Homeric world and one of the most clearly patterned sequences in Homeric narrative), characters can act in ways that compensate for their failure to see through a disguise and that even eventually lead to the removal of that disguise. In what ways and how extensively the patterns of Homeric society and the poem's plot of the hero's disguise and recognition run parallel to one another is the subject of the next chapter.

THREE

Recognition and Hospitality

THE DISCUSSION of the suitors' reception of Odysseus in the preceding chapter outlined a connection between inability to recognize the disguised stranger as Odysseus, and refusal to honor him according to the codes of hospitality that are so highly valued in the Homeric world. Correspondingly, the working out of the *Odyssey*'s plot also establishes a positive connection between recognition and the observance of hospitality. Both in Phaeacia and on Ithaca, Odysseus' hospitable reception leads to his recognition: it is as he attains the status of guest—of the whole Phaeacian community on Scheria and of the loyal members of his household, Eumaeus, Telemachus, and Penelope, on Ithaca—that he is, in each case, revealed to be Odysseus, son of Laertes. This progression confirms the close connection in the Homeric world between identity and social position and between the recognition of identity and other forms of recognition or acknowledgment. The way in which the things a guest typically receives from his host—meals, changes of clothing, baths, conveyance home, guest-gifts—also prove to be the occasions of identification reveals the extent to which identity is expressed in the acknowledging gestures of others.[1] In addition, this dramatized correspondence gives the social institutions that provide for the reception of strangers a powerful

---

[1] For a detailed discussion of the correlation between these forms of hospitable reception and recognition of identity and status, see Sheila H. Murnaghan, "*Anagnōrisis* in the *Odyssey*," 207–224. For a general account of the way gifts that are exchanged in social rituals identify and become identified with the people who exchange them, see Marcel Mauss, *The Gift*, 17–45. On the role of clothing in establishing Odysseus' identity, see Wolfgang Schadewaldt, "Kleiderdinge," and for a detailed recent discussion, Elizabeth Block, "Clothing Makes the Man: A Pattern in the *Odyssey*."

endorsement: the efficacy of these institutions is acted out in their capacity to uncover the truth or, to say the same thing in a different way, properly to acknowledge heroic power.

Because he arrives on Scheria without any outward signs of identity and deliberately withholds his name, Odysseus recovers his identity there entirely through the Phaeacians' recognition of the qualities he displays while he is with them. Since he has never been there before, his recognition by the Phaeacians cannot, like his recognition on Ithaca, take the form of a series of reunions. Nonetheless, it has the same underlying character: it consists fundamentally of the mutual acknowledgment of reciprocal relationships. The difference is that on Scheria, where there are not old relationships of kinship to be reanimated, Odysseus and his hosts enter into new relationships such as can be formed between strangers. And in forming those relationships, Odysseus does, in a sense, undergo a return and a reunion: he returns to, and is reunited with, civilized human society after his years in the unstable and unfamiliar world of the adventures.[2] His achievement of this reunion, in a place where he is unknown, confirms at once his ability to make a place for himself in an extreme version of a peacetime society and the capacity of the social institutions by which strangers are received to counter the annihilating effects of solitude and exposure to the forces of nature.

Odysseus' encounter with Nausicaa on the shore of Scheria begins a process in which his identity is restored through the construction of a series of relationships with the Phaeacians. Nausicaa's initial provision of the various benefits of hospitality—food, clothing, a bath, help in achieving his next destination—springs largely from a sense of what is owed to any suppliant. It is an instinctive, civilized response to Odysseus' assertion of need and to his presentation of himself as also civilized: his covering of his nakedness with a branch, and his tactfully substituting an ingratiating speech for the physical gesture

---

[2] On the general connection between rites of reunion and the exchange of gifts, which is the central ritual of Homeric guest-friendship, see Marcel Mauss, *The Gift*, 17–45.

of grasping her knee (*Od.* 6.206–207). But the effect of her generosity is to turn him into someone especially impressive so that, when he has bathed and put on the clothes she provides him with, he looks to her like a god (*Od.* 6.239–243). Nausicaa's hospitality thus sets in motion the typical events of a recognition scene, but one that occurs without the disguised person actually identifying himself and without any previous relationship to be recovered.[3] Thus, the scene ends, not with the reanimation of an old relationship, but the envisioning of a new one. Nausicaa responds to Odysseus' radiant epiphany with a wish: "αἲ γὰρ ἐμοὶ τοιόσδε πόσις κεκλημένος εἴη / ἐνθάδε ναιετάων, καί οἱ ἅδοι αὐτόθι μίμνειν," "If only a man such as this could live here and be called / my husband, and it should please him to stay here" (*Od.* 6.244–245).

Prompted by her own preoccupation with marriage and her attraction to Odysseus, both of which Odysseus deftly exploits, Nausicaa receives him, in her imagination, into the relationship through which societies of the sort portrayed in the Homeric poems most readily assimilate strangers. In a society organized around the household or extended family (a society, that is, based largely on relations of kinship), marriage, as a way of extending kinship beyond the original family group, is the chief means of incorporating outsiders.[4] The possibility of this conventional, institutionalized relationship provides a means by which Odysseus' seductive appeal to Nausicaa can play an acceptable role in her generous reception of him. It dispels the danger to her and to her community implicit in their meeting.

---

[3] While Odysseus conceals his identity, the identification of Nausicaa is a central feature of the scene. He frames a flattering speech around the question of who she is, and she replies in a ringing statement (*Od.* 6.196–197) that parallels his own announcement of his identity at *Od.* 9.19–20.

[4] It is not, of course, the only one. Phoenix, for example, represents another common type of assimilated outsider, the suppliant who is integrated into a new community after he is obliged to flee his own. But it is noteworthy that his relationship to Peleus is compared to a familial one, that of son to father (*Il.* 9.481). On the parallels between exogamous marriage and sanctuary as institutions that form ties between communities, see Julian Pitt-Rivers, "Women and Sanctuary in the Mediterranean."

And it accords with Odysseus' indications that he is not a threat to Nausicaa, that he is neither the predatory animal to whom he is compared in the simile at 6.103–134 nor the rapacious god who, in a common myth, encounters a girl at play with her friends in a remote place and seduces or abducts her.[5] Instead, he is a civilized member of human society, one who appreciates its values and institutions, marriage in particular.

When Odysseus arrives at the palace, Nausicaa's father Alcinous responds similarly. After he has honored Odysseus' request as a suppliant and promised him conveyance home, he too has reason to be impressed with Odysseus. Alcinous is impressed not because of Odysseus' marvelous appearance but because of both the high regard for propriety and the desire to avoid conflict that Odysseus expresses when Alcinous criticizes Nausicaa for allowing him to come to the city alone (*Od.* 7.303–307). Alcinous acknowledges these qualities by wishing he could incorporate Odysseus into his family as his son-in-law (*Od.* 7.311–316). Like Nausicaa, Alcinous recognizes Odysseus' merits by envisioning the construction of a relationship between them. In both cases the idea is entirely hypothetical; neither Nausicaa nor Alcinous actually expects Odysseus to marry her.[6] But it is hypothetical only because of Odysseus' expressed desire to return to a home that is elsewhere. The possibility of marrying Nausicaa really would exist if Odysseus were

[5] Cf., for example, Hades' abduction of Persephone as told in the *Homeric Hymn to Demeter* and Apollo's rape of Creusa as told in Euripides' *Ion*. This parallel is also noted by Thomas Van Nortwick, "Penelope and Nausicaa," 271.

[6] Note that at *Od.* 7.243 and 581, Alcinous actually refers to the wife he assumes Odysseus has at home. The Alexandrian critics found the idea of a marriage between Odysseus and Nausicaa so alien to the poem that they tried to banish all reference to it from the text: Schol. Hom. *Od.* 6.244, I 324 Di.; Schol. Hom. *Od.* 6.275, I 317 Di.; Schol. Hom. *Od.* 7.311, I 350 Di. For the view that his episode is an adaptation of a story in which a marriage does take place, see W. J. Woodhouse, *The Composition of Homer's Odyssey*, 54–65; G. Vallillee, "The Nausicaa Episode." For discussion of the role of marriage in this episode, but without that assumption, see Richmond Lattimore, "Nausikaa's Suitors."

interested. Phaeacian society, then, is able to acknowledge Odysseus' merits through the benefits of an honored position within it; that such a position confers benefits is clear both from Alcinous' offer of a house and possessions along with his daughter and from Odysseus' praise of marriage to Nausicaa earlier.

The idea that Odysseus should acquire a place in Phaeacian society by marrying Nausicaa is a false start, a way of offering Odysseus a recognition that can only remain hypothetical. But, on the following day, Odysseus is received into another kind of relationship with the Phaeacians that is not inappropriate to his true identity as someone whose home is elsewhere, a relationship of formal *xenia*, "guest-friendship."

In addition to acknowledging his foreignness, this redefinition of Odysseus' relationship to his hosts comes closer to identifying him by more accurately registering his heroic prestige. It is important to note that the marriage projected by Nausicaa and Alcinous is not, like many of the marriages actually portrayed in the Homeric poems, one in which the bridegroom takes the bride away with him to his own home, but one in which the bridegroom becomes a member of the bride's own community. To enter into such a marriage is to take on a role that is prestigious but also subordinate. Someone in such a position is subsumed into his wife's family and derives his identity not primarily from his own qualities and accomplishments but from his membership in that family. When Nausicaa wishes "αἲ γὰρ ἐμοὶ τοιόσδε πόσις κεκλημένος εἴη," "if only a man such as this one could be called my husband" (*Od.* 6.244), and Alcinous says, "ἐμὸς γαμβρὸς καλέεσθαι," "you would be called my son-in-law" (*Od.* 7.313), they are offering Odysseus a pair of titles and an identity based on his relations to themselves. And while this is a substantial honor considering that he appears to be a destitute wanderer, it is not sufficient to identify the great hero that Odysseus actually is. Odysseus' desire to return home invalidates Alcinous' offer, not simply because it means he is unwilling to remain in Scheria but because his homecoming involves laying claim to a more glorious and autonomous role as head of his own household and king of Ithaca.[7]

Furthermore, the tie of *xenia* that Odysseus now forms, while less intimate than that of marriage, is also more difficult and tenuous, and therefore, in this narrative sequence (which has a somewhat artificial, exemplary character) less easily attained.[8] Guest-friendship does not simulate and then lead to kinship, as marriage does; it remains an entirely social and conventional relationship. Nor does a guest-friend have an established place within a stable structure, as a family member does; rather the guest-friend maintains an autonomous and equal status that can easily turn into competition. So this relationship is subject to the difficulty and instability found in relations between peers discussed in the last chapter. Thus, before he can become the guest-friend of Alcinous and his wife Arete, Odysseus must win the acceptance of the whole group of the leading men of Phaeacia. He becomes, in effect, the guest-friend of all of them, for Alcinous arranges for Odysseus to receive guest-gifts from the other leaders of Scheria as well as from himself (*Od.* 8.385–397). Before he achieves this relationship, which both brings him more honor and identifies him more accurately, he must

[7] Other examples of attempts by Homeric heroes to at once honor and subordinate other heroes by subsuming them into their households include Agamemnon's offer to Achilles of marriage to one of his daughters (*Il.* 9.141–148) and Menelaus' desire to have Odysseus abandon Ithaca and settle in one of Menelaus' Argive cities (*Od.* 4.171–182). Not surprisingly, neither of these suggestions is realized. On Agamemnon's offer, see James Redfield, *Nature and Culture in the Iliad*, 16.

[8] Odysseus' fictional progression from bridgegroom to guest-friend could thus be seen as acting out a model of social evolution in which a kinship society, which forms ties largely through marriage, is followed by a more sophisticated society in which ties between non-kin are created through guest-friendship. For the view that this model applies to early Greek society and that this poem reflects a period when the second stage had recently been reached, see M. I. Finley, *The World of Odysseus*, esp. 105. It is also possible to see this narrative sequence as a means of exploring the connection between familial and wholly social relationships but not necessarily a reflection of specific historical events. Odysseus' story fictively replaces the analogy between guest and kinsman, which is articulated by Alcinous at *Od.* 8.546, with an identity.

successfully negotiate an encounter with other men with whom he is potentially in competition.

From the outset the leading men of Phaeacia are cast in the role of Odysseus' competitors. Nausicaa, by characterizing them as her jealous suitors, makes them his opponents in a classic competitive situation, rivalry for the hand of a woman. This is, of course, the context in which he encounters his rivals when he returns to Ithaca as well.[9] The sense that they are dangerous rivals also underlies Athena's action in making Odysseus invisible as he enters the Phaeacian court, "μή τις Φαιήκων μεγαθύμων / ἀντιβολήσας / κερτομέοι ἐπέεσσι καὶ ἐξερέοιθ᾽ ὅτις εἴη," "lest any of the proud Phaeacians, meeting him, / might provoke him with words and ask him who he was" (*Od.* 7.16–17). The danger from which she protects him here is formulated as simply recognition of his identity; she shields him from the combination of provocation and direct questioning that are typically preludes to recognition in the Homeric poems. And that is dangerous precisely because of the connection between recognition of identity and recognition in a broader sense. Asserting one's identity involves making a claim to recognition that might come at the expense of others and for which others might wish to compete. It is, therefore, to Odysseus' advantage for any encounter with the young men of Phaeacia in which recognition is at stake to be forestalled until he has improved his position by winning the sponsorhip of Alcinous and Arete.

---

[9] On the connection between contests and marriage, see Richmond Lattimore, "Nausikaa's Suitors," 95–96. Competition for a woman often occurs in Greek legend as the origin of an oligarchical alliance. Such competition provides an etiology both for the coming together of the group and for the tensions and rivalries that inevitably form within it. The most notable example is, of course, the Achaean expedition against Troy; a less well-known instance is Chariton's *Chaereas and Callirhoe* in which Callirhoe's suitors are so incensed at the victory of someone of lower social status that they band together to destroy the marriage—the opposite of the *Iliad* story in which the unsuccessful suitors fight jointly to uphold the marriage. For the conception of Penelope's suitors as oligarchs and the relative unimportance to them of their suit, see Cedric H. Whitman, *Homer and the Heroic Tradition*, 306–308; Peter W. Rose, "Class Ambivalence in the *Odyssey*," 136–138.

When Odysseus does finally encounter the other Phaeacians, he is able to win their recognition both by his victory in a contest—the orderly form that competition takes in a peaceful society—and by his reluctance to compete at all.[10] Not only does he have to be provoked by the aggressive nonrecognition of Euryalus before he shows off his discus-throwing ability, but he follows his feat with a speech in which he condemns competition between guest and host (*Od.* 8.204–211).

Alcinous responds to this incident by rebuking Euryalus and by offering Odysseus a display of Phaeacian dancing. When Odysseus praises the dancing, Alcinous reciprocates by suggesting that Odysseus be given a *xeineion*, a guest-gift—in other words, that his current status as honored guest be formalized in a permanent relationship of guest-friendship. At this point, Odysseus has been recognized by the Phaeacians through the creation of a relationship that is in accord with his proper identity, and the plot moves swiftly towards the moment of his actual identification. Although he is not to leave Phaeacia until the following day, he now says goodbye to both Euryalus and Nausicaa, as if decisively putting aside his false identity as Nausicaa's bridegroom and Euryalus' rival.[11] The gifts Odysseus receives as tokens of this new guest-friendship play a large part in

[10] Odysseus' declaration of noncompetitiveness reinforces and makes explicit what is implied by his appeal to and reception by Arete. As Julian Pitt-Rivers has shown, the reception of an outsider by a woman at the center of the house has the effect of removing him from the aggressive, retaliatory relations that normally occur between men. "Women and Sanctuary in the Mediterranean," 865–869.

[11] The farewell conversation between Nausicaa and Odysseus at *Od.* 8.457–468 centers on the idea of reciprocal obligation. She asks him to remember her, since he owes his life to her, and he promises to pray to her daily as to a goddess. The extravagance of the comparison of Nausicaa to a goddess here reminds us that it is intended to compensate for the actual relationship of marriage, to which, when first introduced at *Od.* 6.149–152, it seemed a prelude. The faintness with which Nausicaa's disappointment is registered here is indicative of the way in which the poem, like its hero, makes use of Nausicaa, exploiting her position as a potential bride but not entering into any extensive consideration of her feelings.

restoring him to his former status.[12] He begins to assert himself more forcefully; he rewards the singer Demodocus with a piece of meat and asks for a certain song, the story of the fall of Troy, in which he himself played a decisive role. His choice of song hastens his recognition because his mournful response to it inspires Alcinous to ask him who he is, and this time he does not refuse to say.

Both in Alcinous' request and in Odysseus' response, Odysseus' identification of himself is understood to be the fulfillment of their relationship of guest-friendship.[13] Alcinous stops Demodocus' song in the name of friendship and asks that Odysseus identify himself in the same spirit. Alcinous praises the relationship of guest-friendship, saying that to a man of sense a guest is like a brother, and he adds, "τῷ νῦν μηδὲ σὺ κεῦθε νοήμασι κερδαλέοισιν / ὅττι κέ σ᾽ εἴρωμαι· φάσθαι δέ σε κάλλιόν ἐστιν," "Therefore do not now go on concealing with crafty purposes / that which I ask you. It is better that you tell it" (*Od.* 8.542–549).[14] Furthermore, the Phaeacians must know where his home is, one of the chief determinants of his identity, in order to take him there (*Od.* 8.555–556). More broadly, if they

[12] The description of these gifts is intertwined with the account of Odysseus' bath. The gifts seem to absorb from this association the recreative function that baths often have in the *Odyssey*:
8.424–425: Alcinous instructs Arete to bring out a gift for Odysseus and a coffer for all his gifts.
8.426–429: He instructs her to prepare a bath so that "he may bathe and then see all the gifts laid out . . . and rejoice in the feast."
8.430–432: Alcinous himself promises to give Odysseus a cup.
8.432–437: Arete prepares the bath.
8.438–447: Arete gives Odysseus the robe and the coffer and he accepts them and ties them up with a special knot.
8.449–457: Odysseus has his bath.

[13] Similarly, in Odysseus' encounter with the Cyclops, in which the conventions of guest-friendship are travestied, Polyphemus asks Odysseus his name, "ἵνα τοι δῶ ξεινίον, ᾧ κε σὺ χαίρῃς," "so I can give you a guest-gift, in which you would delight" (*Od.* 9.356).

[14] Cf. Stanford's comment on the "τῷ" in *Od.* 8.548, " 'Therefore,' *sc.* because we are in the esteemed relationship of guest and host."

are to have the kind of alliance that guest-friendship involves, both sides must know the identity of their ally. The Phaeacians have not needed to know who Odysseus is to offer him conveyance home and the alliance of guest-friendship. But for Odysseus to take advantage of these offers, he must identify himself. Thus, he claims to tell them his name in order that their alliance may be properly concluded.

νῦν δ᾽ ὄνομα πρῶτον μυθήσομαι, ὄφρα καὶ ὑμεῖς
εἴδετ᾽, ἐγὼ δ᾽ ἂν ἔπειτα φυγὼν ὕπο νηλεὲς ἦμαρ
ὑμῖν ξεῖνος ἔω καὶ ἀπόπροθι δώματα ναίων.

Now first I will tell you my name, so that you too
may know it, and I, when I have escaped the pitiless day of
    death,
may be your host, although I live far away.

(*Od.* 9.16–18)

Odysseus' identification, then, is the inevitable consequence of his reception as the Phaeacians' guest-friend. Through a protracted process in which Odysseus has given displays of his heroic and civilized qualities, and the Phaeacians have responded by receiving him into a series of institutionalized roles—successful suppliant, bridegroom, guest-friend—Odysseus has been recognized so fully that the revelation of his identity naturally follows. The attainment of this moment of revelation vindicates both the hero who has been able to earn this recognition without the help of any external mark of identity and the society whose institutions for the reception of strangers have made it possible. This civilized society has shown itself to be so structured that its conventions naturally bring about Odysseus' proper recognition. In this it differs markedly from the world of the adventures, which is characterized by the Cyclops, whose reception of Odysseus is a travesty of hospitality and to whom Odysseus cannot tell his name without terrible consequences, and by Calypso, who is not capable of forming a relationship of guest-friendship with someone who does not want to stay with her as her lover, and whose nonobservance of the host's duty to allow his guest to leave obscures Odysseus' identity. Odysseus celebrates civilization along with himself in the opening lines of his *apologia*: the revelation of his name and account of his fame are preceded by praise of feasting, the occasion that both epitomizes the benefits of civilized society and provides the setting for his own recognition (*Od.* 9.2–11).

This smooth progression from Odysseus' acceptance into the role of guest-friend to his identification implies an exact match between Odysseus himself and the social role he has attained, between the concealed identity of the destitute and anonymous wanderer washed up on the Phaeacian shore and the attractive figure recreated through Odysseus' ingratiating behavior and the Phaeacians' characteristic responses to it. But this implied equation is an oversimplification. The role constructed for Odysseus on Scheria does not entirely match his many-sided and widely experienced nature. He has certain distinctive characteristics that are not recognized by the Phaeacians, and the poem acknowledges this discrepancy, although it does not emphasize it.

Odysseus has given the Phaeacians a true picture of himself as someone well-spoken, diplomatic, and appreciative of the orderly values of peacetime society. But this is only one side of his character. There is another, harsher side belonging to his years as a wanderer and an adventurer. And while that may be associated exclusively with the past (in this episode he seems to put it behind him and to be reborn as someone well adapted to the peacetime world in which he now finds himself), it is, nonetheless, part of his identity and will reappear when he returns to Ithaca and finds a social situation with which he cannot be at peace.

This other side of Odysseus is distanced throughout the Phaeacian episode. It surfaces only in narratives about the past: in Demodocus' songs, which portray him quarreling at a feast and attacking Troy with both guile and force, and in his own account of his adventures, which contains many aggressive and brutal moments and provides an ambiguous portrait of his relations with his companions. In the present Odysseus responds

101

to these evocations of the past with tears, drawing attention to himself as a sufferer rather than as an imposer of sufferings and even expressing compassion for the victims of his own aggressive actions, as the simile at 8.521–530 implies. Meanwhile, the Phaeacians experience these same narratives solely as entertainment.[15]

These two very different responses to Odysseus' past have in common the way they gloss over or overlook the danger implicit in these stories, the danger that an attractive, aggreeable stranger may also be capable of exploiting and harming his hosts. And yet, not only is this a constant risk of hospitality, but the Phaeacians' reception of Odysseus actually is very dangerous to them. His specific identity as Odysseus,[16] the particular hero who has earned the wrath of Poseidon, makes him the one person whom they can treat hospitably only at the cost of their own destruction. They are destined to suffer for Odysseus' past, in particular for his hostile action against the Cyclops, while he is able, through their help, to arrive home safely. In effect, he takes advantage of them, winning from them favors that, because of their generosity to him has the result of isolating them forever from the rest of human society, he will never be called on to repay.[17]

This darker aspect of Odysseus' identity, while not suppressed, is certainly deemphasized. Just as Alcinous fails to rec-

[15] Alcinous misses the point of Odysseus' tears, interpreting his story of the Trojan War not as evidence of personal participation but as a sign of perhaps having had a friend or brother who fought there (*Od.* 7.581–583).

[16] As George Dimock has pointed out in his essay, "The Name of Odysseus," Odysseus' names itself unites giving pain and suffering pain as inextricable elements of his identity. When the Phaeacians finally hear that name, they are effectively deaf to some of the notes it contains. Cf. also Jenny Strauss Clay, *The Wrath of Athena*, 54–68.

[17] The story of Bellerophon told at *Il.* 6.156 ff is, in a sense, an inverse of this one. There, when the guest is finally questioned and reveals more about himself through a *sēma*, a past enmity is brought to light that leads to danger to the guest from the host rather than danger to the host from the guest. In that instance, the capacity of self-disclosure to turn the automatic friendship of hospitality into enmity is far more marked.

ognize the troublesome aspects of Odysseus' character that emerge from his narrative, responding to Odysseus' story by concluding that he is upright and candid, so he never acknowledges explicitly that Odysseus is the person whose conveyance home brings on the Phaeacians the vengeance of Poseidon that has been prophesied by Nausithous. Although he alludes to this prophecy as he asks Odysseus' name (*Od.* 8.564–571), Alcinous does not recognize, as the Cyclops and Circe do in similar situations, that Odysseus is the person whose arrival will lead to its fulfillment. When Poseidon's revenge is actually carried out, not only is its severity diminished at Zeus' request, but Alcinous, although he realizes that the prophecy has been fulfilled, does not acknowledge that this is because they have given conveyance specifically to Odysseus. The poem, then, reveals the limitations, in this case alarming limitations, to the equation of social and personal identity that the course of its plot affirms, but also plays them down.

The same correlation between social acceptance and recognition of identity shapes the account of Odysseus' actual return to Ithaca. There too Odysseus' identification is brought about through his reception into the roles of bridegroom and guest-friend. In Ithaca, however, circumstances make this a more difficult and complicated process. Because on Ithaca he is recognizable on sight, and the suitors' presence makes premature recognition not only undesirable but dangerous, Odysseus must actively disguise himself. The disguise of a ragged beggar involves a far more overt and challenging declension from his true social status than does his empty-handed anonymity on Scheria.[18]

Furthermore, the capacity of the society Odysseus is reentering on Ithaca to receive him with the proper forms of acknowledgment is genuinely subject to question. A major consequence of Odysseus' absence from his household is a decline in its observance of the laws of hospitality. The house has been taken

---

[18] Cf. Athena's statement that she will dress him in rags that will cause a man to loathe him on sight, thus giving him a disguise that will automatically provoke rejection (*Od.* 13.399–400).

over by the suitors, whose prolonged presence there is itself a sign of their indifference to the rules governing hospitality and who themselves feel no obligation to act hospitably towards strangers. Furthermore, the presence of the suitors inhibits, in various ways, the ability of those who belong to the household to act on their own hospitable inclinations. The same constraints that make Telemachus and Penelope unable to resist the suitors' usurpation of the house prevent them from acting fully as hosts.[19]

The revelation of Odysseus remedies this situation by expelling the suitors from the house, recalling Penelope to her former self, and restoring the practices of civilized society in his household. But, as on Scheria, Odysseus can only be identified after being received into relationships that acknowledge his true status. On Ithaca, however, that necessity is strategic as well as poetic; he cannot identify himself until he has attained the status of guest of Telemachus and Penelope, because until then he is vulnerable to the suitors. It would be not simply inappropriate but actually fatal for his name to be known before that. Therefore, before he can disclose himself and defeat those who disdain the laws of hospitality, Odysseus must overcome this constraint and call forth the capacity to act hospitably in various members of his household.

Finally, because Ithaca is a society in decline as a result of Odysseus' absence, the link between hospitality and his return has a different significance there. On Scheria, society as a whole is vindicated by the capacity of a community of people who have never seen him to elicit the hero's identification by welcoming him according to their conventions of hospitality; on

---

[19] Telemachus, entertaining "Mentes" in Book 1, has to keep him off to the side so he will not be disturbed by the suitors (*Od.* 1.132–134); when he returns from his journey, he must send to friends both the guest-gifts he has received from Menelaus and Helen and his own newly acquired guest Theoclymenus (*Od.* 17.78–83; 16.540–543); nor can he agree to Eumaeus' request that he entertain the stranger (*Od.* 16.69–72). Penelope's mournful response to Odysseus' absence results in neglect of the duties of hospitality, as both she (*Od.* 19.134–136) and Telemachus (*Od.* 15.513–517; 16.73–77) point out.

Ithaca, the connection between hospitality and recognition of identity serves to broaden and reinforce the distinction between good and bad characters that centers on willingness to recognize Odysseus. In godlike fashion, Odysseus provokes the suitors to displays of inhospitality that parallel their inability to recognize him and help to justify the punishment of that inability by aligning it with the transgression of social rules. On the other hand, the willingness of Odysseus' supporters to extend him hospitality serves as an effective substitute for recognition of his identity. Accepting or rejecting the stranger as a guest becomes tantamount to accepting or rejecting Odysseus.

The consequence of Odysseus' self-disclosure to Telemachus in Book 16 is that Telemachus gains the confidence to do what he has only shortly before (*Od.* 16.69–72) said he was too young to do, that is, to assert himself as a host by publicly championing his guest. Odysseus' presence makes possible the final step in the process of growth into heroic adulthood that begins with Telemachus' limited reception of "Mentes." At the same time, Telemachus' sponsorship allows Odysseus to enter his house, to reconnoiter, and eventually to defeat the suitors. Simultaneously, and each with the aid of the other, Odysseus asserts himself and is recognized as a guest, and Telemachus asserts himself and is recognized as a host. In this way they together overcome the aggressive non-recognition of the suitors, of which inhospitality is one manifestation.

The narrative of Odysseus' entry in disguise into his own house takes the form of three successive encounters with the suitors in which they reject him with increasing recklessness— in each case crowning their rejection with the gesture of throwing something at him—while Telemachus acts as his champion with increasing assurance (*Od.* 17.336–488; 18.304–421; 20.257–344.)[20] When the contest of the bow arrives, it is ex-

[20] First, after Antinous throws a footstool at Odysseus as a travesty of a guest-gift at *Od.* 17.405–410, Telemachus responds very tentatively, relying on Eumaeus for inspiration and support and even turning on him instead of the suitors as he tries out his new-found assertiveness (*Od.* 17.393). In the next such episode, just before the duel with Irus, Telemachus identifies himself more

plicitly treated as a test of the appropriateness and viability of Telemachus' championship of the stranger. Odysseus' admission to the contest is seen to depend on his status as Telemachus' guest. Penelope begins the speech in which she declares Odysseus' right to try the bow by saying that he is entitled to respect as a guest of Telemachus (*Od.* 21.312–313).[21] And when Telemachus himself asserts his right to allow Odysseus to compete, he stresses his possession of the bow, which stands for his rightful possession of his father's house, by proclaiming that he could give the bow to the stranger as a gift if he wished (*Od.* 21.348–349). In other words, he grounds his right to determine who will compete for Penelope in his newly asserted capacity to confer a certain status on the stranger by entering into a relationship of guest-friendship with him.[22]

---

forcefully as the stranger's host, although he does so provisionally and depends on the agreement of Antinous and Eurymachus (*Od.* 18.64–65). But after Eurymachus throws the footstool and the suitors say they wish the *xeinos* had died and never come, Telemachus speaks very sharply to them (*Od.* 18.405–411) and is confirmed in his role as host and master of the house by Amphinomus (*Od.* 18.420–421). On the following day, Telemachus attends his guest more assiduously and volunteers that he intends to protect him since this is Odysseus'—and therefore his—house (*Od.* 20.129–133, 257–267); when Ctesippus has thrown the ox hoof, Telemachus speaks up against the suitors even more forcefully, declaring that he is no longer a child and claiming the house for his own (*Od.* 20.304–319). By this point, Odysseus is regularly referred to as Telemachus' guest, both in the sincere statements of Amphinomus (cf. *Od.* 20.295 and 18.416–417) and in the mocking ones of the other suitors (*Od.* 20.294–295, 376), rather than as simply a stranger. See the discussion of these episodes by Bernard Fenik (*Studies in the Odyssey*, 185–187), who notes that, as Telemachus' reaction grows more forceful, the effectiveness of the cast itself decreases. For an analysis of this whole section of the narrative that stresses the way in which Odysseus tests the hospitality of the suitors, see Eric Havelock, *The Greek Concept of Justice*, 167–176.

21 In doing so she uses sincerely the same words Ctesippus uses sarcastically as he throws the ox hoof at Odysseus (*Od.* 20.294–295).

22 In taking on the right of the head of a household to control whom a woman will bring into it through marriage, Telemachus assumes the role Athena has urged on him, should he be assured of Odysseus' death (*Od.* 1.292). The difference in Telemachus brought about by his voyage is reflected in Athena's apparently contradictory commands: before being told to go, he is ad-

When Odysseus has succeeded in stringing the bow and shooting through the axes, he addresses his first words to Telemachus, pointing out that Telemachus' guest has not failed him (*Od.* 21.424–426). Odysseus' demonstration of his extraordinary powers has vindicated Telemachus' treatment of him. The outcome of the trial affirms both Telemachus' prestige as the successful host of a great hero and the value of those hospitable forms of behavior that the suitors neglect and deride. On Ithaca, as on Scheria, Odysseus' reception as a guest leads to his recognition.

Throughout these episodes, Telemachus has been playing a double game, pretending to champion a poor beggar while knowing all along that it is really Odysseus. In other words, the open recognition that he would normally give to his father is disguised as hospitality. But the way in which this hospitable treatment results in Odysseus' public identification implies, as does a similar sequence of events on Scheria, that the open acknowledgment Telemachus suppresses and the hospitable course he adopts are interchangeable forms of recognition with the same underlying significance. Once again, the structure of the narrative suggests that Odysseus' identity and the role of honored guest can be equated.

A similar equation of these two forms of recognition can be detected in the treatment of other characters, especially Eumaeus and Penelope, who are loyal to Odysseus but cannot acknowledge his identity, not because, like Telemachus, they choose not to but because Odysseus chooses not to reveal it to them. In the case of those characters, hospitality serves as a substitute or alternative for recognition of identity. Through their

---

vised to send Penelope home to her father (*Od.* 1.274–278); after his voyage is projected, the advice is changed, reflecting the change it will make on him, and he is told to arrange her remarriage himself (*Od.* 1.292). For the analyst view of this contradiction, including a prosopopoeia of Telemachus complaining at being given contradictory advice, see Denys Page, *The Homeric Odyssey*, 53–64. For another interpretation of this passage that is more sympathetic to what stands in the text, see Mabel Lang, "Homer and Oral Techniques," 160–161. Of course, once it is revealed that Odysseus is not dead, Telemachus has to retreat from that role.

hospitable reception of Odysseus, they confer appropriate honor on him and distinguish themselves from the suitors, who condemn themselves by showing Odysseus no recognition of any kind. This is, then, a specific form of the covert recognition discussed in Chapter 1, a version that corresponds to observing the rules of an established social institution.

An example of a hospitable gesture that is also a covert expression of recognition is the loan of a cloak that comes at the end of the account of Eumaeus' reception of Odysseus in Book 14. Hospitality is, of course, a central issue of this episode. Odysseus, like a wandering god, tests Eumaeus to see if he is hospitable. Eumaeus, who, having isolated himself from the house of Odysseus (*Od.* 14.272–273; 16.465), is not subject to the constraints that affect Telemachus and Penelope, displays exemplary allegiance to the laws of hospitality, despite his humble means. The culmination of this process is Odysseus' hint, through a false tale centering on himself, that he would like to be lent a cloak, and Eumaeus' generous response. Eumaeus' loan of a cloak concludes the episode with a moment of inexplicit recognition, for it signifies not only a host's generosity towards his guest but Odysseus' unstated revelation and Eumaeus' unconscious acknowledgment of him.

Because Odysseus' disguise consists largely of a state of destitution, for him to be given a cloak or any other garment effectively diminishes or removes that disguise. This acquisition brings him closer to this proper status, much as the guest-gifts of the Phaeacians do. Furthermore, Eumaeus' loan is specifically associated with the revelation of Odysseus' identity. It comes as a response to a story in which Odysseus is invoked in his full glory as the clever leader of the Achaeans at Troy. Hinting for the cloak, Odysseus says he wishes he could have it as a token of the youth and strength he no longer possesses.

ὡς νῦν ἡβώοιμι βίη τέ μοι ἔμπεδος εἴη·
δοίη κέν τις χλαῖναν ἐνὶ σταθμοῖσι συφορβῶν,
ἀμφότερον, φιλότητι καὶ αἰδοῖ φωτὸς ἑῆος·
νῦν δέ μ᾽ ἀτιμάζουσι κακὰ χροΐ εἵματ᾽ ἔχοντα."

If only I were now young like that and my strength were firm.
Then one of the swineherds in the hut would give me a cloak,
both out of friendship and out of respect for a good man.
Now they dishonor me because I wear shabby clothes.

(*Od.* 14.503–506)

He characterizes Eumaeus' gesture as not simply an act of hospitable charity but a denial of his, Odysseus', apparent weakness and old age, a denial, that is, of his disguise.

Furthermore, a correspondence between the stranger's acquisition of new clothes and the return of Odysseus has already been established earlier. As soon as Eumaeus identifies his absent master as Odysseus, the stranger encourages him to be hopeful and swears an oath that Odysseus is on his way home, which he follows by saying,

εὐαγγέλιον δέ μοι ἔστω
αὐτίκ᾽, ἐπεί κεν κεῖνος ἰὼν τὰ ἃ δώμαθ᾽ ἵκηται·
ἔσσαι με χλαῖνάν τε χιτῶνά τε, εἵματα καλά·
πρὶν δέ κε, καὶ μάλα περ κεχρημένος, οὔ τι δεχοίμην.

Let me have a reward for good news
at once, when that man, coming back, reaches his house.
Dress me in a cloak and a tunic, in fine clothes.
Before that, much as I need them, I will accept nothing.

(*Od.* 14.152–156)

By specifying that his reward for telling good news that proves also to be true should be a set of new clothes, Odysseus equates the two roles he plays in disguise—destitute beggar and herald of his own return—and suggests that both will come to an end when his return is revealed. By proposing as his reward for the prediction of a happy event something that constitutes that happy event, the removal of his beggar's disguise, he in effect makes the removal of his disguise contingent on the removal of his disguise.

At this point in the narrative, that time of complete and open revelation must be deferred, but Eumaeus' hospitable reception of Odysseus does, through his temporary loan of just one garment, result in a limited and unacknowledged premonition of recognition. The manner of Eumaeus' response serves to contain this necessarily circumscribed recognition. He tells Odysseus that he is glad to give him a cloak, but, because of his poverty, it can only be an overnight loan. But he adds that Telemachus, when he returns, will give the stranger clothes and send him wherever he wants to go (*Od.* 14.508–517).[23] In other words, Odysseus' recognition cannot yet be permanent. In the morning, he must resume his disguise, at least until his encounter with Telemachus. That the loan rather than the gift of a cloak is a narrative stratagem and not simply a realistic detail developing the theme of Eumaeus' generosity despite his slender means is further suggested by the fact that Eumaeus does have an extra cloak after all (*Od.* 14.520–522).[24]

As has already been noted, Penelope's ability to act as host has, like her other good qualities, been obscured by Odysseus' absence. Thus, part of what Odysseus must do as he impresses his presence on her and restores her to her true self is to reawaken her hospitable impulses. In his role as the stranger, he inspires in her hospitable gestures that, like similar gestures elsewhere in the poem, play an important part in bringing about his recognition.

Throughout their encounter in Book 19 Odysseus refuses to tell Penelope who he is and she refuses to believe that Odysseus will ever return, so that any open recognition between them is precluded on both sides. But he does, nonetheless, affect her with his reminiscences and predictions, and she responds by making him her friend and guest. After he convinces her that he once entertained Odysseus on his way to Troy (moving a step

---

[23] The use in *Od.* 14.512 of the word "δυοπαλιξεις," which is very rare and may imply wild waving of extremities (see Stanford's note on this line), is perhaps less puzzling if it is understood as suggesting Odysseus' provocative flaunting of his beggar's disguise.

[24] For discussion of other ways in which Eumaeus' reception of Odysseus as his guest implies Odysseus' identity and promotes his return, see Michael Nagler, *Spontaneity and Tradition*, 125.

closer to identification of himself as Odysseus), she elevates him from the status of poor suppliant to that of friend (*Od.* 19.253–254). The parallelism between recognition of identity and the reception of a stranger is here accentuated by the way this new cordiality follows immediately on what is formally a recognition scene, although the person recognized is ostensibly absent.[25]

Odysseus then tries to convince her that he has reliable information proving that Odysseus is on his way home and even swears an oath that he will return soon. Penelope answers with a denial in terms that equate Odysseus' presence with hospitable treatment for the stranger. She says that if the stranger's words should come true, then he would enjoy her hospitality, but she denies that this will ever happen. In particular, she specifies that in Odysseus' absence the stranger will not receive conveyance home (*Od.* 19.309–316).

But at this point in her speech there occurs a reversal, which proves to be an important turning point in the plot of the poem. Up until this point it has seemed that she is concentrating on conveyance home as simply a representative example of the hospitable services denied to the stranger through Odysseus' absence. But, in the next line, she goes on herself to offer him all the others: she commands her handmaidens to wash him and prepare a bed for him now, and to bathe and anoint him in the morning, so that he can join the feasting in the hall at Telemachus' side, where he will be protected against the abuses of the suitors (*Od.* 19.317–328). As what has seemed to be an example proves to be an exception, Penelope's speech changes from a statement that withholds recognition to one that promotes it. It emerges that conveyance home, rather than being typical of the acts that Odysseus' absence makes impossible, is the only one that Penelope cannot herself perform if she wishes to.[26]

---

[25] Cf. especially the use at *Od.* 19.250 of the formulaic line used elsewhere for face-to-face recognitions: *Od.* 23.206; 24.346.

[26] This change of direction is made smoother by the use of a narrative pattern that typically leads to such a hospitable gesture. Penelope's opening statement at *Od.* 19.309–311 is a deferral, not a denial, of recognition. As William Han-

The choice of conveyance home to serve as this ambiguous gesture is not fortuitous or insignificant. On Scheria, the offer of conveyance home was a logical and expressive stimulus to Odysseus' identification because he was not yet home, and his desire to reach a home located elsewhere was one of his most significant characteristics. On Ithaca, the most important thing is that he is home, and any offer of conveyance elsewhere would be superfluous and redundant; it would interfere with, rather than promote, his proper identification.[27]

Penelope's offer of hospitality is implicitly an offer of recognition. She herself associates it with his recognition of her own superiority to other women in "$\nu\acute{o}o\nu$ $\kappa\alpha\grave{\iota}$ $\grave{\epsilon}\pi\acute{\iota}\phi\rho\sigma\nu\alpha$ $\mu\tilde{\eta}\tau\iota\nu$," "intelligence and thoughtful understanding" (*Od.* 19.326); as has been seen, the recognition of her merits is closely linked to the revelation of Odysseus' return. Furthermore, the forms of welcome that she offers—bath, bed, and protection in the hall—all do eventually lead to his recognition. In fact, the connection between hospitality and recognition works almost too well: the bath that Penelope here offers as a mere preliminary[28] to his appearance in the hall under her and Telemachus' joint sponsorship itself becomes the occasion of his dangerous premature recognition by Eurycleia. Once Penelope has rallied to give the

---

sen has shown by comparing this passage with the two episodes in which such a promise is made to Theoclymenus (*Od.* 15.536–538; 17.163–165), there is a tendency for such deferred acts of hospitality to be followed by the performance of some hospitable act even if directed at someone else (*The Conference Sequence*, 46). It is only the injection of the negative statement that begins at *Od.* 19.313 that temporarily interrupts the operation of this pattern and suggests that Penelope, remaining unaware of the presence of Odysseus, will continue to neglect her duties as a hostess.

[27] It is also the case that, in properly functioning households, it is not the role of the host's wife to provide passage home as it is to provide a bed, bath, and new clothing. See Victoria Pedrick, "The Hospitality of Women in the *Odyssey*." But as Penelope responds to Odysseus' disguised presence, she becomes willing to take on that function in his apparent absence as well (*Od.* 21.342).

[28] The preliminary of a bath through which the hero becomes recognizable before a public appearance at which he is recognized is both narratively and socially indispensable. Both Alcinous at *Od.* 7.427 and Penelope at *Od.* 19.321 refer to a bath as a necessary precondition for such an appearance.

stranger a reception that befits his status (a status defined partly by his acquaintance with Odysseus), it is nearly inevitable that she should recognize his identity, even though that recognition figures neither in Penelope's weighting of these various hospitable gestures nor in Odysseus' plans for the timing of his self-disclosure.

The sequence of events whereby Odysseus gets hold of the bow with which he proves his identity by becoming the guest of both Telemachus and Penelope repeats the process that occurred in Phaeacia, where his attainment to the role of guest also led to his identification. But the final outcome of this process is different and more complicated on Ithaca. For there, finally, the role of guest does not correspond to the identity Odysseus wishes to establish. Thus, on Ithaca the offer of conveyance home cannot serve, as it does on Scheria, as the occasion of his identification, and it must be ruled out as a possible mode of reception. His attainment in other ways to the role of guest does lead to his recognition, but in a way that undoes his identification with that role. On Ithaca his revelation as Odysseus does not complement but replaces his designation as guest: he ceases being Telemachus' guest and Penelope's guest and becomes Telemachus' father and Penelope's husband. Instead of a correspondence between the position he wins for himself as a stranger and his true identity, there is a gap. Father and husband are not roles he can assume on the strength of his attractive qualities and social skills: he can only resume those roles by virtue of being uniquely Odysseus.

For Telemachus, Odysseus' revelation means not only the undoing of Odysseus' role as guest but also the suspension of his own role as host. Once his father's presence is revealed, his own possession of the house, which has been alluded to with increasing emphasis as he has asserted himself as the stranger's host, is no longer a present reality but only a future prospect, and his new-found authority must be suspended for the time being. For Penelope, the transformation of her guest presents her with a claimant to the role of her husband. Although he has gained admission to the contest of the bow in his capacity as guest, by participating in it Odysseus makes a bid to be considered as a possible bridegroom. Thus he tries to reverse the sequence of roles he played in Phaeacia in accord with his desire now to be identified as someone who belongs where he is and as a member of the family rather than as an outsider. But he is thwarted by Penelope. Although she misleads the suitors into thinking so, Penelope is not, like Nausicaa, a potential bride willing to marry whatever man most impresses her with his attractive qualities.[29] She already has a husband and does not want anyone else to play that role.

Penelope's loyalty to Odysseus means that she will not allow the kind of easy mobility between the role of honored guest and the role of husband that was possible in Phaeacia. Until she is satisfied of Odysseus' identity, she insists that he remain firmly in the role of guest. When she demands that he be included in the contest in that capacity, she also makes it clear that he is not to be considered as a serious candidate for her hand (*Od.* 21.314–319, 336–342). These speeches, in which she nullifies the purpose of the contest with respect to the only participant who stands a chance of winning it, are perhaps the clearest indications that she neither recognizes Odysseus nor has abandoned her loyalty to him at this point. Indeed, she retreats here from the measure of recognition that was implicit in the speech in Book 19 analyzed above. She now defines the stranger as someone whose home is elsewhere (*Od.* 21.316) and offers to send him there (*Od.* 21.342). Odysseus has at last reached the point at which his saving ability to make female figures let him go (represented as magic in the case of Circe, Zeus' intervention in the case of Calypso, and an appeal to *xenia* in the case of Arete) no longer helps him to attain what he most desires.

The conflict between the role of guest that Odysseus has earned in Penelope's eyes and the role of husband that he wishes to claim is expressed and then resolved in their sparring over

[29] On the parallels in role and psychological state between Penelope and Nausicaa, see Thomas Van Nortwick, "Penelope and Nausicaa," and the discussions cited there. Van Nortwick notes that ". . . after the footbath, the Nausicaa paradigm fades away" (275–276).

their marriage bed. A bed is one of the forms of hospitality offered by Penelope in 19, but Odysseus refuses it then, choosing to defer the recognition it implies until the confrontation with the suitors is over. But when he is ready to accept Penelope's recognition, he no longer wants it to take the form of hospitality; he no longer is interested in having the identity of a guest or in sleeping in a guest's bed at the periphery of the house.[30] He asks for a bed in exasperation because Penelope has refused to accept him as her husband. It is only when Penelope echoes his command in terms that specify their marriage bed that it becomes clear that she does know him and is prepared to recognize him as Odysseus. The transformation of Odysseus' position from that of welcome guest to that of Penelope's husband is accomplished in the conversion of the bed from hospitable gesture in his command to emblem of their marriage in hers, a change to which the formal parallels in their speeches draw attention (*Od.* 23.166–172, 174–180).

Penelope's willingness to be convinced of Odysseus' identity by the token of the bed but not the bow is related to the way the bow signifies that public role as participant in a network of

---

[30] A visitor sleeps in the outer part of the house, the *prodomos* (*Od.* 3.399; 4.297; 7.345) or *aithousa* (*Od.* 4.302; 15.5; 20.1); in the fullest account of guests being shown their beds, they are said to be led out of the megaron to them (*Od.* 4.301). Notably, the visitor's position is expressly distinguished from that of the host and hostess who sleep "μυχῷ δόμου," "in the innermost part of the house" (*Od.* 3.402; 4.304; 7.346). Thus, to receive a stranger's bed automatically suggests entering a house only partly and being set off from the chamber of the master and mistress that is its core. When Penelope proposes that Odysseus' bed should be placed "ἐκτὸς ἐϋσταθέος θαλάμου," "outside the well-built bedroom" (*Od.* 23.178), she is seemingly not only denying him her bed but relegating him to the periphery of the house in a way that would contradict his successful return and repossession of it. Having recaptured the megaron in his battle with the suitors, Odysseus cannot regress to the *prodomos* where he slept the night before, but must proceed to the very center of the house. By showing that his bed could only be "μυχῷ δόμου," "in the innermost part of the house," he also reclaims his position there. The connection between not being home and sleeping in the outer part of the house emerges very clearly when Athena goes to Sparta to remind Telemachus that he should return home and finds him sleeping in the *prodomos* (*Od.* 15.1–5).

guest-friendships that she finds insufficient to mark him as her husband. The bow that Odysseus uses against the suitors was a gift to him from a guest-friend, Iphitus (*Od.* 21.13–14).[31] It has additional significance as a pledge of future hospitality that was never realized because its donor was killed by an impious host. Thus, it is especially appropriate as the token by which Odysseus reveals himself as someone deserving to be considered a guest-friend and the avenger of the suitors' offenses against hospitality,[32] but it is not associated specifically with Odysseus. It is linked to him by the way it has been kept at his house and by his unique capacity among living men to string it, but he is not its unique owner. Indeed Telemachus raises the possibility that he himself might properly give it to someone else (*Od.* 21.348–349).

The bed, on the other hand, does not come from elsewhere but was made by Odysseus himself. It is literally immobile because it is rooted in the ground, and the thought that it might be moved in unacceptable to both Odysseus and Penelope. Its inalienable quality is essential to its use as a token of Odysseus' identity to Penelope and as a sign of Penelope's fidelity to Odysseus: that quality allows it to signify that Odysseus is not simply an acceptable stranger but Penelope's husband and that Penelope would not accept a stranger in her husband's place.[33]

---

[31] Cf. Sophocles' treatment of the bow of Philoctetes, which is at once Philoctetes' means of survival, the emblem of his special powers, and a guest-gift from Heracles.

[32] Similarly, when Odysseus defeats the Cyclops by giving him wine, he is both outwitting him through his heroic *mētis* and defeating him with an emblem of his participation in the code of hospitality that the Cyclops derides. The wine, as is related in considerable detail, was a guest-gift to Odysseus from Maron (*Od.* 9.196–215). In the Cyclops episode, the connection between guest-gifts and identification persists in inverted form. Tricked by false generosity when Odysseus offers him the wine, the Cyclops makes an insincere offer of a guest-gift; this does elicit a name, but it is a travesty of name, "*Outis*," that matches the Cyclops' subsequent travesty of a guest-gift, promising to eat him last. When Odysseus tells him his real name, the Cyclops promises him guest-gifts again (*Od.* 9.517) but only heaves a rock at him.

[33] The scar, which is the most frequently used token of Odysseus' identity, combines the personal aspect of the bed and the public, social aspect of the bow.

Odysseus' recognition on Ithaca, as on Scheria, confirms the close match between the identity defined in social roles and the self. But both also involve acknowledgment that it is not an absolute correspondence. The disclosure of the stranger's name redefines his relationship to his host, something Alcinous, for whom this redefinition promises trouble, overlooks, but which Penelope, who stands to gain great happiness from it, finally accepts. In each case we are shown that there are aspects of the self that are not accounted for in the social position the hero is able to attain, aspects that testify to the realms, both outside and within civilization, that society cannot regulate. In Phaeacia we are unemphatically reminded of the aggressive, exploitative dimension that makes Odysseus inimical to society, through which he brings home the wildness of the uncivilized world in which he has been traveling. And on Ithaca we are finally confronted with those features of his self that cannot be institutionalized: the ties of blood that make him the unique father of his son, and the personal bond that makes him the unique husband of his wife.

Its history recalls both Odysseus' acquisition of his own unique name and his initiation into social relations, including the bringing home of gifts from abroad (cf. *Od.* 24.334–335).

FOUR

Penelope

AFTER the pivotal events of *Odyssey* 13 in which Athena invests Odysseus with a disguise and they sit down together to plan the suitors' destruction, the second half of the *Odyssey* is governed by what might be called a plot within a plot. The course of events that makes up the plot of the poem conforms to a plot constructed within it by the central character and his divine patron in order to bring about what he desires. While it is his own construct, and its success testifies to his power to control the course of events, Odysseus' plot only works with the cooperation of certain other characters (as was discussed in Chapter 1). In the course of putting his plot into effect, he enlists the aid of Telemachus, Eumaeus, Philoetius, and—inadvertently—Eurycleia. But the one person whose cooperation is most essential to Odysseus' success, Penelope, is not let in on the plot until it is over. Like the suitors, she is a participant in a plot from the knowledge of which she is excluded, even though, unlike them, she shares Odysseus' desire for what this plot effects. She is in the peculiar position of standing outside the plot even though it corresponds to what she wants. This position of outsider to the plot is the role she is assigned and then plays in the action, as she fosters Odysseus' return without knowing that she is doing it; it is also the point of view that she characteristically expresses, as she both directly and indirectly articulates an attitude of suspicion and doubt towards the fulfillment of her own desires.

A considerable point is made of Penelope's exclusion from Odysseus' plot; in fact, the main reason given in the text for his disguise is his need to conceal himself not from the suitors but from Penelope. In Book 13, Athena we are told, covers Ithaca with a mist

. . . ὄφρα μιν αὐτὸν
ἄγνωστον τεύξειεν ἕκαστά τε μυθήσαιτο,
μή μιν πρὶν ἄλοχος γνοίη ἀστοί τε φίλοι τε,
πρὶν πᾶσαν μνηστῆρας ὑπερβασίην ἀποτῖσαι.

. . . till she might make him
unrecognizable and explain everything to him,
so his wife would not recognize him, nor the people of the
    town nor his friends
until the suitors had paid the penalty for all their transgression.

(*Od.* 13.190–193)

This emphasis on Penelope as the object of Odysseus' disguise is puzzling, since Odysseus is aware, as we are, that Penelope remains loyal to him: he has been told so by his mother in the underworld (*Od.* 11.181–183) and learns it now again from Athena (*Od.* 13.333–338). Concealing his return from Penelope makes Odysseus' strategy against the suitors harder rather than easier to effect; it means he cannot enlist her aid as he enlists the aid of Telemachus, Eumaeus, and Philoetius. Furthermore, it causes her unnecessary pain as it prolongs the grief and uncertainty with which she is afflicted because of Odysseus' absence. Thus it is one of those illogical or contradictory features of the *Odyssey*'s plot that has aroused the suspicion of commentators.[1]

One answer to this suspicion is to point to the positive effects of this admittedly illogical feature of the plot, some of which have already been touched on in Chapter 1. Odysseus' delay in revealing himself to Penelope means that their recognition comes as the joyous sequel to the suitors' removal; it is thus placed at the point when the marriage that most decisively defines the identity of each is no longer threatened, and they are truly in a position to celebrate the happy conclusion of their trials. Furthermore, the account of their earlier encounters allows for effects of irony and for a compelling portrait of the growing psychological sympathy between Penelope and the

[1] For a recent discussion of this problem, see Chris Emlyn-Jones, "The Reunion of Penelope and Odysseus," 1–2.

stranger[2] and for Penelope's recovery in response to the stranger's presence. But, although the inconsistency may be, in this sense, redeemed by the kinds of thematic development it allows, it is still itself a significant element in the *Odyssey*'s plot and worth investigating for the role it plays.

The paradox that Odysseus disguises himself from Penelope even though she remains loyal to him is not simply glossed over for the sake of the poetic effects it leads to. The inconsistency of Odysseus' action is acknowledged within the text, most strikingly in Athena's response to Odysseus' attempt to disguise himself from her with a false tale. Athena translates Odysseus' show of wiliness into a program for his return, in effect imposing this paradoxical course of action on him. She announces that the caution Odysseus has shown will be applied particularly to Penelope, even though she acknowledges that Penelope is loyal to him.[3]

ἀσπασίως γάρ κ᾽ ἄλλος ἀνὴρ ἀλαλήμενος ἐλθὼν
ἵετ᾽ ἐνὶ μεγάροις ἰδέειν παῖδάς τ᾽ ἄλοχόν τε·
σοὶ δ᾽ οὔ πω φίλον ἐστὶ δαήμεναι οὐδὲ πυθέσθαι,
πρίν γ᾽ ἔτι σῆς ἀλόχου πειρήσεαι, ἥ τέ τοι αὔτως
ἧσται ἐνὶ μεγάροισιν, ὀϊζυραὶ δέ οἱ αἰεὶ
φθίνουσιν νύκτες τε καὶ ἤματα δάκρυ χεούσῃ.

Any other man coming happily home from such wandering
would be eager to see his children and wife in his house.
But it doesn't suit you to expose yourself by asking questions
until you test your wife, but she, as always,
stays in the house, and always bitter nights
and bitter days waste away for her as she weeps.
(*Od.* 13.333–338)

[2] The development of sympathy between Penelope and the stranger has been studied most extensively by Norman Austin, *Archery at the Dark of the Moon*, 200–238.

[3] Because of the way in which Athena seems to speak for Odysseus here, attributing intentions to him that he has apparently not had, the authenticity of this passage has been questioned since antiquity. For references and discussion, see Wolfram Krehmer, "Zur Begegnung zwischen Odysseus und Athene," 218–219.

As Athena praises Odysseus for the wariness that distinguishes him from other heroes, she evokes two ways in which a hero's wife can represent a threat to the success of his enterprise. First, his desire for her can distract him from the task with which he is faced, luring him into a premature enjoyment that costs him the achievement of his true goal; and, second, she can herself betray him. These two dangers are neatly linked in the story Menelaus tells about how Helen (a figure who epitomizes both female seductiveness and female treachery) tried to subvert the Achaean strategy of the Trojan Horse by calling out in the voices of their wives to the various heroes who were hidden inside (*Od.* 4.264–289): her feigned behavior is distracting while her actual behavior is treacherous.

Of these threats, the capacity of women to distract heroes from their task is emphasized in the *Iliad* with its focus on battlefield achievement, especially in the account of Hector's visit to the city in *Iliad* 6, and in the parts of the *Odyssey* dealing with Odysseus' struggle to reach home.[4] On the other hand, the second half of the *Odyssey*, with its focus on Odysseus' reception into the home he has now reached, emphasizes the danger that arises from the possible treachery of wives. Athena's words make it clear that the poem is concerned with this possibility even if its hero's own wife is entirely loyal, for she congratulates Odysseus for adopting a course of action that is, in principle, correct, although in this instance unnecessary. Wives are in general not to be trusted, and most men are too incautious to remember this. Odysseus' procedure of disguising himself from Penelope should therefore be understood as an expression of the general treacherousness of wives that does not reflect on the character of Penelope, whose fidelity is not in doubt.[5] The direction of Odysseus' disguise against Penelope is comparable to the destitution and old age that constitute it: both are manifes-

[4] On this point, see Johannes Th. Kakridis, "The Role of Women in the Iliad," 68–75.

[5] Cf. *Od.* 15.20–23, where Athena motivates Telemachus to return to Ithaca from Sparta by invoking the general tendency of women to forget their husbands.

tations of the circumstances in which he could be expected to find himself, but which he manages to escape; both are expressions of general limitations on human success that the story this poem tells, the story of Odysseus, transcends.

Odysseus' concealment of his return from Penelope, however illogical, dramatizes the way the hero's success is threatened by his need to depend on his wife. To return to a point made already in Chapter 1, Odysseus' marriage is at once the most crucial and the most vulnerable of the relationships that allow him to recover his former position. His identity as Penelope's husband stems from a socially assigned role that could have been played by someone else and in which, in light of his long absence, he could be replaced. Thus, it is through his marriage that Odysseus, having survived all the dangers of the world beyond his home, is still threatened with annihilation. It is as her suitors that his competitors are able to challenge his position; they can legitimately pretend to the role of Penelope's husband, as they cannot to the role of Odysseus' son and heir. That Odysseus should have to participate in a suitors' contest for Penelope in order to regain his own home emphasizes the way the artificiality of marriage imports the instability of identity characteristic of the battlefield into the center of his home. His identity as her husband is not an indisputable fact but an honor to be won by proving himself to be "best of the Achaeans."[6] And this challenge is intensified by the poem's suggestion, in contradiction to its own predominant vision of social life, that whoever marries Penelope will inherit Odysseus' house.

The possible instability of any marriage can only be countered by the continued allegiance of both husband and wife to the idea—which always remains only an idea—that it is permanent. The durability of a marriage, its resistance to the pressures of separation and change, cannot derive from the natural permanence of a blood tie but depends solely on the steadiness of mind of its participants, on the continuity of such inherently volatile qualities as desire, affection, and loyalty. Thus, this so-

---

[6] Gregory Nagy, *The Best of the Achaeans*, 38–39.

cially instituted relationship depends for its success on qualities that cannot be institutionalized. Even within the bounded realm of peacetime civilization, society cannot guarantee the irrational and idiosyncratic preferences that are necessary to lasting ties between people. This is dramatized by the brief but suspenseful gap between Penelope's reception of Odysseus as a guest and her identification of him as her husband, with which the previous chapter's discussion ended. Odysseus can pass a series of social tests of his eligibility to be Penelope's husband, showing himself to be a worthy guest and winning the contest of the bow, but he is still not her husband if she is not willing to acknowledge him.

Odysseus' return would be impossible if it were not for the steadiness of Penelope's mind, her determination that the role of her husband is an inalienable aspect of Odysseus' identity and not something that could be transferred to someone else. While his own loyalty to Penelope, his refusal to have her replaced even by a goddess, is what motivates him to undertake the risks of his homeward journey,[7] his achievement in reaching home would be nullified if she were not loyal to him. That is what happens to Agamemnon, who reaches the shores of his home but loses both *kleos* and *nostos* because his wife has shifted her loyalty to another man, and the congruence between the official tie of marriage and her own affections has been ruptured. Thus the *Odyssey*, which focuses on the conditions of *nostos*, places a strong emphasis and high value on the fidelity of the hero's wife. This is expressed in the speech in which Agamemnon, in the underworld, responds to the story of Odysseus by congratulating him for having a wife who had a virtuous mind and who never forgot her husband (*Od.* 24.191–202).

[7] The story of Odysseus' homecoming finds both its chronological starting point and its motivating force in Odysseus' refusal to accept Calypso as a substitute for Penelope. At his first appearance in the poem we are told that Odysseus is weeping and wasting away because Calypso no longer pleases him (*Od.* 5.151–153). This condition inspires Athena's appeal to Zeus, which sets Odysseus' return in motion (*Od.* 1.59). Later, of course, Odysseus also refuses to accept Nausicaa as a substitute for Penelope.

Odysseus' success is finally attributed to Penelope's virtue, and her virtue takes the form of the same strength of mind and constancy of memory, the same willed mental endurance that is essential to Odysseus' survival of his adventures. As John Finley comments, Agamemnon's statement "comes near making our *Odysseia* a *Penelopeia*."[8] In this poem, in which the recovery of Ithaca rather than the homeward journey is the main subject of the narrative, Penelope's steadfastness becomes a more prominent element in Odysseus' success than his own. Not only does Penelope provide the most powerful potential threat to Odysseus' enterprise, but she threatens to usurp his poem as well.

But even though Penelope's loyalty is essential to Odysseus' success, there is a danger that it may not be sufficient. Her determination to view Odysseus as her unique husband creates a serious vacuum at the center of power in Ithaca and so obstructs the orderly continuity of society over time, which is only possible if certain stable roles can be assumed successively by different individuals. Thus Penelope is subject to powerful social pressures, represented in a sinister form by the suitors, who would like to usurp Odysseus' place by marrying her, but also more legitimately by Telemachus, who would like to succeed to Odysseus' place lawfully and cannot if Penelope remains Odysseus' waiting wife. It is through these pressures on Penelope that the vulnerability of Odysseus' cause to the passage of time becomes most critical.

The mistrust of women that underlies Odysseus' disguise is one response to this challenge. While the *Odyssey*'s portrait of Penelope is one of the most sympathetic treatments of a female character in Greek literature, that portrait is also placed in a wider context of misogyny through the presentation of Penelope as an exception to a general rule. The poem self-consciously depicts the formation and authorization of a tradition of misogyny even as it places a counterexample at the center of its story. This can be seen in the way in which the Agamemnon story is invoked as justification for Odysseus' concealment of his return from Penelope.

[8] John H. Finley, Jr., *Homer's Odyssey*, 3.

The *Odyssey*'s sense of its own story as extraordinary is expressed throughout in its use of the Agamemnon story, not just as a foil to the story of Odysseus, but as a norm from which the story of Odysseus departs. Even as the poem opens, Zeus is drawing general conclusions about human behavior from the Agamemnon story, and other characters are seen to do so throughout the poem. Similarly, it is Agamemnon himself who is given the opportunity to make a final comment on the story of Odysseus in the underworld speech referred to above (*Od.* 24.191–202). The consequences of this bias for the reputation of women are made explicit in that speech as Agamemnon predicts that Penelope's virtue will win undying *kleos* for her while Clytemnestra's treachery "χαλεπὴν δέ τε φῆμιν ὀπάσσει / θηλυτέρῃσι γυναιξί, καὶ ἥ κ᾽ εὐεργὸς ἔῃσιν," "gives an evil reputation / to all women, even to one who does what is right" (*Od.* 24.201–202). Agamemnon here looks ahead to the formation of a tradition of misogyny that, as he acknowledges, is based on paying attention to some examples and not to others.[9]

The *Odyssey* in its depiction of Odysseus concealing his return from Penelope makes it clear that he is treating Penelope as if she were like Clytemnestra even though he knows that she is not and suggests that that is an appropriate course of action.[10] Although Odysseus is not depicted as internalizing the information he receives during his visit to the underworld, he is in effect following the advice given him there by Agamemnon. Agamemnon advises him to apply the lesson of his, Agamemnon's, experience to his own situation. He tells Odysseus not to be gentle and open with his wife but to conceal his true thoughts from her, although, like Athena in Book 13 but even more explicitly, he goes on to say that, in Odysseus' case, this caution is

[9] Compare a surviving fragment of Euripides' *Melanippe the Captive*, in which the speaker, presumably Melanippe herself, complains that men blame all women if one is found to be evil. Denys Page, ed., *Select Papyryi* (Loeb Classical Library), III.13.20–21.

[10] In the mythological tradition outside the *Odyssey*, Penelope is, in fact, identified with Clytemnestra in two ways: her father Icarus is the brother of Clytemnestra's father Tyndareus, and in a number of later stories she does not remain faithful to Odysseus. See W. H. Roscher, *Ausführliches Lexicon der griechischen und römischen Mythologie*, III.2.1908–1911.

unnecessary: "ἀλλ' οὐ σοί γ', 'Οδυσεῦ, φόνος ἔσσεται ἔκ γε γυ-
ναικός," "And yet you, Odysseus, will never be murdered by
your wife . . ." (*Od.* 11.444).[11]

Odysseus listens to this advice rather than trusting the picture
given him by his mother when he asks her about conditions at
home: she stresses Penelope's steadfastness, her "τετληότι
θυμῷ," "enduring heart," and tells him, presumably projecting
from the situation when she died, before the suitors' arrival,
that Telemachus is happily administering his possessions (*Od.*
11.181–187). What makes it appropriate for Odysseus to follow the general lesson to be derived from Agamemnon's experience with his notably different wife rather than the specific
picture drawn by Anticleia is the fact Athena tells him before
disguising him, a fact Anticleia did not live long enough to
know and failed to foresee: the arrival of the suitors. As soon as
Odysseus hears it, his response is to compare himself with Agamemnon, "ὢ πόποι, ἦ μάλα δὴ 'Αγαμέμνονος 'Ατρεΐδαο / φθίσε-
σθαι κακὸν οἶτον ἐνὶ μεγάροισιν ἔμελλον," "Oh, surely I was
on the point of perishing in my palace / by the evil fate of Atreus'
son Agamemnon . . ." (*Od.* 13.383–384).

Despite her difference of character, which is repeatedly
stressed, Penelope is as dangerous as Clytemnestra because the
nature of her position as Odysseus' wife means that, whether
she wants to or not, she eventually attracts his enemies to his
house. Even if she is entirely loyal to Odysseus, she is nonetheless associated with the suitors and must therefore be treated
with caution. Odysseus' gesture of disguising himself from Penelope shows how the artificial character of marriage makes
women systematically unreliable to their husbands so that any

---

[11] This interchange between Odysseus and Agamemnon itself illustrates the
formation of a generally misogynistic outlook on the basis of the misfortunes of
the Atridae: Agamemnon concludes his own story, which stresses Clytemnestra's treachery, with a statement, like the one he makes in 24, that Clytemnestra's actions will bring shame on all women (*Od.* 11.432–434); Odysseus comments that Zeus has, in general, cursed the Atridae with female treachery and
refers to the way this curse has spread to the many others who died because of
Helen (*Od.* 11.436–439); and Agamemnon makes this the basis for his warning to Odysseus not to trust his wife (*Od.* 11.441–443).

woman, no matter what her character, can be regarded as treacherous. The construction of the plot articulates the general nature of the relationship in which these figures are located without regard for their individual characters or motives. Odysseus' disguise is in many ways characteristic of him, but its use to conceal his presence from Penelope does not answer either to her fidelity or to his sympathy for her sufferings.[12]

The consequence of Odysseus' illogical tactic of concealing himself from Penelope is an illogically constructed plot in which the crucial step—the setting of the contest of the bow—must come from a character who is not in on the plot. In this way, the vulnerability that lies behind Odysseus' gesture of disguising himself from Penelope becomes an essential element of the action. Odysseus is forced to rely on someone whose mind is unknown to him and who cannot herself perceive the direction of events. The postponement of his revelation to her until after the suitors' destruction puts him in a position in which, while her cooperation is crucial to his success, he cannot gain it directly. He must remain a stranger to her, and he must deal with her as if she were a stranger to him. His disguise artificially creates a state of estrangement between them that simulates the genuine possibility of estrangement that is latent in marriage and is aggravated by separations such as they have just endured.

In its account of Penelope's encounters with her disguised husband the poem gives us a complex depiction of someone involved in a plot of which she is unaware. Penelope's unawareness during her encounters with Odysseus in Books 18 and 19 is highlighted by the several ways in which the *Odyssey*'s text emphasizes the plotted nature of the action: Odysseus' presence in disguise; the operation beneath the surface of the action of the recurrent narrative patterns of recognition scenes (discussed in Chapter 1); the characters' participation in the codes of hospitality; Athena's particularly intrusive interventions in Books 18

[12] The way typical plot patterns, of which the returning hero's disguising himself from his wife is certainly one, may override the depiction of character is borne out by Vladimir Propp's observation that the characters' motivations are the most variable and fluid elements in folktales. *Morphology of the Folktale*, 68.

and 19; and a series of omens, portents, and prophecies announcing Odysseus' return. These indications make Penelope's role an especially pointed, ironic depiction of the difference between a character's actions when they are seen as part of a coherent and finished plot and as experienced by that character as events unfold.

The figure of Penelope in the *Odyssey* exemplifies with particular clarity the double life led by most characters in literary plots, as both figures in an orderly artistic design and as representations of human beings making their way through experiences whose patterns they cannot perceive or predict. In Penelope's case these two aspects of her role in the poem yield perspectives on her character and behavior that are so different that they cannot easily be reconciled. If her behavior is seen as leading up to the culminating event of her story, her recognition of Odysseus, it is consonant with an action that defines her as unshakably loyal,[13] clear-sighted, and in control of her destiny; all of her previous actions can then be understood as anticipations or preliminary versions of this destined recognition, anticipations that reveal this same combination of traits.

But if her actions are seen as reflecting the fact that she cannot know where events are leading, they no longer seem to reveal those same supposedly unvarying characteristics; in fact they show that it may be impossible to act in ways that reveal those characteristics in circumstances such as Penelope's. Her behavior raises the same questions about the relationship of character

[13] The link between recognition of identity and marital fidelity is a manifestation of the connection between recognition of identity and willing assent to the claims involved in a gesture of self-identification or self-description, which was discussed in Chapter 1. It is reflected in a somewhat displaced way in the episode of Odysseus' recognition by Helen in *Odyssey* 4. Helen's recognition of Odysseus signals not only her identification of him but also her willingness to view him as an accomplice and her renunciation of her adulterous behavior (Cf. *Od.* 4.259–264, and especially the acknowledgment of Menelaus' merits in *Od.* 4.264). This can be expressed thorough recognition of someone other than her husband because her adultery has touched men to whom she has not been married, men who, although they once wished to marry her, are now allied politically to her husband.

and circumstance that are countered by Odysseus' disguise. And the presentation of Penelope as also emerging from a kind of disguise when she recognizes Odysseus also counters those questions in relation to her behavior, but only retrospectively, only in connection with a global view of the action. The presentation of her experience as she experiences it testifies to the powerlessness and vulnerability to fortune that call heroic identity into question. Odysseus' continued absence prevents her from remaining loyal to the idea that he is her only husband, and she cannot perceive the true nature of events as long as they are deliberately hidden from her. In light of Odysseus' disguise she must continue to respond to the circumstances that that disguise at once reflects and perpetuates, circumstances that require her inevitably to choose another husband. If Odysseus' disguise testifies to aspects of her role as wife that transcend her character, it also puts her in a position where, seemingly against her character, she necessarily acts out that role.

The presentation of Penelope's double role is complicated by the way she herself is portrayed as duplicitous: like Odysseus, she is a maker of plots. As Athena explains to Odysseus when she meets him on the shore, Penelope is engaging in a strategy of deliberate duplicity towards the suitors. She behaves in ways that lead them to believe she will marry one of them, although, as Athena puts it, "$\nu\acute{o}os$ $\delta\acute{e}$ $o\acute{i}$ $\ddot{a}\lambda\lambda\alpha$ $\mu\varepsilon\nu o\iota\nu\tilde{a}$," "her mind is intent on other things" (*Od.* 13.379–381). Penelope's deceitful behavior, then, imitates the possibility that Odysseus' deceit points at less directly, the possibility that she might marry one of the suitors. It also suggests, as does Odysseus' disguise, superiority over the suitors, an ability to outwit them that nullifies their threat.

In the course of the story, Penelope takes a series of actions that seem to represent capitulation to the pressures on her to abandon her loyalty to Odysseus, but which in fact promote his return: weaving and unweaving a shroud for Laertes, appearing before the suitors to solicit gifts, setting the contest of the bow, and ordering Eurycleia to move the marriage bed. But while this pattern of duplicity runs through her actions, both the way this doubleness is incorporated into each action and the relationship between her outer gestures and inner intentions shift as the narrative develops. As a result, it is not automatically possible to interpret all of her actions in the same way even though they possess this fundamental similarity. The degree to which Penelope seems to understand and to control the ambiguity of her own actions grows less with successive realizations of this pattern, and this development raises questions about the continued capacity of even someone as crafty as Penelope to control a situation as difficult as hers.

The first of Penelope's duplicitous actions, the weaving and unweaving of Laertes' shroud is the most easily intelligible and the most clearly deliberate. It takes place before the *Odyssey*'s action begins, and, by the time the poem's story opens, it is fully understood by everyone. It is in any case an action that, once detected, is inherently intelligible. It is not only duplicitous but outwardly double, since it consists of two complementary gestures, weaving and unweaving. Penelope forestalls the suitors' understanding by concealing one of those gestures from them, but once they catch her unweaving, her purposes are clear to them.

But the two such actions that she takes during the time Odysseus is in disguise, appearing before the suitors in Book 18 and setting the contest of the bow in Book 19, are more difficult to make sense of. Their correct interpretation depends not on catching her out in a secret activity, but on an understanding of her state of mind as she performs them, yet the text makes her state of mind hard to assess. Nor can her intentions be assumed to be the same as they were during the weaving episode that sets the pattern these two actions follow. The eventual detection of the trick with the shroud points to the way in which what that trick represents—an attempt to hold out against the passage of time—cannot work forever. Its very intelligibility is a sign of its failure. When what is at issue is steadiness of mind, the continued ability of the will to resist circumstances, the events of the past cannot provide a reliable guide to the present. Precisely because they come later, Penelope's subsequent appearances of giving in to the pressures of time cannot be assumed to share the deliberate insincerity of that earlier action.

Nor can the significance of these other actions be determined retrospectively by the latest one, her trick with the bed. By then the removal of Odysseus' disguise has entirely changed the situation: it means both that she acts in the knowledge of his presence, so that the issue of her capitulation can be wholly fictional and hypothetical, and that she speaks openly to him, providing an explanation that allows her deceitful gesture to be interpreted. Through successive manifestations of a stable pattern of behavior, but with shifting implications for our understanding of the character involved, the *Odyssey* highlights the disturbing effects of the passage of time on the notion of stable character.

Throughout the events of Books 18 and 19, Odysseus, from the vantage allowed by his disguise, responds with a kind of assurance that anticipates the successful outcome of his enterprise. On the other hand, Penelope, who is excluded from the knowledge of Odysseus' return and whose ability to control events is slipping away, offers a far more confused and uncertain response inspired by the contradictory influences of her hopes for Odysseus' return and her awareness that, as time passes, his return becomes less and less likely. Her behavior suggests a dynamic mixture of motives that corresponds to the variable and unpredictable nature of her situation as she perceives it, and that even includes an element of pleasure in the presence of the suitors, with whom she has no choice but to come to terms.[14] And when she speaks of her situation to the stranger during their long private meeting, describing the painful division she experiences as she faces an increasingly certain remarriage to which

[14] Penelope's positive interest in the suitors, which need not be inconsistent with a preference for Odysseus' return, can be seen in her impulse to appear to them in 18 and especially in her dream. For the view that her dream expresses attachment to the suitors, see Georges Devereux, "The Character of Penelope." Devereux's view is followed by A. V. Rankin, "Penelope's Dreams in Books XIX and XX of the *Odyssey*," and Joseph Russo, "Interview and Aftermath."

she would prefer death, she testifies to the constraints and uncertainties of human life that the plot she stands outside attempts to deny.[15]

This contrast between Odysseus and Penelope's perspectives is most evident in the episode of her appearance to the suitors in Book 18. There Odysseus, seeing Penelope for the first time since his return, treats her with none of the suspicion that underlies his disguise even though she is behaving in a way that ought certainly to arouse his suspicion, encouraging the suitors and soliciting gifts from them. Yet he confidently concludes that she is tricking them. He rejoices at her overtures to the suitors because "νόος δέ οἱ ἄλλα μενοίνα," "her mind was intent on other things" (*Od.* 18.283). His interpretation, which echoes Athena's divine perspective, accords well with Penelope's faithful character and with the way events turn out, which he is in a better position than anyone else to foresee. As he manipulates events from a position of superior knowledge and control, he assumes that she is doing the same.

But Odysseus' interpretation is also contradicted by the account of Penelope's decision to make this appearance, especially her speech to her nurse. This speech suggests that she has no clear plan to deceive the suitors, but rather that her intentions are confused and that she herself hardly understands them (*Od.* 18.164–168). The result is a discrepancy between Odysseus' conviction about her state of mind and the hints we are given by the text. Odysseus' interpretation, which is made possible by his own disguised presence, is a proleptic understanding of events as part of a larger strategy. Penelope's perception, which is governed by the concealment from her of what Odysseus knows, represents the sense of events as unfolding haphazardly and without direction that is experienced by those who see only

---

[15] The contrast between Penelope's perspective and the divine perspective of those who know how events will turn out is nicely expressed by Athena when she first tells Odysseus that Penelope is constantly mourning his absence and then goes on to say that *she*, however, never doubted that he would come home (*Od.* 13.339–340).

what is apparent at the moment, by those who are not in on the plot.[16]

This same double perspective is at play in the account of Penelope's decision to set the contest of the bow, strategically the most important development of the *Odyssey*'s plot. The contest has an ambiguous character similar to that of her other actions, but the particular form of its ambiguity is once again different. It is not that her public gesture is contradicted by a private action, as with the trick of the shroud, or that her public gesture is possibly contradicted by her private intentions, as with the appearance in the hall (at least by Odysseus' theory of it) and with the trick of the bed; here her public action is self-contradictory. She sets as a condition for a new husband the performance of a feat of which only her old husband is capable. The feature of the contest that makes it seem most threatening and disloyal to Odysseus, the way it is designed to find someone who is truly his match, is actually what makes it the means of recovering his unique identity. The contest does not, after all, result in the kind of discrimination among the suitors that is incompatible with Odysseus' triumph. Because the suitors are blind to their own inferiority to Odysseus, they are tricked into accepting a condition for marriage to Penelope that automatically disqualifies them and seals their fate.

But Penelope herself seems unaware that she is tricking the suitors: when she first describes her plan to the stranger, she sees it as bringing about her departure from the house and brushes aside his claim that Odysseus will be back before the contest begins. And when she fetches the bow from the storeroom, she weeps. The wonderful duplicity of her action seems to be out of her control and out of her mind, to be, from her

---

[16] This discrepancy has been explained in neo–analytic terms by Uvo Hölscher. According to Hölscher, those things in Penelope's behavior that seem flirtatious or duplicitous are vestiges of an earlier folktale version, while her evident innocence reflects the epic poet's reworking of that version in line with a conception of Penelope as a modest and dignified heroine. "Penelope vor den Freiern." Cf. also "The Transformation from Folk-Tale to Epic," 62–63.

point of view, fortuitous. The expectations with which she proposes the contest are thus entirely contrary to the prospects Odysseus foresees when he encourages her to go through with her plan.

This crucial step in the *Odyssey*'s plot is brought about neither by Odysseus' nor Penelope's cleverness in devising a strategy against the suitors, but rather by the lucky chance that at the point when Penelope feels she can no longer hold out against the suitors, Odysseus is there to take advantage of the means she devises to replace him. The solution to their difficulties emerges from a fortuitous combination of her despair and his improvisation. The result is an exhilarating twist in the narrative, but also a more self-conscious and disturbing use of chance for the resolution of a plot than the improbable coincidences on which so many plots, including those of the folktale tradition lying behind the *Odyssey*, depend. This reliance on chance is disturbing because it contradicts the poem's dominant and more comforting assumptions. Both Penelope's action in setting the contest and the words with which she expresses her intentions counter the notions that clever and strong-willed characters like Odysseus and Penelope can make events turn out as they want them to and that the passage of time represents inevitable progress towards the fulfillment of their desires.

Penelope's speech to the stranger announcing her decision is a compelling portrait of someone sadly, reluctantly facing the realization that she can no longer hold out against the ineluctable pressures of time, that she can no longer shape her circumstances so as to leave open the possibility of having what she wants (*Od.* 19.560–581).[17] With this depiction of its heroine courageously facing her own apparent loss of happiness, the *Odyssey* courageously acknowledges the real limitations on human happiness that its own conclusion transcends. Indeed, the courageousness of this acknowledgment can be measured in the

[17] For an appreciative account of the effects of irony and pathos produced by Penelope's action if it is understood in this way, see Bernard Fenik, *Studies in the Odyssey*, 45–47.

way this portrait has recurrently been found unsatisfactory and has been rejected in a variety of ways.

Within the poem itself, Penelope's decision attracts the moral censure of Ithacan public opinion. When, during his reunion with Penelope, Odysseus perpetuates the fiction of his absence through the false wedding feast, the response of passers-by is to condemn Penelope.

ἦ μάλα δή τις ἔγημε πολυμνήστην βασίλειαν·
σχετλίη, οὐδ᾽ ἔτλη πόσιος οὗ κουριδίοιο
εἴρυσθαι μέγα δῶμα διαμπερές, ἧος ἵκοιτο.

Surely someone has married the much-wooed queen.
Hard-hearted, she could not endure to keep the great house of her own husband unceasingly, until he should come back.

(*Od.* 23.149–151)

Penelope's remarriage (which even Odysseus could plausibly be said to endorse, as Penelope's words at 18.256–273 suggest)[18] is here treated as a betrayal of Odysseus.[19] Once again the text points to the misogynistic tendency of general human opinion, the inclination to blame women for the circumstances by which they are constrained.

The emphasis on Penelope's lack of endurance expressed in the phrase "οὐδ᾽ ἔτλη," "could not endure," suggests another way in which her gesture represents a betrayal of Odysseus: it betrays the contention that the *Odyssey* is asserting through its portrayal of Odysseus' unique success, the contention that the mind and will are sufficient to win out against circumstances, that Odysseus can control events through his strategic plotting of them.

Like Amphimedon in the underworld, who constructs from his experience of Odysseus' story a conspiracy theory according

[18] Cf. also the way Odysseus anticipates Penelope's remarriage in his question to Anticleia at *Od.* 11.179.
[19] Cf. *Od.* 16.75, where Telemachus suggests that the *dēmos*, the people, would be offended if Penelope were to remarry.

to which Penelope was explicitly instructed by Odysseus to set the contest, critics have felt that the events of the story only make sense if Penelope is aware of what she is doing, if those who benefit from the turn of events have also shaped them. They find in the text, as it stands, a breach of literary propriety that offends them as much as Penelope's supposed breach of faith offends her Ithacan observers. Penelope's surrender (or even, as it is sometimes called, her collapse)[20] is viewed as unmotivated and inconsonant with her characterization as intelligent.[21] In a variety of ways, these critics have tried to explain the text away by claiming that something different is going on, that Penelope really (in one of a number of senses) recognizes Odysseus before she sets the contest.

One example of this type of explanation is the analyst argument that the *Odyssey*'s text reflects the imperfect adaptation of an earlier version of the story in which, as in Amphimedon's telling, Odysseus does reveal himself to Penelope before the contest.[22] In this view, Penelope's action really belongs to a context in which she does understand what she is doing, from which it has been transplanted. What lack of control is registered in the text can be attributed to the composer rather than to the characters.[23] Penelope is the victim not of her own cir-

---

[20] E.g., by Woodhouse, *The Composition of Homer's Odyssey*, 80 ff.

[21] E.g., Philip Harsh writes: "Either Penelope is stupid or by this time [midway through Book 19] she suspects this man's identity (unless, of course, the poet is manipulating his characters as puppets)." "Penelope and Odysseus in *Odyssey* XIX," 11. This statement reacts against two related phenomena: the poem's rendition of the fact that Penelope cannot see what is disguised from her, and its depiction of the role of chance in giving her action a meaning other than what she intends. For an equally forceful statement of the view that "the poet could not possibly have chosen a worse moment for Penelope's surrender," see Denys Page, *The Homeric Odyssey*, 123 ff.

[22] For a recent summary of this position, see G. S. Kirk, *The Songs of Homer*, 245–247. This view is also held by Wilamowitz (*Die Heimkehr des Odysseus*, 87), Schwartz (*Die Odyssee*, 110), Woodhouse (*The Composition of Homer's Odyssey*, 80–91), and Page (*The Homeric Odyssey*, 119–129).

[23] Cf. especially Woodhouse's remarks: *The Composition of Homer's Odyssey*, 87–88, 90.

cumstances but of the circumstances of the poem's composition.

Another version of this type of explanation is the interpretation advanced by Philip Harsh—that Penelope recognizes Odysseus even though he does not deliberately reveal himself and that she keeps her recognition a secret. Harsh's reading is a logical development of the poem's portrayal of Penelope as capable of duplicity; it exploits the text's reminder that her motives cannot positively be determined from what she does or even from what she says as a means, again, of giving her intentions that are in harmony with the outcome of her actions. It gives Penelope control not only of her destiny, but also of the poem's persuasive imitation of an act of despair. But, although this interpretation cannot be disproven, its complete abandonment of the evidence of the text as a control, however logical, has caused it to be almost universally rejected.[24]

Another version of the view that Penelope really does recognize Odysseus is the theory that she recognizes him subconsciously.[25] This approach has yielded a series of sensitive interpretations of Penelope's behavior that are, by contrast to analyst treatments, highly sympathetic to what is in the text and that reconcile her responses with the many signs of Odysseus' return that she receives. By locating control over events in Penelope's

[24] Philip Harsh, in his article "Penelope and Odysseus in *Odyssey* XIX," was the first modern critic to propose that Penelope consciously recognizes Odysseus during their encounter in Book 19 but keeps her recognition secret until their open reunion in Book 23. But the question of whether she suspects Odysseus' identity before she openly recognizes him was already being debated in antiquity: see Seneca, *Epistles*, 88, 8. Harsh's interpretation is adopted by Douglas Stewart, *The Disguised Guest*, 103 ff.

[25] The idea that Penelope recognizes Odysseus subconsciously is most fully stated by Anne Amory in "The Reunion of Odysseus and Penelope." Amory's interpretation is shared by many critics, including: Alice J. Mariani, "The Forged Feature," 141–142; Norman Austin, *Archery at the Dark of the Moon*, 235 ff; Cedric H. Whitman, *Homer and the Heroic Tradition*, 303–304; Joseph Russo, "Interview and Aftermath: Dream, Fantasy, and Intuition in *Odyssey* 19 and 20."

subconscious, this interpretation successfully integrates both versions of her experience into her character, drawing on a theory of human behavior in which all people are more in control of their destinies than they realize and are in a sense kept unaware of the plots of their own lives.

But this view tends to gloss over the ways in which the poem shows us that Penelope's behavior is imposed on her by her impossible role as faithful wife of a man who is absent. It is always a simple step to reinterpret Homeric depictions of characters affected by forces outside them, such as divine interventions, as representations of internal psychological forces;[26] but what gets lost in that move is the epics' sensitivity to the painful, disorienting rifts that can exist between character and social role. The view that Penelope recognizes Odysseus subconsciously harmonizes the contradictory elements in the text at the cost of playing down the extent to which Penelope's obliviousness is the result of her circumstances; this view tends to involve, instead, the construction of a portrait of Penelope as innately irrational, impulsive, and passive, a portrait that is often identified as typically feminine.[27] Penelope emerges in this reading as lacking, rather than sharing, the mental power that is so central to Odysseus' success.

One critic, Anne Amory, thus describes Odysseus and Penelope as having intrinsically different ways of viewing the world: "In contrast to the way Odysseus reasons about his experiences and reaches out to become master of his circumstances, Penelope is passive and intuitive. She looks at things only intermittently; she is always holding a veil in front of her

---

[26] For an especially influential statement of this view, see E. R. Dodds, *The Greeks and the Irrational*, Chapter 1, esp. 14–15.

[27] Joseph Russo sums up this view when he writes of her decision to set the contest of the bow: "Since Penelope is a woman of strong intuitions, as Amory and Austin have nicely shown us, she now decides to take a certain leap into the unknown, because she 'feels' the time has come." "Interview and Aftermath," 10–11. Cf. Charles Taylor's summary of Amory's treatment of Penelope in her essay, "The Reunion of Odysseus and Penelope": "She shows that her responses, though complex, are understandably feminine." *Essays on the Odyssey*, ix.

face, or looking away from things."[28] This characterization obscures the way these differences are determined both by a feature of the plot, the fact that Odysseus knows what is happening and is concealing it from Penelope,[29] and by the social role of women, which lies behind that plot. When Penelope is allowed to know that Odysseus has returned, she can be as clear-sighted and resourceful as he is. But as long as Odysseus deprives Penelope of the knowledge of his return, she remains vulnerable to the effects of his absence, which include uncertainty about the future and the impossibility of remaining Odysseus' wife forever.

When Odysseus, having defeated the suitors, stops disguising himself from Penelope, the terms of his interaction with her change. He no longer feels the need to conceal his presence from her and so can enjoy at last the reunion he has so much desired—except that the smooth fulfillment of Odysseus' envisioned scenario is frustrated because Penelope refuses to recognize him. When he finally brings her into his plot, she is not automatically willing to participate in it, and this raises the possibility that her exclusion from it was not, after all, inconsistent with her nature. The removal of Odysseus' disguise signals his defeat of the suitors and thus his conquest of the threat Penelope has involuntarily subjected him to. But his loss of that protective distance from her also forces him to face the more difficult and challenging question of what she herself really wants, and she actively confronts him with that question through her slowness to acknowledge him.

Penelope's unparalleled and unexpected reluctance to recognize Odysseus once he has disclosed himself to her[30] causes him

[28] Anne Amory, "The Gates of Horn and Ivory," 55.

[29] Significantly, Amory cites as exceptions to the view that Odysseus "has a firm grip on what is true and what he is inventing, and . . . is master both of the actual situation and of his own lies with which he deceives others" most of the events preceding his plotting with Athena: his adventures and his failure to recognize Ithaca on arrival. "The Gates of Horn and Ivory," 55.

[30] Other characters, such as Telemachus and Laertes, resist recognizing Odysseus briefly until they are presented with proofs, but Penelope's failure to recognize him continues after she has been presented with proofs that have con-

to experience directly that complete dependence on another person's attitude of mind that was evoked indirectly and impersonally through his disguise. The advantage represented by his mastery of disguises, the ability to control the timing of his self-revelations, proves useless in the face of Penelope's unwillingness to recognize him. The implication of his being in disguise—that he is in control of the action of the plot—proves false when he surrenders his disguise and still does not get what he wants. The hero's success depends finally on the willing assent of his wife. His lack of control over her is linked to the specific danger of sexual betrayal as her passive non-recognition takes on the form of an active suggestion of infidelity in her command to Eurycleia to move the bed. At this point Odysseus faces as a real possibility the betrayal by Penelope that, even as he disguised himself from her, he did not really believe in.

Odysseus' vulnerability to Penelope receives its most direct and painful expression in the spontaneous outburst in which he gives voice to the sense of wounded honor her suggestion evokes. Notably, he expresses pain, not at the thought that she has had another lover, but at the thought that another man has outdone him. No one, he says, could move that bed without the help of a god (*Od.* 24.184–187); in building it around a rooted tree, he has ensured that no other man could move it. This response well defines the role played by Odysseus' marriage in his sense of self. The fixity of the bed can be seen as symbolizing the permanence of marriage in a variety of suggestive ways; for Odysseus it does so specifically because it represents a permanent achievement that cannot be challenged by any rival. Even this most intimate token of identity has an agonistic significance.

---

vinced others: Odysseus' success against the suitors, and, especially, the scar. Her stubborn resistance in the face of these proofs frustrates all expectations. This frustration is registered successively by Eurycleia, when Penelope is unconvinced by her report of Odysseus' return (*Od.* 23.69–72); by Telemachus, when Penelope does not recognize Odysseus once she is in his presence (*Od.* 23.96–103); and by Odysseus himself, when she remains unmoved even by his epiphany as his younger self (*Od.* 23.167–172).

Odysseus' outburst effects a resolution that clarifies the doubts and reverses the suspicions raised in the narrative that leads up to it. No man has moved Odysseus' bed, and Penelope has always wanted his return. When Odysseus and Penelope both finally give up their disguises, they recover a quality of *homophrosynē*, "like-mindedness," that is expressed in the text in a variety of ways. One is the formal parallelism of the two speeches, each beginning "*daimoni-*," "strange one," in which Odysseus asks for a stranger's bed, and Penelope commands Eurycleia to make up his own bed outside the bedroom. Another is the reverse simile that compares Penelope's experiences to Odysseus', suggesting an imaginative sympathy that transcends their difference of gender. Yet another is the way in which the bed functions as a token between them. Unlike the bow, which takes on its significance from Odysseus' unique ability to string it, no matter what it means to Penelope, the bed derives its value as a token entirely from the meaning it has for both of them. Odysseus has made it immobile, rooted always in his house, but he has also gone away and left his house in Penelope's control. The immobility of the bed does not by itself guarantee the stability of the marriage: in Odysseus' long absence Penelope could easily have invited another man to share it. It is only because she allows no one else to know about the bed's fixity and thus can use it to test him that this secret fact signifies either Odysseus' identity or Penelope's fidelity. It is only because of what is in Penelope's mind that what Odysseus describes as a *sēma*, a "mark," of the bed (*Od.* 23.188, 202) can function as a *sēma* of another type—a token that convinces her of his identity (*Od.* 23.206).

As Penelope finally acknowledges Odysseus, she also explains what has caused her to hold up their reunion. She says that she was afraid that someone would trick her, and then goes on to talk about Helen, whom she exonerates on the grounds that Helen did not foresee the consequences of her actions and that she was compelled to act as she did by a god. Penelope and Helen are so different, at least where sexual fidelity is concerned, that it is hard at first to see how they could be at all comparable, and, indeed, the passage has been questioned since Alexandrian times for that reason.[31] But there is an underlying analogy between what Helen actually did and what Penelope has feared she might be doing by recognizing Odysseus. Penelope has been afraid that her recognition of the stranger as Odysseus might be based on desire rather than true knowledge, that, even though her acceptance of him would spring from his similarity to Odysseus, it would repeat Helen's action of accepting an attractive stranger as a substitute for her husband.

Like Odysseus' disguise, Penelope's caution stems from fear of her own susceptibility to desire, a fear that she might not, after all, be distinguishable from Helen and Clytemnestra. But while Odysseus' disguise acknowledges that fear with a certain conscious insincerity, Penelope, it turns out, feels it much more directly and acutely. Penelope's suspicion of the fulfillment of her own desire[32] is intensified by a clear-sighted sense of its improbability. Even as she longs for Odysseus' return, she knows that it would be a miraculous event, and this makes her slow to recognize it when it happens. Her first instinct is to connect what is happening around her with the more probable patterns of human experience. Thus, she is quicker to see the stranger's resemblance to Odysseus when he is wearing the disguise that represents the state in which Odysseus could be expected to be found than when that disguise has been removed. When Eurycleia comes to tell her that Odysseus has returned and has killed the suitors, Penelope refuses to believe it, even though she admits that that is what she wants. Instead she attributes this superhuman act of retribution to those who could be expected to perform it, the gods (*Od.* 23.58–68). And when she feels herself moved to accept the stranger as Odysseus, she compares herself to Helen who, along with her sister Clytemnestra, provides in this poem the paradigm of probable female behavior.

[31] For a well-stated defense of the passage, see Arthur Platt, "Notes on the *Odyssey*," 383–384. Cf. also the discussion by Anne Amory, "The Reunion of Odysseus and Penelope," 120.

[32] On Penelope's reluctance to believe what she wishes to be true, see Anne Amory, "The Reunion of Odysseus and Penelope," esp. 105.

Finding it hard to believe that Odysseus could be an exception, a hero who returns even after so long an absence, Penelope cannot believe that she might herself be an exception, a wife who in no sense betrays her husband even after so long a separation.

Penelope holds up her reunion with Odysseus by exercising what is ordinarily treated in the poem as a virtue: attention to the analogies provided by the experiences of others. Penelope's attention to the example of Helen and consequent hesitation to recognize Odysseus corresponds to his attention to the example of Agamemnon and consequent hesitation to identify himself to Penelope. In each case this course of action is both a sign of merit and, because of the merit of the other, because of Odysseus' ability to return and Penelope's fidelity, unnecessary.[33] In this way the *Odyssey* simultaneously upholds the importance of learning from the examples of others and recounts a story in which the hard truths embodied in these examples are suspended.

Penelope's explanation of her nonrecognition broadens the significance of her brief but powerfully frustrating resistance to Odysseus' return: her nonrecognition represents not simply the threat of infidelity—the power of the hero's wife to undermine his success at the very center of his home—but a more general awareness of the violence to the normal conditions of human life his return requires. As she is depicted interfering with its smooth completion, it is her role to assure that the story of Odysseus is not told without any acknowledgment of its miraculousness. The awareness of normal experience that lies behind his concealment from her now emerges, in a new way, as a feature of her own outlook.

Once she has recognized Odysseus, Penelope plays this role in another and more explicit way, for she refuses to celebrate

---

[33] Odysseus and Telemachus are both too foolish to see that Penelope's hesitation expresses a virtue that sets her apart from other women; thus each chides her for not rushing to recognize her husband as any other woman would (*Od.* 23.96–103, 166–170). The foolishness of this censure is underscored by the contrast with Athena's praise of Odysseus for not rushing to be reunited with his wife as any other man would (*Od.* 13.333–336).

their extraordinary good fortune without articulating the ways in which it is limited by the normal constraints of human life. Her very first words as she acknowledges Odysseus counter the claim, implicit in the manner of Odysseus' homecoming, that it represents the obliteration of the passage of time, that somehow Odysseus can return from his adventures at Troy and elsewhere and begin again as the young man he was when he left. Her words serve as a reminder that, for mortals, the loss of time can never be made up.

θεοὶ δ᾽ ὤπαζον ὀϊζύν,
οἳ νῶϊν ἀγάσαντο παρ᾽ ἀλλήλοισι μένοντε
ἥβης ταρπῆναι καὶ γήραος οὐδὸν ἱκέσθαι.

The gods gave us misery
since they begrudged us the chance of being always together
to enjoy our youth and arrive at the threshold of old age.
(*Od.* 23.210–212)

Finally, just before Odysseus and Penelope go to bed to experience at last the realization of their desires, she chooses one more delay for the sake of confronting another, even more severe challenge to the poem's happy ending. Just as Athena has held back the day so that Penelope and Odysseus can celebrate their reunion unconstrained by the passage of time, Odysseus announces that his trials are not over and his return is not permanent, referring vaguely to the further toil prophesied to him by Teiresias in the underworld (*Od.* 23.247–253). After making this announcement, he tries to brush it aside, closing his speech with a gesture towards bed (*Od.* 23.254–255). But Penelope resists his evasion, postponing their going to bed until he has told her in detail what he means.

εὐνὴ μὲν δὴ σοί γε τότ᾽ ἔσσεται ὁππότε θυμῷ
σῷ ἐθέλῃς, ἐπεὶ ἄρ σε θεοὶ ποίησαν ἱκέσθαι
οἶκον ἐϋκτίμενον καὶ σὴν ἐς πατρίδα γαῖαν·
ἀλλ᾽ ἐπεὶ ἐφράσθης καί τοι θεὸς ἔμβαλε θυμῷ,
εἴπ᾽ ἄγε μοι τὸν ἄεθλον, ἐπεὶ καὶ ὄπισθεν, ὀΐω,
πεύσομαι, αὐτίκα δ᾽ ἐστὶ δαήμεναι οὔ τι χέρειον.

You will have your going to bed whenever you wish it
in your heart, since after all the gods have made you return
to your well-built house and your fatherland.
But since you thought of this and a god put it in your mind,
come, tell me that trial, since later on, I think,
I will learn of it, and knowing it at once will be no harder.

(*Od.* 23.256–261)

Penelope characteristically resists the segregation of awareness
of the hardest truths of their situation from celebration of their
supreme good fortune, and this assures that these two aspects
of the story are seen together. Odysseus himself comments on
the strangeness of Penelope's willingness to sacrifice complete
happiness at the moment of their reunion for the sake of knowing the truth.

δαιμονίη, τί τ᾽ ἄρ᾽ αὖ με μάλ᾽ ὀτρύνουσα κελεύεις
εἰπέμεν; αὐτὰρ ἐγὼ μυθήσομαι οὐδ᾽ ἐπικεύσω.
οὐ μέν τοι θυμὸς κεχαρήσεται· οὐδὲ γὰρ αὐτὸς
χαίρω . . .

Strange one, why now do you urge me on and bid me
tell you? But I will tell you and hide nothing.
But your heart will not rejoice in it, nor do I myself
      rejoice . . .

(*Od.* 23.263–267)

This conversation acts out on a small scale the postponement
of Odysseus' return that is its subject. As Odysseus must tell Penelope about Teiresias' prophecy before they can celebrate their
reunion, so he must take another journey, evidently to placate
Poseidon, before he can truly enjoy his old age and the prospect
of an easy death at home. And the revelation of this destiny, in
addition to showing that other challenges remain in the future,
shows that Odysseus cannot yet put his past adventures behind
him. Although he has survived the adventures of his homeward
journey and found his way home to a world that is quite remote
from them, it turns out that he is not unscathed by them. Odysseus' need to placate Poseidon means that he is still subject to

the consequences of his encounter with the Cyclops. Even after returning home, he has not escaped the consequences of his journey outward in search of *kleos*, of his activity in another realm in which self-assertion brings inescapable danger, in which destruction of an enemy can arouse the anger of a god who favors him, where the gods do not intervene to punish breaches of hospitality. Penelope, the figure who represents the potential unruliness at the heart of social organization, requires Odysseus to acknowledge the unruliness outside that always threatens to intrude on the bounded realm of peacetime civilization.

Penelope, the figure against whom Odysseus' disguise is primarily directed and the one who is slowest to believe that it is a disguise and not the truth, places what that disguise represents, awareness of the inescapable limitations of human life, at the center of Odysseus' return. She does this in a variety of ways that become more overt as the plot moves towards greater openness between her and Odysseus, until finally she causes that awareness to be articulated directly as they prepare to revel in their good fortune. Her role in the narrative is a retarding one: she causes a series of delays to the poem's happy ending that correspond to qualifications of it. In winning her acceptance of his return, Odysseus achieves a success that is qualified, but also strengthened, by acknowledgment of the odds against it.

But if Penelope is characterized by her knowledge of the odds against Odysseus' return, she also shares his desire for it. And this desire inspires the extraordinary loyalty that finally assures a happy ending that is only possible because it is delayed. When she is convinced that Odysseus really has returned, she is as willing to rejoice as he is. Having postponed their reunion by insisting on hearing about the postponement of Odysseus' return, she puts this obstacle behind them by referring to the way in which even that will one day be behind him. "εἰ μὲν δὴ γῆράς γε θεοί τελέουσιν ἄρειον, / ἐλπωρή τοι ἔπειτα κακῶν ὑπάλυξιν ἔσεσθαι," "If the gods are bringing about a better old age / then there is hope for an escape from troubles" (*Od.* 23.286–287). She abandons herself to a reunion with Odysseus that is at once mental and physical. Not only does it turn out that she has always wanted what he wants, but she also at last joins him in believing that it has come true.

FIVE

Recognition and Song

BETWEEN the lovemaking that marks their complete reunion
and their parting to take up their separate tasks, Odysseus and
Penelope engage in an activity typical of newly reunited characters in Homeric poetry: they exchange stories, each telling the
other what he or she has suffered in the course of their long separation.[1] Penelope's account is described only briefly, but Odysseus' is reported on at some length in an indirect and somewhat
stylized narrative that amounts to an encapsulated and updated
version of the narrative of his adventures that he has already
given at the Phaeacian court.[2] This repetition has seemed dull
and inartistic to some readers of the *Odyssey*, especially those inspired by the Alexandrian critics' designation of 23.296 as the
telos, the "goal" or "point of fulfillment," of the poem to find
everything after that line unhomeric and extraneous to the action.[3] But the repetition can also be seen as establishing a significant parallel between the two very different recognition
scenes that are the climactic events in the two main sections of

---

[1] E.g., *Od.* 17.67–70; 17.108–149, where much is made of having Telemachus report to Penelope on the events of his journey; 19.462–466; *Homeric
Hymn to Demeter*, 405–433. When Nestor and Menelaus tell their experiences
to Telemachus, they tell what happened since they were separated from Odysseus, with whom they are now, in a sense, reunited in the person of Telemachus.
William F. Hansen makes a similar observation when he points out that there is
a tendency for characters in the Homeric epics to tell how they got to wherever
they are. *The Conference Sequence*, 39.

[2] On these two stories as retellings of the *Odyssey* within the *Odyssey*, and on
the progressive updating of versions of its own story throughout the *Odyssey*,
see William G. Thalmann, *Conventions of Form and Thought in Early Greek Epic
Poetry*, 161–163.

[3] For a helpful summary of these problems, see Stanford, *The Odyssey of Homer* II:404–407.

the narrative: Odysseus' public self-proclamation to a community of strangers who know him only by reputation and his private reunion with his wife. In both cases, Odysseus' establishment of his identity is followed by the experience of serving as his own poet.[4] In the first case, the analogy between Odysseus' narrative and a poet's song is very marked: he delivers it at a banquet, at which a singer has just been performing, and is compared to a singer by his host (*Od.* 11.363–369). In the second case, the analogy is suggested more subtly[5] and derives, to a large extent, from the reminiscence of the earlier instance.

The inclusion of representations of song in these climactic episodes of the *Odyssey*'s plot, like the *Odyssey*'s preoccupation generally with poetry and narration, engages an issue basic to all literary representation. Any narrative re-creation of events, like any mimetic work of art, is necessarily distinct from the events it re-creates. It is later in time, elsewhere in space, and different in form. In the world portrayed by the Homeric epics, this disjunction becomes an important concern in the lives of the characters because poetic narrative is the most valued medium for the preservation of *kleos*, the glorious reputation or fame which is the goal of heroic action.[6] The achievement of *kleos* provides the best approximation of immortality available to a mortal hero: it is a record of his existence that is communicated to people living in places he has never been and in times he is not able

---

[4] Among discussions of the comparison between Odysseus and a poet that is developed in the *Odyssey*, see especially Alice J. Mariani, "The Forged Feature," esp. 77–86; Carroll Moulton, *Similes in the Homeric Poems*, 145–153; Peter W. Rose, "Class Ambivalence in the *Odyssey*, 145–149; Charles Segal, "*Kleos* and Its Ironies in the *Odyssey*"; Douglas Stewart, *The Disguised Guest*, 146–195; William G. Thalmann, *Conventions of Form and Thought in Early Greek Epic Poetry*, Chapter 6.

[5] One feature of the version delivered to Penelope that assimilates it to such poems as the *Iliad* and the *Odyssey* is the way attention is drawn to the choice of starting point with "ἄρξατο," "he began," in 310.

[6] For the range of meanings of *kleos*, see James M. Redfield, *Nature and Culture in the Iliad*, 31–33; Gregory Nagy, *The Best of the Achaeans*, 16. For *kleos* as the term that expresses "the very notion of epic poetry within epic poetry," see Nagy, *The Best of the Achaeans*, 95; *Comparative Studies in Greek and Indic Meter*, 244–255.

to survive into; it is the closest he can come to transcendence of the normal mortal restriction to a certain time and place.

A hero's *kleos* becomes an imperishable substitute for his transitory self, and thus it is a prize for which he is willing to risk even his life. And yet the prizing of *kleos* is also a symptom of the mortality that makes it necessary, so that the song that takes his place when he is dead also becomes a token of his death. The inextricability of *kleos* from mortality is intensified in the heroic world by its association with premature death. The actions that win *kleos* do so because they involve the risk of life, and so *kleos* is almost always won at the cost of an early death. This cost is expressed in the opposition, made explicit in the terms of Achilles' choice, between *kleos* and *nostos*.

The winning of *kleos* precludes survival and removal to a sphere in which death is no longer a constant threat. It therefore also means exclusion from the sphere in which heroic actions are celebrated in song, for the recital of poetry is a feature of peacetime societies, like those of Phaeacia and Ithaca, and not of the arenas in which those actions take place. On the battlefield, where most heroes are destined to die, there are no poets and no occasions for singing heroic song. In the *Iliad* the only exception to this is Achilles singing "κλέα ἀνδρῶν," "the fames of men," when Agamemnon's ambassadors find him in Book 9 (*Il.* 9.189), and there the point is precisely that he has withdrawn from the world of heroic action; he is re-creating, at the edge of the Achaean camp, a small facsimile of the peacetime world to which he cannot quite bring himself to return. Nor is he, presumably, singing his own *kleos*. His singing indicates the choice he has temporarily made to forego personal glory for the sake of enjoying a long life, to yield *kleos* to others. The same point is made by Odysseus' encounter with the Sirens, in which the chance to hear himself and others sung about represents a temptation that would cost him his life and consign him to oblivion. The enjoyment of song can only distract a hero from performing the actions that earn him glory.

Thus the heroic world is governed by a paradox from which very few heroes escape: to experience the *kleos* for which all heroes strive is to forego it. In most cases heroic song is like the glorious tomb that may also commemorate a hero's achievement, a mark of honor that he cannot himself enjoy because he is dead, whose very existence signifies his death.[7] The disjunction that always exists between a narrative and its subject becomes, in this world, a token of mortality, of the larger and final rupture that defines and darkens mortal life.

Not only is the setting of heroic song removed from that in which its events take place, but the bards who sing it and the audiences who listen to it are also marked by their distance from heroic life and action.[8] In their disengagement from the mortal struggle that heroic action represents, poets and their audiences are somewhat inhuman, resembling at once the gods and the dead. In the *Iliad*, the gods themselves do serve as an audience for the action,[9] and the human audience portrayed most prominently in the *Odyssey* consists of the Phaeacians, people who lead a quasi-divine life free of normal toil and strife. The suitors, who also take special pleasure in song, foolishly emulate this state, thinking that they can also live the effortless life of the gods. Furthermore, listening to song involves a suspension of activity and a suspension of consciousness that makes those who do it resemble the dead. It is perhaps significant that the point at which Alcinous breaks into Odysseus' narrative to call attention to himself as its audience occurs during the account of the underworld.

Poets also tend not to represent normal human life; their condition is that of the wandering beggar who is without fixed ties and a fixed place in society, a condition that verges on nonexistence.[10] The characters in the Homeric poems who either are

[7] On the connection between *kleos* and tomb markers, see James M. Redfield, *Nature and Culture in the Iliad*, 34; Dale S. Sinos, *Achilles, Patroklos and the Meaning of Philos*, 48.

[8] Similar points are made by George Walsh, *The Varieties of Enchantment*, 14–16.

[9] On this point see Jasper Griffin, *Homer on Life and Death*, Chapter 6.

[10] The link between low social status and closeness to death is illustrated by Laertes' condition before his recognition of Odysseus.

professional poets or behave like poets are all (with the notable exception of Odysseus) figures who are, in some other way, disqualified from heroic action: Demodocus is blind; Phemius is ineffectual; Helen is a woman;[11] Nestor is old; and Achilles only acts as a poet at the point at which he has deliberately taken himself out of the action.[12] Furthermore, poets are inhuman in another way, for their words are not composed by themselves but inspired by the gods. They sing not of their own knowledge, but of that of the gods, who never die. And this divine perspective, which assures the accuracy of what poets say, makes their words more like those of the dead, who also tell the truth (*Od.* 11.148), than like those of living mortals.

Odysseus' successive experiences of acting as his own poet, first for an audience of strangers and then for his wife, are expressions of just how rare and complete his success in the *Odyssey* is. For those occasions eliminate the gap that normally exists between the hero's own experiences and the songs in which they are commemorated. They permit an unparalleled coincidence of the hero who is the subject of song and the song itself, a coincidence that is stressed by their situation within scenes of recognition, which center on an emphatic assertion of the hero's presence. This repeated depiction of a songlike narrative as the sequel to identification puts the connection between the recognition of identity and the recognition of heroic achievement into poetic terms. The result is a powerful statement of this hero's extraordinary ability to survive, to achieve the evasion of death, the delayed mortality, that is the closest he can come to the direct experience of immortality. With that survival comes a confrontation with the version of his experience that will be immortal, that will survive when he is dead.[13]

---

[11] For Helen's special association with song in the *Iliad*, see Linda L. Clader, *Helen*, 5–9; Alice J. Mariani, "The Forged Feature," 29–30. Mabel Lang notes that in the *Odyssey* Helen plays a role that is elsewhere in the poem that of a bard. "Homer and Oral Techniques," 162.

[12] Cf. Anchises in the *Homeric Hymn to Aphrodite* who plays the lyre while all of his companions are off tending the herds (78–80).

[13] This aspect of Odysseus' achievement is also dramatized by his unparal-

It is Odysseus' singular achievement to survive the war and the challenges of his homeward journey and to arrive in Phaeacia, where he has the opportunity both to hear himself commemorated in song for his deeds in Troy and to add to his own *kleos* by telling the part of his story that has previously been unknown.[14] There he experiences the reward that heroes die for but normally do not themselves experience: he witnesses and participates in the transmission of his own fame to far-flung people who, until he reveals himself to them, do not know him in person. But for him this turns out to be not a pleasant but a painful experience. While the Phaeacians listen with pleasure to Demodocus' songs, Odysseus weeps. And when he himself takes over the part of the singer and tells his own story, he gains no more pleasure from his participation in his own fame; he begins his narrative by telling his audience it will cause him grief to tell it (*Od.* 9.12–13).

Odysseus is prevented from enjoying these narratives because of his own involvement with their events, events which form part of a larger story that is for him still painfully unconcluded. His own struggles are not yet over; while he has survived to witness his own achievement of *kleos*, he has not yet achieved *nostos*. And this experience of *kleos* without *nostos* makes him no better off than if he were still back in the battlefield world of struggle and early death, where that trade-off is usually met. Thus he hears songs about what happened there without any of the usual detachment experienced by members of audiences. His own present inactivity creates no sense of distance; rather, he suffers an acute grief, which is compared in a simile to the grief of a widow lamenting over her husband who has just died in

---

leled success in hearing the Sirens' song and yet remaining alive. The Sirens' spontaneous recognition of Odysseus is followed by a summary of a song. As Pietro Pucci has pointed out in his essay, "The Song of the Sirens," the affinity of this song to traditional poetic narrative is enhanced by the Sirens' resemblance to the Muses and by their use of diction that refers specifically to the *Iliad*. In addition to Pucci's discussion, see Charles Segal, "*Kleos* and its Ironies in the *Odyssey*," 38–43.

[14] On this aspect of Odysseus' narration at 9.19 ff., see also Charles Segal, "*Kleos* and Its Ironies in the *Odyssey*," 24–26.

battle (*Od.* 8.523–529). This simile points up Odysseus' difference from other members of the audience by transposing his response to the battlefield—the setting to which the song, in effect, returns him. The change of gender turns the listener's inactivity into the helpless passivity suffered by women. Not only does the widow confront the premature death that is the hallmark of the battlefield as an irremediable personal catastrophe, but she is defenseless against the enemy, who are about to carry her off into slavery.[15]

Only when Odysseus repeats the same narrative at home to Penelope is he able to enjoy telling it. Only then has he reached the point when he no longer needs to act to secure his own achievement, when taking pleasure in song is no longer a distraction from the struggle to win fame.[16] Only in the context of his successful homecoming, and therefore out of the impersonal context where formal song is found, is Odysseus finally able to find the pleasure that song characteristically conveys. If the *Odyssey* celebrates the power of song in its portrayal of the meeting of subject and audience in Phaeacia, it also acknowledges a distance between them that can never be completely removed. Odysseus' meeting with his audience only emphasizes the impersonality of the recognition won by far-flung fame: while he may have survived, he is still as much separated from the people he cares about as he would be if he were dead or still at Troy. While his audience comes to know him through his legend, its members have no actual involvement with him, and their pleasure in the song is detached and purely aesthetic; they are pleased by his story, but not because it is specifically about him.

Odysseus' narrative to Penelope marks not only the first time he can enjoy telling his story but also the first time she can enjoy hearing it. Penelope's uncompromising desire for Odysseus' re-

[15] Cf. Pietro Pucci's observation that the Sirens' dangerous overture to Odysseus represents, in effect, an invitation to return to the *Iliad*. "The Song of the Sirens," 125.

[16] It should be noted that this episode of storytelling is framed by two other activities that are usually portrayed in the *Odyssey* as dangerous distractions: making love and sleeping.

turn makes her hostile to the possibility that Odysseus might no longer exist as a man but only as the subject of song. In particular, she is distressed at the possibility that Odysseus' story might be over, that it might have the finished quality that would turn it into a proper narrative, assimilating it into the poetic tradition that commemorates dead heroes.

This distress motivates her first appearance in the poem, when she descends from her bedroom to ask Phemius to sing a different song. Phemius is singing "'Αχαιῶν νόστον . . . λυγρόν, ὅν ἐκ Τροίης ἐτετείλατο Παλλὰς 'Αθήνη," "of the Achaeans' bitter homecoming / from Troy, which Pallas Athena had inflicted upon them" (*Od.* 1.326–327). This brief indication of the contents of the song establishes as its subject a general pattern of experience without specifying which heroes are involved in it. It suggests the pattern into which Odysseus' story is likely to fall while leaving open the question of whether it does. To Penelope, with her strong sense of the probable, the song inevitably evokes the likelihood that Odysseus' *nostos* can be conclusively labelled *lugros*, "bitter," and so affects her as an unbearable reminder of his absence. As she says to Phemius, she derives no pleasure from Odysseus' *kleos*, but only longing, "τοίην γὰρ κεφαλὴν ποθέω αἰεὶ / ἀνδρός, τοῦ κλέος εὐρὺ καθ' Ἑλλάδα καὶ μέσον Ἄργος," "Such a man do I long for as I think constantly / of him whose fame is spread far and wide throughout Hellas and the center of Argos" (*Od.* 1.343–344). Penelope here shows herself to be like Odysseus in Phaeacia and like other characters in the Homeric epics who cannot enjoy songs as other people do because they are personally involved in the story.[17] Her reluctance to hear this song expresses that refusal to give up her personal attachment to Odysseus that inspires her resistance to the idea of marrying someone else.

Penelope's request to Phemius involves her in a quarrel with Telemachus. Telemachus speaks harshly to her, rebuking her for her response to the song and ordering her to return to her quarters and her weaving (*Od.* 1.346–359). He urges Penelope

---

[17] On this point, see Gregory Nagy, *The Best of the Achaeans*, 98–102.

to adopt a more detached and aestheticized response to the song of the Achaeans' return, telling her first that she should distinguish the song from the events it recounts. He says that Zeus, not the singer, is responsible for those events, and that the song is valued for its novelty rather than the acceptability of its contents. Furthermore, she should reconcile herself to the song's contents, viewing Odysseus' loss, which he here treats as certain, as part of an inescapable larger pattern rather than as a personal catastrophe, "οὐ γὰρ Ὀδυσσεὺς οἶος ἀπώλεσε νόστιμον ἦμαρ / ἐν Τροίῃ, πολλοὶ δὲ καὶ ἄλλοι φῶτες ὄλοντο," "For it wasn't only Odysseus who lost his day of homecoming / at Troy. Many other men also perished" (*Od.* 1.354–355). She should give up her grief and enjoy the song for what it is.

With this speech Telemachus behaves surprisingly both by asserting his right to the household and by quarreling with his mother, and these are closely related developments. Telemachus' maturity interferes with Penelope's determination to wait for Odysseus to return in person (as is recognized in her account to the suitors in Book 18 of Odysseus' instructions to wait for him only until Telemachus should grow a beard); it is specifically in conflict with her determination that Odysseus not be replaced. For even if she prevents him from being replaced as her husband, she cannot prevent him from being replaced by Telemachus as head of his house. That Telemachus' first display to her of his new maturity comes in this dispute over a song shows how poetry is also implicated in this conflict. Telemachus is willing to have his father's physical presence replaced by his *kleos*, the fame that lives after him in the form of song, while Penelope is not.[18]

To return to a point made in Chapter 1, Telemachus, as we see him in the *Odyssey*, is learning to act successfully in a world in which his father is not present and is known only by his *kleos*, by his reputation and the songs and other monuments that preserve it. His conflict with Penelope over Phemius' song marks

---

[18] On the different responses of Telemachus and Penelope to Phemius' song as reflections of their different situations, see Klaus Rüter, *Odysseeinterpretationen*, 208–209.

the beginning of his formation of a new attitude appropriate to the time when his father has already died, an attitude of respect for his father's memory but willingness to have his father be only a memory.[19] Consequently, he goes on a journey in the course of which he is repeatedly recognized as his father's son and of which the purpose is not to bring his father back but to create the conditions that will allow him to take his father's place. He does not search for his father but for the ending to his father's story, the conclusion to the narrative that will at once testify to his father's life and confirm that it is over. His aim is to recover his father's *kleos* both so that that *kleos* is available to be transferred to him[20] and so that it is clear that the time has come for that transfer to be made. Thus Athena, when she first meets Telemachus, instructs him to go in search not of Odysseus but of information about whether Odysseus is dead or alive, and she suggests that he might behave comparably to Or-

[19] This new attitude can also be seen in other of Telemachus' statements towards the end of Book 1. He thanks Athena for her advice by saying that she has treated him as a father would a son (*Od.* 1.308), thereby acknowledging that people other than his father can serve the function of helping him to claim his inheritance. One of the most important ways in which Athena helps Telemachus is by telling him the story of Agememnon's homecoming, a story that Menelaus later assumes he would have heard from his father (*Od.* 4.94–95). When Eurymachus suggests that Athena may have brought him a message from his father, he answers that there is no longer any hope of Odysseus' return and identifies Athena as one of his father's friends—that is, as someone who, like the heroes he visits on his journey, can supply him with the knowledge of his father that he needs in the absence of any prospect of seeing his father again (*Od.* 1.413–419).

[20] When a hero dies in circumstances in which there are no friends present to commemorate his life through the proper rites of burial, either at the hands of enemies, like Agamemnon, or in obscurity, as it seems Odysseus has, his *kleos* is not preserved and cannot be handed on to his son. Thus Telemachus says that he wishes for the sake of his own *kleos* that Odysseus had died in Troy or in the presence of his companions afterwards (*Od.* 1.236–243). Similarly, Achilles in the underworld expresses pity for Agamemnon because his death took place under circumstances that did not allow for the transfer of *kleos* to his son. These losses become the starting points for accounts of the son's successful efforts to restore the father's *kleos*, accounts that dramatize the notion of inherited excellence that underlies the *Odyssey*'s aristocratic outlook.

157

estes, whose father was already dead before he took action (*Od.* 1.279–302).

The relationship between Telemachus' journey and the issues raised by Phemius' song is made clear when Telemachus arrives at the court of Nestor and explains his presence in terms that recall his earlier rebuke to Penelope. He says that he is looking for his father's *kleos*, noting that the sad fates of all the other Achaean warriors are well known, while "κείνου δ᾽ αὖ καὶ ὄλεθρον ἀπευθέα θῆκε Κρονίων," "The son of Cronus has made even that man's death unknown" (Od. 3.88). Thus he asks Nestor for a story about Odysseus that would align his fate with those of the other Achaeans who fought at Troy and would include an account of his death, which he assumes has already taken place. He then goes on to assure Nestor that he (unlike Penelope in Book 1) is not deterred by its personal significance from wanting to hear it, "μηδέ τί μ᾽ αἰδόμενος μειλίσσεο μηδ᾽ ἐλεαίρων, / ἀλλ᾽ εὖ μοι κατάλεξον ὅπως ἤντησας ὀπωπῆς," "And do not soften your story out of consideration or pity for me, / but truly tell me whatever you have seen" (*Od.* 3.96–97).[21]

Telemachus' desire to learn about his father's death points to the peculiar position of the *Telemachy* in the *Odyssey*.[22] This subsection of the narrative is inspired by an assumption, the assumption that Odysseus will not return, that is in conflict with the central message of the poem as a whole. Thus it tells a story, the story of Telemachus' preparation to take his father's place, of which the conclusion is postponed to a time beyond the *Od-*

[21] The relationship between the kind of account Telemachus is asking for and the poetic tradition is also suggested by the way his request resembles a poet's prayer to the Muses for authoritative, eyewitness information about distant events (e.g., *Il.* 2.484–492).

[22] David Bynum's statement of the main scholarly problem raised by the *Telemachy* captures well the issue of how advantageous its presence is to the figure of Odysseus. "The problem of the initiatory story has long existed in Homeric scholarship in the form of a question: Why did the *Odyssey*, ostensibly about the old hero's obstructed return from the Trojan War, actually begin with an extended account of his son Telemachus' seemingly pointless adventures in seeking to learn his lost father's fate?" "Themes of the Young Hero in Serbocroatian Oral Epic Tradition," 1300.

yssey's scope. Because the *Telemachy* is subordinated within the larger structure to the story of Odysseus' return, just as Telemachus himself is subordinated to the more glorious figure of his father, it has a different conclusion, Telemachus' reunion with his father, than the one to which it seems to be leading, the one its central character expects. Consequently, when that reunion does take place, Telemachus is no longer prepared to believe it, and Odysseus has some difficulty persuading him that he really has returned.

Because Odysseus is destined to return, Telemachus cannot succeed in the specific goal of his journey. He hears a variety of instructive stories from Nestor, Menelaus, and Helen, stories that provide him with an education in what his father's heritage represents and in what he might himself be expected to accomplish. But he does not find a reliable version of Odysseus' story that is similar to the stories of the destruction of the Achaeans that he already knows and that comes to a neat conclusion with Odysseus' death. Neither Nestor nor Menelaus knows the end to Odysseus' story; the best information they can offer is Menelaus' report of what he heard some time ago from Proteus, that Odysseus was alive but was detained by Calypso and had no way of getting home. This information leaves Odysseus' story in the same unconcluded but frozen state that it is in when the *Odyssey* begins.

Telemachus, like Penelope in the poem's later books, negotiates a series of events that are leading to the opposite outcome from the one he quite reasonably foresees. Consequently, the narrative of his experiences is also characterized by a double, or ironic, perspective, although the ironies of his situation are far less painful. The actions he takes out of conviction that Odysseus will never return earn him approbation rather than accusations of infidelity and promote a fate to which he can look forward with pleasure—his own accession to his father's place. Telemachus' new-found certainty that Odysseus will not return comes through as a sign of his inexperience and a youthful tendency to extreme positions. When Athena on one occasion rebukes him for voicing that certainty, she is expressing the more experienced and open-minded perspective of Mentor, whose persona she adopts, as well as that of the goddess who manipulates and foresees the poems' events. She reminds Telemachus that miracles are possible, "ῥεῖα θεός γ᾽ ἐθέλων καὶ τηλόθεν ἄνδρα σαώσαι," "With ease a god can save a man, if he wishes, even one who is far away" (*Od.* 3.231), although she also goes on to acknowledge that not even the gods can save a man from death when his destined end has come (*Od.* 3.236–238).

The inescapable mortality that Athena here acknowledges is the key to the place of this seemingly irrelevant narrative in the story of Odysseus' return. The *Telemachy* is an exposition of the forms of immortality a hero enjoys in the normal course of experience: not the transcendence of normal mortal limitations that Odysseus enjoys with Athena's aid, but the forms of immortality that come through children and through celebration in song. The poem acknowledges the similarity of these forms of metaphorical survival by making them depend on one another: Telemachus becomes a hero who truly carries on his father's tradition by hearing songlike stories about him, and the poetic tradition of the life of Odysseus becomes available on Ithaca because Telemachus goes out to learn about it and brings it back with him.

Although Telemachus is frustrated in his search for the definitive conclusion to his father's story, and his journey is in that sense a practical failure, it contributes in another way to the completeness with which the story of Odysseus is told in the *Odyssey*. The reminiscences of Nestor and Menelaus help to link the figure who left for Troy with the figure who returns. In particular, Nestor's recollections of the return journey leave off at a point very close to where the story Odysseus tells begins. By hearing those reminiscences, Telemachus closes the narrative gap between the hero of Troy and the survivor who returns. These two extensions of the hero into times and places from which he himself is absent, which are made in this narrative to depend on one another, are linked intrinsically by the similarity of their relationship to him: both are versions of the hero that also inevitably differ from him, not least because another person is involved in their creation.

The *Telemachy* is a celebration of the forms of continuity available in ordinary life. It depicts the most realistic hope for a happy solution to the troubled situation in Ithaca. This solution does not depend on a miracle, the conquest of time through the return of Odysseus, but only on a certain measure of good fortune, Telemachus' intrinsic worthiness to carry on his father's legacy and his ability to make contact with men like Nestor and Menelaus who can instruct him in that legacy. This measured good fortune is expressed in the kind of divine help that Telemachus enjoys—not the gift of a magic plant or a totally transforming disguise, but the advice and support of Athena in the guise of an old family friend—and in the essentially ordinary character of his experiences, which consist primarily of routine rituals of hospitality and conversations. This set of unremarkable experiences is endowed with value through analogies with other, more demanding achievements: Odysseus' journey, to which it is related by structural parallels, and Orestes' avenging of his father's death, to which it is explicitly compared. Telemachus is able, by his successful negotiation of adult social life, to save his father's endangered *kleos* and to establish himself as Odysseus' proper successor.

While this section of the poem celebrates the ways in which Odysseus can live on in his own absence, it also demands reconciliation to Odysseus' loss, acceptance of the idea that he will not return in person. This is the spirit in which Telemachus undertakes his voyage, as his appeal to Nestor indicates, and it is the underlying basis of the world that he visits, a world of life going on without Odysseus there. The narrative of the *Telemachy*, in particular the account of Telemachus' encounter with Menelaus with its stress on the conquest of grief, acts out the process of reconciliation to loss that is a condition of the world in which it is set.[23] The very capacity of the figures Telemachus

---

[23] At the beginning of their encounter, Menelaus declares himself unable to enjoy his own survival because he so bitterly mourns the loss of his companions (*Od.* 4.90–112); but Peisistratus, the son of one of those companions, speaks of the value of consolation (*Od.* 4.190–202). Then the entire party experiences consolation through Helen's drug, which creates instantaneously the detachment from loss that ordinarily comes with time. Then Menelaus and Helen both

encounters to reminisce about Odysseus testifies to their accommodation to his loss, for reminiscences are signs of con-
quered grief. As James Redfield points out, the formal lamen-
tations that in funerals give voice to grief at the dead person's
loss "do not speak of the dead man as he was in life; rather they
speak of how things are now that he is gone, the difference
made by his absence."[24] Until Odysseus returns to Ithaca and
makes his presence felt, his dependents there do not reminisce
about him but rather speak of what they are suffering because
of his absence.[25] The only characters who reminisce about
Odysseus before he is recognized are Odysseus himself in the
guise of the stranger and the characters who help Telemachus
emerge from his state of helpless mourning: "Mentes," Nestor,
Menelaus, and Helen.[26] The story of Telemachus' education
shows how even personal memories can turn into narratives
that have the capacity to remove care possessed by the drug they
resemble, and in this narrative accompany.[27]

---

show their detachment from the pain of the past in their reminiscences of Troy,
hers of her recognition of Odysseus and his of Odysseus' endurance in the Trojan Horse. At the end of these reminiscences, Telemachus shows his own accommodation to his father's fate and his appreciation of the comforts that go
with consolation. He comments that the endurance described in these stories
has not saved Odysseus from death, and he suggests that they go to bed to take
pleasure in sleep (*Od.* 4.292–295). This account of one evening recapitulates
the gradual process of accommodation to loss that lies behind Menelaus' getting
on with life, which is already expressed in the marrying off of his daughter and
son in which he is engaged when he first appears in the poem (part of a general
emphasis on marriage throughout the episode; cf. *Od.* 15.125–129). The artificial way in which a process that depends on the passage of time is presented in
a single episode is reflected in the motif of Helen's drug, which works as an artificial substitute for the passage of time by creating instantaneous reconciliation to loss (and is not, as many critics have suggested, a sign of the shallowness
and decadence of life in Sparta).

[24] James M. Redfield, *Nature and Culture in the Iliad*, 180.

[25] E.g., Telemachus at *Od.* 1.157–168; Penelope at 18.251–256; Eumaeus
at 14.61–71; Laertes at 24.281–296.

[26] Thus one of the effects on Telemachus of his encounter with Athena in
Book 1 is that he remembers his father more than before (*Od.* 1.321–322).

[27] On the relationship between Helen's drug and poetry, see William G.
Thalmann, *Conventions of Form and Thought in Early Greek Epic Poetry*, 166.

The *Telemachy* contributes to the *kleos* of Odysseus as a heroic figure both by filling in his legend and by showing that he is destined to be followed by a worthy son. But, as a glimpse of a world colored by acceptance of loss, it is uncongenial both to Odysseus and to Penelope as characters in the poem, for they refuse to be satisfied with anything other than Odysseus' return. Thus it makes sense that, while Odysseus is the one character in the *Odyssey* who visits nearly every one of the scattered and various realms it contains (which gives him a mastery of the range of experiences represented that is like the poet's), he does not visit the world of the *Telemachy*, the world that represents the ability to get along without him.[28] Nestor and Menelaus could be said to be figures who work against Odysseus' interests. Because they are able to remember Odysseus as someone distinctly in the past and therefore to help Telemachus, they contribute to making Odysseus' return superfluous. Furthermore, their presence in the poem compromises Odysseus' glory by diminishing his singular quality. They, too, are heroes who have fought at Troy and have managed to return home.[29]

Similarly, it makes sense that Telemachus should conceal his journey from Penelope, and that the independence he displays in taking it should contribute to a general pattern of friction between them. Her hostility to the forms of replacement for Odysseus represented by the *Telemachy*—his replacement by his son and by his reputation or *kleos*—springs from her absolute fidelity. The absoluteness of her fidelity makes her generally hostile to the principle of substitution that is necessary to the kind of social continuity that the *Telemachy* celebrates. The extension of society beyond the restricted and transitory lives of individuals depends on social conventions whereby nonidentical re-

---

[28] Furthermore, from the standpoint of strategy, Telemachus' journey does not help, but rather endangers, Odysseus' cause. As Karl Reinhardt points out, Athena's efforts only keep Odysseus and Telemachus further apart. "Homer und die Telemachie," 44.

[29] On Menelaus as a figure who provides Telemachus with a possible image of Odysseus and his fate, see Friedrich Klingner, "Über die vier ersten Bücher der Odyssee," 76–77.

placements are accepted for those who are absent or lost; it requires those who participate in it to relax their strict allegiance to the precise form of what is distant or past so that they can find a version of it here and now.

This process is illustrated in the Homeric epics in particular by their focus on two forms of social institution, the payment of ransom, which is a central theme in the *Iliad* and allows the continuity of society over time, and hospitality, which is a prominent element in the *Odyssey* and allows the continuity of society over space. In the *Iliad* the acceptance of even the palpably nonidentical and inadequate substitute of material goods as consolation for the irreplacable loss of someone loved represents the relinquishing of the past necessary to survival in the present.[30] In the *Odyssey*, the extension of social ties beyond the family represented by hospitality depends on the acceptance of a stranger in the place of a relative.[31]

Penelope, however, holds out against all of the fictions of identity that underlie social institutions. She cannot find consolation in any substitute for Odysseus and draws the line at letting her guest take the place of her husband until he has proved that he is Odysseus. This inflexibility brings her inevitably into conflict with Telemachus, whose interests lie with the creation of a new situation for the future.[32] He becomes exasperated with her suspicion of new arrivals, whether of Phemius' song or of the stranger who claims to be Odysseus, but whom she continues to view as an imposter.[33]

---

[30] This point is articulated most clearly in Ajax's speech during the embassy to Achilles (*Il.* 9.632–636).

[31] Cf. *Od.* 8.546, where Alcinous says that a guest is "ἀντὶ κασιγνήτου," "in the place of a brother."

[32] This divergence of interests is neatly reflected in the version of events on Ithaca, omitting the presence of the suitors, given by Anticleia: while Penelope and Laertes languish, Telemachus flourishes in Odysseus' place (*Od.* 11.181–196).

[33] Thus, when Penelope refuses to recognize Odysseus once he has declared himself to her, Telemachus accuses her of having an "unfeeling spirit" ("ἀπηνέα θυμὸν") and a heart harder than stone (*Od.* 23.97–103). Earlier, however, he had urged her to harden her heart to listen to Phemius' song, "σοὶ δ᾿ ἐπιτολμάτω

Telemachus' exasperation with Penelope points to the anti-social aspect of her behavior. When Penelope holds out for the miraculous solution to the situation on Ithaca, she is also impeding the more ordinary one. Her glorious fidelity is not only inconvenient to Telemachus as Eurymachus notes when he tells Telemachus that "*μέγα μὲν κλέος αὐτῇ / ποιεῖτ', αὐτὰρ σοί γε ποθὴν πολέος βιότοιο*," "She is creating great glory [*kleos*] for herself, but for you the loss of much livelihood" (*Od.* 2.125–126), but seriously at odds with the social continuity Telemachus stands for. This conflict generates some moments of tension between them, moments in which the relations of the characters recapitulate the underlying conflicts between the story told in the *Telemachy* and that told in the second half of the poem. But on the whole, the poem easily accommodates both characters and both stories and its happy ending is extended and strengthened as a result.[34]

The *Telemachy* is a section of the *Odyssey's* narrative that belongs not only in time but also in spirit to the period of Odysseus' absence. It is in harmony with the piece of information about him that Telemachus does come up with, his concealment by Calypso, a form of obscurity that might as well be death from the point of view of those left behind. This depic-

---

κραδίη καὶ θυμὸς ἀκούειν," "Let your heart and spirit endure to listen" (*Od.* 1.353). In the *Iliad*, Achilles' stubborn attachment to what he has lost—first the honor connected with Briseis and then Patroclus—involves the same combination of softheartedness towards someone lost to him and hardheartedness towards someone present. He is criticized for this by Ajax (*Il.* 9.630–638) and by Apollo (*Il.* 24.44–52), and by the end of the poem he learns to give up his attachment to what is irretrievably lost. He relinquishes his attachment to Patroclus, which has caused him to hold on to Hector's body, in favor of sympathy for the living, even in the person of his enemy Priam. The difference in spirit between the two epics can be measured in the way the figure who learns that same lesson in the *Odyssey*, Telemachus, does so far less painfully, and the figure who refuses to learn it, Penelope, is rewarded by Odysseus' return.

34 The conflict between Telemachus and Penelope is also softened by the fact that each is behaving appropriately to his or her gender. Fidelity is a female virtue, just as lamentation is a female activity, while the continuity of society is a male concern. This distinction lies behind Telemachus' statement to Penelope that *mūthos*, "storytelling," is the business of men (*Od.* 1.358–359).

tion of absence that is really only concealment is reformulated when Odysseus returns in disguise and explores his home unrecognized while everyone on Ithaca believes that he is dead. Odysseus' disguise is reinforced by a series of narratives that reiterate the connection between storytelling and absence that is revealed by the *Telemachy*.

The ambiguity of Odysseus' disguised presence, which signifies at once his presence and his absence, is expressed in narratives that have an ambiguous relation to the central fact governing this part of the poem: Odysseus' presence, or, to put it another way, the stranger's identity. Under their surface falseness, which is designed to maintain the fiction of Odysseus' absence, these narratives tell indirectly the truth of Odysseus' presence. They involve him as a character, they prophesy his return, and they reproduce his actual experiences in fictional form.[35] These stories are twice compared explicitly to poetry, once by Eumaeus, who attributes to them the enchanting quality of song (*Od.* 17.513–521), and once in the poet's comment on one of Odysseus' tales to Penelope: "ἴσκε ψεύδεα πολλὰ λέγων ἐτύμοισιν ὁμοῖα," "He dissembled, telling many false things resembling true things" (*Od.* 19.203), which closely resembles the Muses' characterization of their own art to Hesiod at *Theogony* 27. Furthermore, the indirection with which he asserts himself makes Odysseus like a poet, whose role it is to speak in voices not his own of experiences he never had, telling of others' achievements and making no claims for himself (except perhaps indirectly, as in Homer's portrait of Demodocus). This affinity may account for the similarity between Odysseus' disguise as a homeless wanderer and the role given to poets in various early legends.[36]

---

[35] On the false tales as recast versions of Odysseus' own adventures, see Alice J. Mariani, "The Forged Feature," 285–312; Karl Reinhardt, "Die Abenteuer der Odyssee," 51–53. This is acknowledged ironically within the poem when the stranger, promising to tell Penelope about Odysseus, says, "οἶδα γὰρ εὖ περὶ κείνου, ὁμὴν δ' ἀνεδέγμεθ' ὀϊζύν," "For I know well about him, and we have received the same painful suffering" (*Od.* 17.563).

[36] Cf. especially the pseudo-Herodotean life of Homer, which itself is based

Odysseus' false tales, because they recast his actual experiences in the ways mentioned above, simulate the gap between storyteller and subject that is characteristic of all song, however sincerely composed. Their deliberate falsity represents simply a more apparent version of the distance from the experience recounted that characterizes every narrative. They testify overtly to the inevitable differences between actual experiences and their retelling in song. In particular, as they preserve Odysseus' disguise, they retain narrative's inability ever to be telling about the present. This feature is mimicked very pointedly by the way in which Odysseus' narratives project what is actually happening in the present, his return, into the future.

These narratives, true to the mixture of truth and falsehood they involve, succeed as evocations of Odysseus as someone absent, as someone remembered in the past or hoped for in the future, but not as indications of his presence. Only Athena, who cannot be fooled by a disguise, sees through one of Odysseus' lying tales. Other characters respond to what is false in them, their seeming truth, and remain unconvinced by what is true. Those characters are unable to make the temporal transpositions that would reveal that what is ascribed to past or future is actually occurring in the present.

Not only does Eumaeus find Odysseus' stories enchanting, but he is moved by an account of how Odysseus cleverly arranged the loan of a cloak to lend Odysseus a cloak himself and thus participates unwittingly in a present reenactment of this "past" event. But he repeatedly rejects the stranger's assurances that Odysseus will return, unable to believe it until he sees it and unable to see it because of Odysseus' disguise. Penelope responds to the stranger's claim to have met Odysseus in the past with a demand for tokens, by which she is then convinced. Thus she acts out a recognition scene with a fictional, absent, and past version of Odysseus instead of with the actual Odysseus who is before her.[37] Laertes responds to Odysseus' account of how he

partly on the *Odyssey* (see the discussion by Norman Austin, *Archery at the Dark of the Moon*, 248–249) but also probably reflects typical legends about poets.

[37] Penelope's unwillingness to believe indirect accounts of Odysseus' pres-

entertained Odysseus, something that could never have happened, as the truth. He cannot see that it represents an inversion of the truth, that if Odysseus becomes the host and the time is transposed to the future, the story becomes true. Thus he sadly denies that the stranger could ever be received by Odysseus.

Like the partial epiphanies of gods, these distanced evocations of Odysseus cannot bring about his specific identification. To the extent that they promote his recognition, inspiring Eumaeus' loan of a cloak or Penelope's extension of hospitality, they do so by arousing a generalized courtesy in response to the general truths that make his fictions plausible: the hardness of life, the instability of fortune, the likelihood that a stranger turning up on Ithaca would be a homeless wanderer. And while these gestures double for recognition in significant ways, as has been seen, they also fall finally short of it. The receptivity of these characters to Odysseus' tales is not the acknowledgment of his extraordinary achievement that he seeks. Rather, it reflects their awareness of the unlikelihood of what he has accomplished, their readiness to believe tales that are far less glorious and impressive than the one he will tell when he is acknowledged as Odysseus.

As long as Odysseus tells narratives designed to conceal his presence and protect him from confrontation with his enemies, those narratives replicate the distance between all stories told about heroes and the actions that make them heroic. He can only commemorate the great Odysseus as a figure from the past and can only himself be recognized as a luckless wanderer who has lost his claims to greater stature. As long as he remains in disguise Odysseus is committed to the self-effacement of the poet. The many moments of irony generated by these tales, which show Odysseus' inventiveness and versatility and point unmistakably to a foregone conclusion to his story, are a source of pleasure to the poem's audience, but it is not a pleasure that Odysseus himself shares. His return means nothing to him un-

---

ence is seen in her noncommittal response to her dream and in her rejection of Eurycleia's announcement at the beginning of Book 23. That announcement is, specifically, like a poet's song, not an eyewitness account (*Od.* 23.40–41).

less he can make it known and acknowledged by others, and so he is no more able to enjoy his return until it is made public than his friends are.[38]

Odysseus can only establish his presence on Ithaca by putting aside his disguise and taking action against the suitors, by re-creating a battlefield in his own house. Just as reminiscences of what he did in the past do not serve to indicate his presence, so his bow identifies him, not because it once belonged to him, but because of what he does with it in the present. He can only make himself recognized through physical actions, shooting through the axes and then at the suitors, which are finally distinct from speech. This is reflected in the simile that immediately precedes those actions, in which Odysseus is compared as he strings his bow to a poet stringing his lyre (*Od.* 21.404–409). Odysseus is like a poet not as he takes the action that reveals his identity, but as he prepares to take it. This simile marks the culmination of his disguise as a poet and the moment when he abandons it to act and to reveal himself.

Only when all significant dangers are past and Odysseus is reunited with Penelope can storytelling be associated with open self-revelation, and only then can both storytelling and self-revelation be enjoyable experiences. And one of the pleasures of self-disclosure for Odysseus is that he can tell a much more glorious and more interesting version of his past experiences than he has told while in disguise. As he sheds his disguise, he also sheds the relatively undistinguished history that went with his false persona and tells a story that suits him much better. Odysseus' success in surviving to experience his own celebration in narrative gives him the chance to create a legend that corresponds to this glorious achievement. He not only witnesses his own *kleos*, but he also shapes it.

The first-person narrative that Odysseus delivers to the Phaeacians and then recapitulates for Penelope is designed not simply to convey information but also to amplify the effect of his self-identification. This is clear from the way, the first time

---

[38] Cf. the exchange between Odysseus and Athena at *Od.* 20.30–53.

he tells it, it originates in and grows out of the declaration of his own name. While the *Odyssey* hardly registers the interested quality of Odysseus' narrative through the slant of his narrative voice, which remains very similar to that of the poet, it is apparent from the shape of the story he tells, the portion of his history to which it corresponds.

Jenny Strauss Clay has recently pointed out that Odysseus' tale differs from a poet's in its focus on his own exploits and lack of specific reference to divine activities, but this difference may not be as much to his disadvantage as she implies.[39] Odysseus' ignorance of divine activities means that he has little occasion to acknowledge divine involvement in his success. This advantage is reflected in the subject of the narrative as well. The section of his story that he tells corresponds to the period of time during which he is deprived of divine assistance, during which the credit for his successes really does belong largely to him.

The starting and ending points of Odysseus' narrative are similarly significant. It begins at the point at which he is separated from the other great Achaean heroes, who figure in his story only as dead men, and ends with his reception by a goddess. The history of earlier events, in which he was obliged to share the glory with other Achaean leaders, is the province of the professional bard Demodocus, who is not committed to glorifying only Odysseus. Indeed, the prominence of several rival heroes in the tradition Demodocus recounts is thematized in his account of the rivalry between Odysseus and the *Iliad*'s hero, Achilles.[40] Subsequent events, including his near-annihilation

---

[39] Jenny Strauss Clay, *The Wrath of Athena*, 8.

[40] Gregory Nagy has pointed out that Demodocus' first song represents, for Odysseus, a gain in *kleos* relative to the tradition reflected in the *Iliad*; here he shares with Achilles the title "best of the Achaeans," that, in the *Iliad*, is reserved to Achilles alone. *The Best of the Achaeans*, 40–41. Nonetheless, Demodocus' song does involve a need for Odysseus' glory to be shared with Achilles, a need that Odysseus' own narrative avoids. Cf. Odysseus' account of the underworld in Book 11 (where Achilles refuses Odysseus offer of *timē* and claims that Odysseus' fate is preferable to his own) with the poet's account of the underworld in Book 24, (where Achilles and Odysseus are both honored with a narrative— Agamemnon's account of Achilles' funeral and Amphimedon's account of

while alone at sea, have been told through his less glorious false persona as a bereft and unrecognized wayfarer. The part of his story that is associated with Odysseus-identified-as-Odysseus is the part that glorifies him the most.

The *Odyssey* indicates what is at stake in the selection of a particular piece of the tradition with Odysseus' request to Demodocus for the song of the Trojan Horse. Odysseus moves towards self-disclosure and with it control over the contents of the songs that claim the Phaeacians' attention by asking Demodocus to sing of an episode that occurred after Achilles' death, an episode in which Odysseus himself plays the sole leading part. In doing so, as George Walsh has recently pointed out, he asks him "to sing not *kata kosmon*, following the 'order' of the Trojan story as a whole, but *kata moiran*, giving the part its due."[41]

The progression from the first of Demodocus' songs to the second and then to Odysseus' own story dramatizes the *Odyssey*'s awareness that it and other poems like it are informed by two somewhat divergent aims: the aim of presenting an account of events that is not partial, both in the sense that it is complete and in the sense that it is unbiased, and the aim of glorifying individual heroes. This duality has already been acknowledged at the beginning of the poem, where a distinction is established between the proem, delivered in the poet's own persona, in which the poet's partisanship for Odysseus is revealed, and the rest of the poem, which is attributed to the Muses.[42] When this

---

Odysseus' return—and with Agamemnon's prediction of eternal *kleos*). Despite their differing conclusions, the various recent discussions of the relationship between Demodocus' song and the *Iliad* all help to confirm that the presence of this song in the *Odyssey* reflects the prolem of how songs designed to praise individual heroes can be accommodated within a larger tradition about a large-scale, joint undertaking like the Trojan War. This literary issue recapitulates the issue of competition over honor that forms the subject, presumably, of Demodocus' song, certainly of the *Iliad*. In addition to the discussion by Nagy, see Clay 96–112, 241–246; Walter Marg, "Das erste Lied des Demodokos"; Klaus Rüter, *Odysseeinterpretationen*, 247–254.

[41] George B. Walsh, *The Varieties of Enchantment*, 17.

[42] This distinction is pointed out by Jenny Strauss Clay, *The Wrath of Athena*, 34.

distinction is acted out in the contrast between Demodocus and Odysseus as storytellers, it is also related to the issue of the kinds of claims to truth that narratives can make.[43]

Because his words come directly from the Muses, Demodocus' songs are unquestionably accurate, even though he himself has not been an eyewitness to the events he describes. This is affirmed when Odysseus compliments Demodocus for singing about the struggles of the Achaeans as if he had been there himself or had heard about them from someone who had been present (*Od.* 8.491). When Odysseus tells a story that is, by contrast to Demodocus', mediated by specific human concerns and interests, he receives a similar compliment from Alcinous, who concludes from the shapeliness of Odysseus' narrative that not only is Odysseus' story true but that Odysseus himself is not a deceptive person.[44] The misguidedness of this conclusion highlights the fact that Odysseus' narrative cannot be counted on to be true in the way that Demodocus' can. Alcinous' assessment testifies not to the story's truth but to the impressiveness of Odysseus' self-presentation. The *Odyssey*'s depiction of its notably manipulative hero as a storyteller points to the potential for deceit that derives from narrative's inevitable distance from what it tells, a problem that arises once narrative is viewed as a human as well as an exclusively divine art.[45]

This problem is resolved—to the extent that it can be—when

[43] Cf. George Walsh's discussion of the two kinds of truth—one comprehensive and the other more pointed—attributed to poetry in the *Odyssey*, which touches on related issues. *The Varieties of Enchantment*, 13–21.

[44] Notably, Alcinous also misses the story's focus on Odysseus, describing it as an account of the sufferings of all the Achaeans as well of those of Odysseus (*Od.* 11.369).

[45] While Demodocus' song is an unmediated gift of the Muses and is thus supposed to be utterly accurate, Phemius' art is portrayed in a more complex manner. He claims, in one breath, that he is *autodidaktos*, "self-taught," and that his skill has been implanted by the gods (*Od.* 22.347–348). Thus the poem itself, like the actions it describes, results from an inseparable conjunction of human and divine activity; the less overtly poetic narratives of the Ithacan section are equally as important to the *Odyssey*'s representation of its own poetics as is the portrayal of Demodocus.

Odysseus tells the same story for the second time, for that second rendition follows on the most rigorous possible verification of his self-presentation, his recognition by Penelope. Both Penelope's situation as Odysseus' wife and her own cautious nature make her a far more exacting judge of the truth of Odysseus' story than Alcinous. In winning her assent to his claim to have returned after so many years, Odysseus is able to unite impressiveness, for that is after all an extraordinary claim, and truth. Shortly after that, when he repeats to her the version of his past adventures that he has told the Phaeacians and she accepts it as readily as she does his claim to be Odysseus, the story's authenticity receives the most powerful guarantee possible.[46]

When Penelope listens with conviction to a story that is both novel and marvelous, Odysseus is able to canonize the fantastic version of what he was doing between his departure from Troy and his return—the version he told the Phaeacians—rather than the more realistic versions he has been telling on Ithaca.[47] He is able to make the version of his story that suits him best the authoritative one—the version that has the enchanting qualities of romance and that begins with his independence from the other heroes he fought with at Troy and ends at the moment of its own telling, looking no further into the problems of the future. The yielding of realism to romance involved in Penelope's recognition is recapitulated in poetic terms as she becomes his willing audience.

One of the ways the *Odyssey* registers the inevitable disjunction between poems like itself and the heroes whom they de-

---

[46] Penelope's guarantee is not, however, absolute. Odysseus' capacity for deceit, in general, and Alcinous' blunder, in particular, serve as reminders that there is no internal mark of truthfulness that can authenticate the stories human beings tell one another. Even the narrative with which Odysseus establishes his identity, the narrative of how he built the bed, is not intrinsically authoritative. Its authority derives from the spirit in which it is told and heard and from the like-mindedness of teller and listener.

[47] In this context it is worth remembering that the parts of the story that are contained in Odysseus' narrative are the parts that were most persistently associated with him in later tradition.

scribe is in the contrast between the two occasions on which Odysseus tells this story. The occasion that brings the hero the most gratification is the one that resembles a poetic performance less. When he tells his story to Penelope, he no longer has an audience whose attention represents far-flung fame, but he is also, finally, home. He has reached the point at which his achievement is secure, the point at which the claims that he makes for himself merge with the indisputable facts of his identity.

The story that Odysseus tells about himself to Penelope may not be as neatly finished off as a professional singer's song, but that is because he is still alive to tell it. Because he has reached the point at which he can pause to experience his own survival, the telling of Odysseus' story can be removed from his struggles and yet he can be its teller. And, because it does not serve as a substitute for his presence, as an impersonal survival, Penelope can listen to it with pleasure. She can now finally take pleasure in a narrative about Odysseus, for the question of his fate has been happily resolved. Because the subject of the story is the same as the person telling it, there is no danger it will end with the unwelcome closure of its hero's death. Odysseus and Penelope have achieved the only conditions under which it is possible to hear a song about someone to whom one is personally tied with rejoicing rather than tears, conditions in which that person is actually and recognizably present. Odysseus' is not a narrative that corresponds to the fixed *sēma*, or monument, to Odysseus that Athena tells Telemachus to build if he learns that Odysseus is dead. It is, rather, a story that allows for something comparable to the year of continued waiting that she prescribes if he finds that Odysseus is still alive: continued life, at least for a time—the happiest ending a mortal hero's story can have.

Even Odysseus, the most successful hero in Homeric epic, the hero whose story is characterized by recurrent evasions of death, cannot know the *Odyssey*, the account of his glorious return from Troy through which his fame survives him. The versions of the story of Odysseus that the *Odyssey* depicts serve in various ways to dramatize this fact. The stories that Telemachus hears on his voyage are stories told in Odysseus' absence, in anticipation of his death. Those that Odysseus himself hears and tells in Phaeacia are incomplete, for they cannot include his return. Those that he tells when he does return are designed to conceal his return, to keep it still a projected future event rather than a present reality. But at the moment of his reunion with Penelope, when his return is assured and he can pause to enjoy his own success, he is able to take pleasure in a narrative that echoes and resembles the poem in which it occurs. The occasion of its telling is very different from those on which songs are sung, but it provides him with the satisfaction that those occasions never can.

Conclusion

BY THE END of the *Odyssey*, the plot jointly hatched by Athena and Odysseus at the end of Book 13 has been successfully concluded. The story of Odysseus has been enacted in a way that makes good the claims this poem puts forward for its uniquely successful hero, claims that are given a new force in that pivotal encounter with its emphasis on Odysseus' assumption of a disguise. The second half of the poem unfolds in a way that fulfills the promise implicit in that disguise. It is a narrative characterized by a heightened sense of events moving towards an assured and desired conclusion as part of an overall strategy or design. It is governed by Athena's unprecedentedly overt and continuous intervention on her favorite's behalf, and it is colored by the premise that Odysseus is always in control.

Odysseus' maintenance of a disguise throughout this narrative shows his control over himself and over the impression he makes on others and gives him an automatic advantage over other characters, allowing him to convert their uninformed words and actions to his own use. This advantage is replicated in the ironic perspective on the action that is communicated to the poem's audience as a consequence of the hero's disguise. The words of characters who are fooled by Odysseus' disguise lose their straightforward authority: the suitors' expressions of contempt for the beggar in their midst become unwitting acknowledgments of Odysseus' presence; Penelope's, Telemachus', and Eumaeus' expressions of grief and despair over Odysseus' loss become wonderfully misconceived denials of the happiness that lies before them. Our perception of a story told about characters responding to Odysseus' absence is always colored by our awareness of his presence.

But, as the foregoing discussion has shown, this story is not told without qualification. Its optimism about the possibility of human happiness and success, and its celebration of its excep-

176

tional hero, are qualified in a variety of ways that spring from the inherent ambiguity of disguise. Any account of disguise implies the plausibility, or even probability, of the vision of reality that the disguise falsely projects, but the *Odyssey* is especially scrupulous in acknowledging the power of what Odysseus' disguise denies.

One form this scrupulousness takes is the poem's explicitness about the divine machinery that drives its plot. The elaborate dialogue between Odysseus and Athena in *Odyssey* 13 spells out the way in which Odysseus' disguise depends on divine favoritism that can only be exercised fully at the point at which he reaches his home; this is reinforced by Athena's role at the end of the poem, where Odysseus' attempt to press his claims beyond his home loses him her undivided support. Odysseus' interactions with both friendly and hostile characters on his return reveal that the idea that makes his disguise acceptable, the idea that it represents a falsification, is only tenable in the setting of his home. Only there does his disguise represent the falsification of an inalienable claim to a certain position, and only there can it be safely and conclusively lifted. Only there does the idea expressed in the name Odysseus correspond to a series of roles that no one else can fill. And only there can the efforts of others to compete for the position Odysseus claims be viewed as criminal transgressions, so that their defeat becomes not just an individual triumph but the operation of divinely sanctioned justice. Away from home, in contexts in which self-realization is rooted in competitive performance rather than in well-defined roles, the obscurity allowed, but also enforced, by disguise can never be shed without danger, as Odysseus' experience with the Cyclops attests.

Another means by which the poem qualifies its dominant optimism is through the voices and actions of sympathetic characters who remain deceived by Odysseus' disguise and therefore continue to testify to the undeniable effects of Odysseus' long absence. The poem gives weight to the experiences of such characters by leaving the most decisive action in its plot, the setting of the contest of the bow, in the hands of one of them, Penelope, with the result that its presentation of its hero is tempered and complicated in a number of ways.

Some of the results of Odysseus' absence that are depicted in this way are unrelievedly painful, in particular the increasing grief and despair suffered by Laertes and Penelope. The depiction of these characters challenges the implication that the hero's return can miraculously erase the effects of his long absence. Other results are more ambiguous and challenge the absolute necessity of the hero's return rather than its power to nullify all the consequences of his absence. While Odysseus' influence is essential to any acceptable solution to the situation on Ithaca, the poem depicts ways in which over time his influence has begun to work in his absence to bring about a solution that may not depend on his presence.

While still in disguise as a poor beggar, Odysseus reactivates codes of hospitable behavior that work towards the restoration of order on Ithaca; furthermore, the interactions of two surrogate versions of Odysseus—his son Telemachus and his reputation—hint at a form of continued order secured by social institutions rather than by the unending survival of an individual hero. In one sense, this underscores the degree to which the poem celebrates its hero, for it points to ways in which he remains a potent figure even after his death. But it also diminishes his individual importance and threatens the depiction of personal happiness that is essential to the poem's theme of *nostos*. These impersonal survivals may memorialize Odysseus, offering him one version of the approximation of immortality that is the reward of human action, but their efficacy does not help, and may even hinder, his success in enjoying his own personal survival—the reward that makes his life richer even than Achilles'.

The story that the *Odyssey* tells of its hero's disguised return serves as a medium for holding two contrasting visions in suspense. One is a vision of the difficulties and limitations of human life. It is eloquently expressed by Odysseus when he is in disguise, especially in his warning to Amphinomus; it is embodied in the hardluck stories that make up Odysseus' false tales and the biography of Eumaeus; it is voiced by Penelope in her expressions of despair; and it is exemplified in the world of the *Telemachy*, a world of valued but also ordinary social rituals, in which all the excitement is found in stories of the past, and in which legendary heroes appear in a diminished light. The harshness of this vision is tempered by its celebration of the various means through which these hardships can be alleviated or contained: social institutions, the continuity of the generations, the adaptability of the human heart, the vicarious pleasures of song.

The other is a vision that treats all of these realities as a form of disguise, as a screen masking the true story, which is the heroic tale of Odysseus' glorious return. It answers the realism of the first vision with fantasy and wish-fulfillment. The interplay of these two visions creates the *Odyssey*'s peculiar texture, which is at once more realistic and more fantastic than that of the *Iliad*. This opposition is cast into self-consciously literary terms in the *Odyssey* as it raises the question of which of its internal songlike narratives of Odysseus' experiences between Troy and his return to civilization is the true one, the romantic version told to the Phaeacians, or the realistic version found in Odysseus' Ithacan tales.

Through its accommodation of these two visions, the *Odyssey* represents two avenues to happiness, one that is anomalous and miraculous and one that is within the range of what can reasonably be hoped for in human life. But in the end, the poem does not give these solutions equal weight. The exigencies of narration—the need to present one event as following another and to arrive eventually at a conclusion—also allow for the establishment of hierarchies among divergent possibilities. In the logic embodied in the *Odyssey*'s plot, disguise is not only the opposite to recognition, it is also its prelude. Eventually Odysseus' disguise, with all that it signifies, gives way to his recognition. This recognition is certainly qualified by its dependence on factors that it would seem to deny: Telemachus' new-found self-sufficiency, Penelope's inability to hold out any longer, the fortuitous circumstance that Odysseus is there to convert her gesture

179

of despair into the means of his triumph, but it is nonetheless the definitive conclusion to the *Odyssey*'s plot. Telemachus steps aside as master of the house to allow for the revelation of Odysseus' return, Penelope's reluctant attempt to replace Odysseus becomes a means of bringing him back, her guest becomes her husband, the past is restored in the present, and Odysseus' unique achievement is finally secure.

Bibliographical References

Adkins, Arthur W. H. *Merit and Responsibility: A Study in Greek Values*. Oxford: Clarendon Press, 1960.

Amory, Anne. "The Gates of Horn and Ivory." *Yale Classical Studies* 20 (1966): 3–57.

———. "The Reunion of Odysseus and Penelope." In *Essays on the Odyssey*, edited by Charles H. Taylor, Jr., 100–121. Bloomington: Indiana University Press, 1963.

Arend, Walter. *Die typischen Szenen bei Homer*. Problemata 7. Berlin: Weidmann, 1933.

Aristotle. *Poetics*. With commentary by D. W. Lucas. Oxford: Clarendon Press, 1968.

Athanassakis, Apostolos N., trans. *The Homeric Hymns*. Baltimore: The Johns Hopkins University Press, 1976.

Auerbach, Erich. *Mimesis: The Representation of Reality in Western Literature*, translated by W. Trask. Princeton: Princeton University Press, 1953.

Austin, Norman. *Archery at the Dark of the Moon: Poetic Problems in Homer's Odyssey*. Berkeley: University of California Press, 1975.

———. "Name Magic in the *Odyssey*." *California Studies in Classical Antiquity* 5 (1972): 1–19.

Basabe, Enrique. "Las últimas anagnōrisis de la Odisea." *Helmantica* 1 (1950): 339–361.

Belmont, David E. "Early Greek Guest–Friendship and Its Role in Homer's *Odyssey*." Ph.D. dissertation Princeton University, 1962.

Block, Elizabeth. "Clothing Makes the Man: A Pattern in the *Odyssey*." *Transactions of the American Philological Association* 115 (1985): 1–11.

Büchner, W. "Die Penelopeszenen in der Odyssee." *Hermes* 75 (1940): 129–167.

181

Burnett, Anne Pippin. "Pentheus and Dionysus: Host and Guest." *Classical Philology* 65 (1970): 15–29.

Bynum, David E. "Themes of the Young Hero in Serbocroatian Oral Epic Tradition." *Publications of the Modern Language Association* 83 (1968): 1293–1303.

Calhoun, G. M. "Classes and Masses in Homer." *Classical Philology* 29 (1934): 192–208, 301–316.

Chantraine, Pierre. *Grammaire homérique.* 2 vols. Paris: Librairie C. Klincksieck, 1958, 1963.

Clader, Linda L. *Helen: The Evolution from Divine to Heroic in Greek Epic Tradition.* Leiden: Brill, 1976.

Clarke, Howard W. *The Art of the Odyssey.* Englewood Cliffs, N.J.: Prentice-Hall, 1967.

Clay, Jenny Strauss. *The Wrath of Athena.* Princeton: Princeton University Press, 1984.

Damon, Philip. "Dilation and Displacement in the *Odyssey.*" *Pacific Coast Philology* 5 (1970): 19–23.

D'Arms, Edward F., and Karl K. Hulley. "The Oresteia-Story in the *Odyssey.*" *Transactions of the American Philological Association* 77 (1956): 207–213.

Dekker, Annie F. *Ironie in de Odyssee.* With summary in English. Leiden: Brill, 1956.

Detienne, Marcel. *Les maîtres de vérité dans la Grèce archaïque.* 2nd ed. Paris: F. Maspero, 1973.

————, and Jean-Pierre Vernant. *Cunning Intelligence in Greek Culture and Society.* Translated by Janet Lloyd. Atlantic Highlands, N.J.: Humanities Press, 1978.

Devereux, Georges. "The Character of Penelope." *Psychoanalytic Quarterly* 26 (1957): 378–386.

Dietz, G. "Das Bett des Odysseus." *Symbolon* 7 (1971): 9–32.

Dimock, George E., Jr. "The Name of Odysseus." In *Essays on the Odyssey,* edited by Charles H. Taylor, Jr., 54–72. Bloomington: Indiana University Press, 1963.

Dodds, E. R. *The Greeks and the Irrational.* Berkeley: University of California Press, 1951.

Edwards, Mark W. "Type-scenes and Homeric Hospitality."

Transactions of the American Philological Association 105 (1975): 51–72.

Emlyn-Jones, Chris. "The Reunion of Penelope and Odysseus." *Greece & Rome* 31 (1984): 1–18.

Erbse, Hartmut. *Beiträge zum Verständnis der Odyssee.* Berlin: De Gruyter, 1972.

Evelyn–White, H. G. *Hesiod, the Homeric Hymns and Homerica.* Cambridge, Mass.: Harvard University Press, 1914.

Fenik, Bernard, *Studies in the Odyssey.* Hermes Eizelschriften 30. Wiesbaden: F. Steiner, 1974.

Ferrucci, Franco. *The Poetics of Disguise: The Autobiography of the Work in Homer, Dante, and Shakespeare,* translated by Ann Dunnigan. Ithaca, N.Y.: Cornell University Press, 1980.

Finley, John H., Jr. *Homer's Odyssey.* Cambridge, Mass.: Harvard University Press, 1978.

Finley, M. I. *The World of Odysseus.* 2nd ed., rev. New York: Viking Press, 1978.

Foley, Helene P. " 'Reverse Similes' and Sex Roles in the *Odyssey.*" *Arethusa* 11 (1978): 72–76.

Frame, Douglas. *The Myth of Return in Early Greek Epic.* New Haven: Yale University Press, 1978.

Fränkel, Hermann. *Early Greek Poetry and Philosophy.* Translated by Moses Hadas and James Willis. New York: Harcourt Brace Jovanovich, 1973.

Greene, Thomas M. *The Descent from Heaven: A Study in Epic Continuity.* New Haven: Yale University Press, 1963.

Griffin, Jasper. *Homer on Life and Death.* Oxford: Clarendon Press, 1980.

Hansen, William F. *The Conference Sequence: Patterned Narrative and Narrative Inconsistency in the Odyssey.* University of California Publications in Classical Philology 8. Berkeley: University of California Press, 1972.

Harsh, Philip W. "Penelope and Odysseus in *Odyssey* XIX." *American Journal of Philology* 71 (1950): 1–21.

Havelock, Eric A. *The Greek Concept of Justice: From Its Shadow in Homer to Its Substance in Plato.* Cambridge, Mass.: Harvard University Press, 1978.

Heatherington, M. E. "Chaos, Order, and Cunning in the *Odyssey*." *Studies in Philology* 73 (1976): 225–238.

Hölscher, Uvo. "Die Atridensage in der Odyssee." In *Festschrift für Richard Alewyn*, edited by Herbert Singer and Benno von Wiese, 1–16. Cologne: Böhlau Verlag, 1967.

―――. "Penelope vor den Freiern." In *Lebende Antike: Symposion für Rudolf Sühnel*, edited by Horst Meller and Hans Joachim Zimmermann, 27–33. Berlin: E. Schmidt, 1967.

―――. "The Transformation from Folk-Tale to Epic." In *Homer: Tradition and Invention*, edited by Bernard Fenik, 51–67. Leiden: Brill, 1978.

―――. *Untersuchungen zur Form der Odyssee*. Hermes Einzelschriften 6. Berlin: Weidmann, 1939.

Holtsmark, Erling B. "Spiritual Rebirth of the Hero—*Odyssey* 5." *Classical Journal* 61 (1966): 206–210.

Houston, George W. "Θρόνος, Δίφρος, and Odysseus' Change from Beggar to Avenger." *Classical Philology* 70 (1975): 212–214.

Jacoby, Felix. "Die geistige Physiognomie der Odyssee." *Die Antike* 9 (1933): 159–194 *Kleine philologische Schriften* I: 107–138. Berlin: Akademie–Verlag, 1961.

Jaeger, Werner. "Solons Eunomie." *Sitzungsberichte der Preussischen Akademie der Wissenschaften, Phil. hist. kl.* 11 (1926): 69–85. *Scripta Minora* I: 314–337. Rome: Edizione di Storia e Letteratura, 1960.

Jörgensen, Ove. "Das Auftreten der Götter in den Buchern ι-μ der *Odyssee*." *Hermes* 39 (1904): 352–382.

Kakridis, Hélène J. *La notion de l'amitié et de l'hospitalité chez Homère*. Bibliotheke tou Philologou 9. Thessaloniki, 1963.

Kakridis, Johannes Th. "The Role of the Woman in the *Iliad*." In *Homer Revisited*, 68–75. Publications of the New Society of Letters at Lund 64. Lund: Gleerup, 1971.

Kearns, Emily. "The Return of Odysseus: A Homeric Theoxeny." *Classical Quarterley* 32 (1982): 2–8.

Kilb, Hans. *Strukturen epischen Gestaltens im 7. und 23. Gesang der Odyssee*. Munich: Fink, 1973.

Kirk, G. S. *The Songs of Homer*. Cambridge: Cambridge University Press, 1962.

Klingner, Friedrich. "Über die vier ersten Bücher der Odyssee." In *Studien zur griechischen und römischen Literatur*, 39–79. Zurich and Stuttgart: Artemis, 1964.

Krehmer, Wolfram. "Zur Begegnung zwischen Odysseus und Athene." Inaugural-Dissertation, University of Erlangen-Nürnberg, 1973.

Lang, Mabel L. "Homer and Oral Techniques." *Hesperia* 38 (1969): 159–168.

Lattimore, Richmond. "Nausikaa's Suitors." In *Studies Presented to Ben Edwin Perry*, 88–102. Urbana: University of Illinois Press, 1969.

Lesky, Albin, "Göttliche und menschliche Motivation im homerischen Epos." *Sitzungsberichte der Heidelberger Akademie der Wissenschaften, Phil. hist. kl.* 4 (1961): 1–52.

Levine, Daniel B. "*Odyssey* 18: Iros as Paradigm for the Suitors." *Classical Journal* 77 (1982): 200–204.

Levy, Harry L. "The Odyssean Suitors and the Host–Guest Relationship." *Transactions of the American Philological Association* 94 (1963): 145–153.

Lord, Albert B. *The Singer of Tales*. Cambridge, Mass.: Harvard University Press, 1960.

Lord, Mary-Louise. "Withdrawal and Return: An Epic Story Pattern in the *Homeric Hymn to Demeter* and in the Homeric Poems." *Classical Journal* 62 (1966–67): 241–248.

MacIntyre, Alasdair. *After Virtue: A Study in Moral Theory*. Notre Dame, Ind.: University of Notre Dame Press, 1981.

Marg, Walter. "Das erste Lied des Demodokos." In *Navicula Chiloniensis: Festschrift für Felix Jacoby*, 16–29. Leiden: Brill, 1956.

Mariani, Alice Jane. "The Forged Feature: Created Identity in Homer's *Odyssey*." Ph.D. dissertation Yale University, 1967.

Mattes, Wilhelm. *Odysseus bei den Phäaken: Kritisches zur Homeranalyse*. Würzburg: K. Triltsch, 1958.

Mauss, Marcel. *The Gift: Forms and Functions of Exchange in Archaic Societies*, translated by Ian Cunnison. New York: Norton, 1967.

Monro, D. B. *Homer's Odyssey: Books XIII to XXIV*. Oxford: Clarendon Press, 1901.

Moulton, Carroll. *Similes in the Homeric Poems*. Hypomnemata 49. Göttingen: Vandenhoeck und Ruprecht, 1977.

————. "The End of the *Odyssey*." *Greek, Roman and Byzantine Studies* 15 (1974): 153–169.

Muellner, Leonard Charles. *The Meaning of Homeric EYCHOMAI Through Its Formulas*. Innsbruck: Inst. f. Sprachwissenschaft d. Univ. Innsbruck, 1976.

Murnaghan, Sheila H. "*Anagnōrisis* in the *Odyssey*," Ph.D. dissertation The University of North Carolina, 1980.

Nagler, Michael N. "Dread Goddess Endowed with Speech." *Archaeological News* 6 (1977): 77–85.

————. *Spontaneity and Tradition: A Study of the Oral Art of Homer*. Berkeley: University of California Press, 1974.

Nagy, Gregory. *Comparative Studies in Greek and Indic Meter*. Cambridge, Mass.: Harvard University Press, 1974.

————. *The Best of the Achaeans*. Baltimore: The Johns Hopkins University Press, 1977.

————. "On the Death of Sarpedon." In *Approaches to Homer*, edited by Carl A. Rubino and Cynthia W. Shelmerdine, 189–217. Austin: The University of Texas Press, 1983.

————. "Sēma and Noēsis: Some Illustrations." *Arethusa* 16 (1983): 35–55.

Page, Denys. *Greek Literary Papyri*. 2 vols. The Loeb Classical Library. Cambridge, Mass.: Harvard University Press, 1942.

————. *The Homeric Odyssey*. Oxford: Clarendon Press, 1955.

Parry, Milman. *The Making of Homeric Verse*. Edited by Adam Parry. Oxford: Clarendon Press, 1971.

Pedrick, Victoria. "The Hospitality of Women in the *Odyssey*." Forthcoming article.

Pfister, F. "Epiphanie," *Realencyclopädie der classischen Altertumswissenschaft*, suppl. 4: 227–323.

Pitt-Rivers, Julian. "Honour and Social Status." In *Honour and Shame: The Values of Mediterranean Society*, edited by J. G. Peristiany, 21–77. Chicago: University of Chicago Press, 1966.

―――. "Women and Sanctuary in the Mediterranean." In *Échanges et Communications: Mélanges offerts à Claude Lévi-Strauss*, edited by Jean Pouillon and Pierre Maranda, II, 862–875. The Hague: Mouton, 1970.

Platt, Arthur. "Notes on the *Odyssey*." *Classical Review* 13 (1899): 382–384.

Podlecki, A. J. "Guest-Gifts and Nobodies in *Odyssey* 9." *Phoenix* 15 (1961): 125–133.

―――. "Omens in the *Odyssey*." *Greece & Rome* 14 (1967): 12–23.

Powell, Barry. *Composition by Theme in the Odyssey*. Meisenheim am Glan: Hain, 1977.

Propp, Vladimir. *Morphology of the Folktale*, translated by Laurence Scott. 2nd ed., rev. Austin: The University of Texas Press, 1977.

Pucci, Pietro. "The Proem of the *Odyssey*." *Arethusa* 15 (1982): 29–62.

―――. "The Song of the Sirens." *Arethusa* 12 (1979): 121–132.

Rankin, A. V. "Penelope's Dreams in Books XIX and XX of the *Odyssey*." *Helikon* 2 (1962): 617–624.

Redfield, James. *Nature and Culture in the Iliad*. Chicago: The University of Chicago Press, 1975.

Reinhardt, Karl. "Homer und die Telemachie." In *Tradition und Geist*, 37–46. Göttingen: Vandenhoeck und Ruprecht, 1960.

―――. "Die Abenteuer der Odyssee." In *Tradition und Geist*, 47–124. Göttingen: Vandenhoeck und Ruprecht, 1960.

Richardson, N. J. *The Homeric Hymn to Demeter*. Oxford: Clarendon Press, 1974.

Rose, Gilbert P. "The Unfriendly Phaeacians." *Transactions of the American Philological Association* 100 (1969): 387–406.

Rose, H. J. "Divine Disguisings." *Harvard Theological Review* 49 (1956): 63–72.

Rose, Peter W. "Class Ambivalence in the *Odyssey*," *Hermes* 24 (1975): 129–147.

Russo, Joseph. "The Inner Man in Archilochus and the *Odyssey*." *Greek, Roman and Byzantine Studies* 15 (1974): 139–152.

———. "Interview and Aftermath: Dream, Fantasy, and Intuition in *Odyssey* 19 and 20." *American Journal of Philology* 103 (1982): 4–18.

Rüter, Klaus. *Odysseeinterpretationen*, edited by Kjeld Matthiessen. Hypomnemata 19. Göttingen: Vandenhoeck und Ruprecht, 1969.

Saïd, Suzanne. "Les crimes des prétendants, la maison d'Ulysse et les festins de l'*Odyssée*." *Études de littérature ancienne*, Paris (1979): 9–49.

Schadewaldt, Wolfgang. "Kleiderdinge: Zur Analyse der Odyssee." *Hermes* 87 (1959): 13–26.

———. "Neue Kriterien zur Odyssee–Analyse: Die Wiedererkennung des Odysseus und der Penelope." *Sitzungsberichte der Heidelberger Akademie der Wissenschaften, Phil. hist. kl.* 2 (1959) 1–28.

Schein, Seth L. "Odysseus and Polyphemus in the *Odyssey*." *Greek, Roman and Byzantine Studies* 11 (1970): 73–83.

Schwartz, E. *Die Odyssee*. Munich: M. Hueber, 1924.

Segal, Charles P. "*Kleos* and Its Ironies in the *Odyssey*." *L'Antiquité Classique* 52 (1983): 22–47.

———. "The Phaeacians and the Symbolism of Odysseus' Return." *Arion* 1 (1962): 17–64.

———. "Transition and Ritual in Odysseus' Return." *La Parola del Passato* 40 (1967): 331–342.

Sinos, Dale S. *Achilles, Patroklos and the Meaning of Philos*. Innsbruck: Inst. f. Sprachwissenschaft d. Univ. Innsbruck, 1980.

Snell, Bruno. *The Discovery of the Mind*, translated by Thomas G. Rosenmeyer. Cambridge, Mass.: Harvard University Press, 1953.

Sowa, Cora Angier. *Traditional Themes and the Homeric Hymns.* Chicago: Bolchazy-Carducci, 1984.

Stanford, W. B. *The Odyssey of Homer.* 2nd ed. 2 vols. London: Macmillan, 1958.

———. *The Ulysses Theme: A Study in the Adaptability of a Traditional Hero.* 2nd ed. Oxford: Basil Blackwell & Mott, 1983.

Stewart, Douglas J. *The Disguised Guest: Rank, Role, and Identity in the Odyssey.* Lewisburg, Pa.: Bucknell University Press, 1976.

Strasburger, Hermann. "Der soziologische Aspekt der homerischen Epen." *Gymnasium* 60 (1953): 97–114.

Suerbaum, Walter. "Die Ich-Erzählungen des Odysseus: Überlegungen zur epischen Technik der Odyssee." *Poetica* 2 (1968): 150–177.

Taylor, Charles H., Jr. "The Obstacles to Odysseus' Return." In *Essays on the Odyssey,* edited by Charles H. Taylor, Jr., 87–99. Bloomington: Indiana University Press, 1963.

Thalmann, William G. *Conventions of Form and Thought in Early Greek Epic Poetry.* Baltimore: The Johns Hopkins University Press, 1984.

Thornton, Agathe. *People and Themes in Homer's Odyssey.* London: Methuen, 1970.

Todorov, Tzvetan. "Primitive Narrative." In *The Poetics of Prose,* translated by Richard Howard, 53–65. Ithaca, N.Y.: Cornell University Press, 1977.

Vallillee, G. "The Nausicaa Episode." *Phoenix* 9 (1955): 175–179.

Van Nortwick, Thomas. "Penelope and Nausicaa." *Transactions of the American Philological Association* 109 (1979): 269–276.

Vernant, Jean-Pierre, *Mythe et société en Grèce ancienne.* Paris: F. Maspero, 1974.

Vester, H. "Das 19. Buch der Odyssee." *Gymnasium* 75 (1968): 417–434.

Vidal-Naquet, Pierre. "Valeurs religieuses et mythiques de la terre et du sacrifice dans l'*Odyssée*." In *Problèmes de la terre en Grèce ancienne*, edited by M. I. Finley, 269–292. Paris: Mouton, 1973.

Walsh, George B. *The Varieties of Enchantment: Early Greek Views of the Nature and Function of Poetry*. Chapel Hill: University of North Carolina Press, 1984.

Wender, Dorothea. *The Last Scenes of the Odyssey*. Mnemosyne Supplement 52. Leiden: Brill, 1978.

Whitman, Cedric H. *Homer and the Heroic Tradition*. Cambridge, Mass.: Harvard University Press, 1958.

Wilamowitz-Moellendorf, U. von. *Die Heimkehr des Odysseus*. Berlin: Weidmann, 1927.

Woodhouse, W. J. *The Composition of Homer's Odyssey*. Oxford: Clarendon Press, 1930.

Index of Names
and Subjects

191

Index of
Passages Cited

Library of Congress Cataloging-in-Publication Data

Murnaghan, Sheila, 1951–
Disguise and recognition in the Odyssey.

Bibliography: p.   Includes index.
1. Homer. Odyssey. 2. Disguise in literature.
3. Recognition in literature. 4. Identity
(Psychology) in literature. 5. Odysseus (Greek
mythology) in literature. I. Title.
PA4167.M8 1987   883'.01   87–2296
ISBN 0–691–06716–3 (alk. paper)